i

New Mexico Magazine's

ENCHANTED TRAILS

by Ruth Armstrong
and the staff of
New Mexico Magazine

New Mexico Magazine, Santa Fe, NM
USA

Library of Congress Catalog Card Number: 80--82644

ISBN 0-937206-01-6

© New Mexico Magazine, 1980

Designed by Richard Sandoval and Dick Hogle
Edited by Sheila Tryk and Scottie King
"Ghost Towns" by Scottie King; "Rockhounding" by Mike Pitel.
Maps by Peter Clapp
Cover photograph by Sheila Tryk
Photography by Mark Nohl

CONTENTS

FOREWORD

This book is intended as a companion to those of you who already know the joy of exploring New Mexico as well as to first-time visitors who, we hope, will soon experience that sense of discovery that continually surprises and delights us.

We've tried to design this guide to be easy to use. The contents page can give you a clue to the many things to see and do in the state, whatever the season. Under the chapter called Cities & Towns, we've listed most of the major towns in alphabetical order. But if you can't find the spot you're looking for, check the index. The place may be listed with a larger nearby town.

And if the city where Great-Grandpa used to mine for gold isn't in the Cities & Towns chapter, it may just be in the Ghost Towns chapter!

The numbers to the right of the city names refer to the coordinates on the official state map. You can get a copy of one from most chambers of commerce, Tourist Welcome Centers or the State Highway Department (PO Box 1149, Santa Fe, MM 87501).

And when you find a town you want to know more about, remember that the local chamber of commerce will be able to provide you with all the information you want.

We hope you have as much pleasure visiting New Mexico as we have had writing about it. Have a happy and safe journey.

WEATHER

New Mexico's weather is dramatic, exciting and capricious. We don't promise you'll always love it, but we promise it will never bore you.

Many cities and towns in New Mexico are more than a mile high. Elevations range from 3,030 feet (923.54 metres) at Jal in the southeast corner of the state to 8,750 feet (2,667 metres) at Red River in the north-central part. Most mountain recreation sites are at elevations between 7,500 (2,286 metres) and 10,000 feet (3,048 metres). The highest peaks rise to more than 13,000 feet (3,962 metres). Elevation has a great deal of influence on the weather.

New Mexico's spectacular natural beauty embraces plateaus, mesas, pine-clad mountains, alpine meadows and valleys, and high desert country. It includes six of the seven life or vegetation zones found in the United States — Arctic-Alpine, Hudsonian, Canadian, Transition, Upper Sonoran and Lower Sonoran. (Sorry, no Tropical.)

The state's southern latitude and high elevations make a sunny, relatively mild, dry climate. The sun is often hot, but the air is usually cool. Typical summer daytime temperatures range from the 80s and 90s F (26 to 38 C) at lower elevations to the 70s and 80s (20s to 30s C) at higher elevations. Remember, 80 degrees F (26 C) with low humidity is crisp and invigorating, a far cry from 80 degrees in a humid climate. Your clothes won't stick to you in New Mexico.

Nighttime temperatures usually drop 20 to 40 degrees, making sleep a pleasure. Usual winter daytime temperatures range from the 50s and 60s (the teens C) at lower elevations to the 40s and even the 50s (4 to 14 C) at higher elevations. Above 7,000 feet (2,133 metres) considerable snow falls, which makes it possible for New Mexico to have 12 developed ski and winter sports areas.

Let the weather be part of your fun as you travel New Mexico. Watch big cumulus clouds pile up like whipped cream on mountain peaks. In the summer, watch and listen to the drama of lightning and thunder rip the clouds apart until they drop their cooling showers. Marvel at the perfect double rainbows, nature's promise to "be good." Any time of year, see the unbelievable colors of the sky — turquoise, azure, even purple. At sunrise and sunset the brilliance makes your heart ache — it is more than man deserves. Enjoy it.

CLOTHES

The basic rules are be comfortable and be casual. Perhaps this month-by-month breakdown of the "usual" weather may help you.

January— Warm clothing, coats, sweaters, ski jackets, wool suits, gloves or mittens, hats, boots, walking shoes. Thermal underwear if you're going to the mountains.

February — About the same as January. There is usually a false spring in February, but it lasts only a few days. When that happens you can shed a coat and wear a sweater.

March — Still on the cold side, but warming up, especially at lower elevations. Snow is not uncommon, but it won't last long. At the high elevations, it may snow one day and be 60 degrees F (15 degrees C) the next. Windy. You will need warm clothing, but may have to shed some of it at times.

April — The green-up month. Sweaters, all-weather coats and jackets, lightweight slacks, suits.

May — Settling into summer, but still has a touch of spring. Ordinary summer clothing is usually comfortable, such as summer pants suits, slacks, jackets, jeans, but you will always need a sweater or lightweight coat or jacket for nights, or even days sometimes. In the mountains there will still be snow on the ground in many places.

June — Summer is here. Days will be warm except in the mountains, nights comfortable. No rain yet, usually. Summer-weight slacks, shorts, dresses, jeans (practically a uniform for outdoor recreation), and always a sweater or light coat.

July — Summer temperatures prevail, but the thundershower season begins the last part of the month, and the brief, scattered showers can drop temperatures 20 degrees in a few minutes. In the mountains these thunderstorms are often cold and the rain may turn to hail. For a summer family-style vacation in the outdoors, jeans, shirts, sweaters or jackets are standard, with sneakers, hiking boots or other comfortable walking shoes. If your plans include the opera, theater or elegant restaurants you will want something a little dressier.

August— Similar to July. Thundershowers continue.

September — There's a snap in the air that says fall is on its way, but it's not really here yet. Days continue to be warm.

Summer clothing will usually do for September, so long as you have a sweater or jacket. But in the high mountain communities nighttime temperatures may drop below freezing.

October — Geese flying overhead say fall has arrived. Aspen, cottonwood, maple and woodbine spill their paint pots in hills and valleys. Days are crisp and golden with cobalt skies, about 10 degrees cooler than summer, colder in the mountains. Medium-weight suits, slacks, jackets and dresses will be comfortable. You won't need your heaviest coats yet.

November — Fields, hillsides and fallen leaves are the color of a Siamese cat. Weather usually remains sunny and crisp, but there is a noticeable bite in the air, and storms can hit. Winter clothing will feel good. Ski areas will begin to open around Thanksgiving.

December — Some snowstorms, especially at higher elevations, but many days continue warm and sunny. Winter clothing needed.

ROADS AND SERVICES

Interstate highways 40 and 10 cross New Mexico east-west, Interstate 25 runs north-south, but you should get off the interstates to discover and explore the scenic, historic, geological and archeological sites that make this such an intriguing state. We hope this book will help you plan your trips in New Mexico to see not only the towns along the highways, but the interesting places near them.

New Mexico is a large state — fifth largest of all the United States — and sparsely populated, which often means long distances between towns and service stations. A good rule is to try to travel on the top half of your gas tank.

All major highways between all major towns are paved, but many interesting places are reached only by unpaved roads. Don't let this keep you from exploring. Most unpaved roads are graveled, graded and safe. In the section where we discuss towns and their nearby points of interest, we will note bad roads. Because of the clay in the soil, unpaved roads can be very slick when wet, but summer showers are usually brief, and if the roadway has any elevation it will drain quickly.

If your adventuring takes you into four-wheel-drive country where you must cross or follow arroyo beds (gullies), be extremely cautious if there are dark clouds over the mountains in any direction. A wall of water from a rainstorm miles away can be deadly, the flash flood rushing down the confines of a dry arroyo bed or canyon.

For your own safety as well as for the protection of the land, please obey all signs prohibiting off-road vehicles.

New Mexico State Highway rest stops are located near all ports of entry and along major highways. Some have good exhibits on the history or geology of the area, as well as picnic and rest facilities. Because of the long distances between towns, freeway driving sometimes becomes hypnotic. The American Automobile Association recommends stopping every two hours. If you feel drowsy or sluggish at anytime please stop at one of these rest stops. Pull off the road and get a little exercise and fresh air. We want you to live to see ALL of New Mexico.

Welcome Centers are found throughout the state. Permanent centers are located in Anthony, Chama, Lordsburg and Glen Rio, 30 miles (48 kilometres) east of Tucumcari. Summer centers are found at Gallup, Hobbs, Santa Fe, Carlsbad, Raton, Aztec, and Clovis. They provide the tourist with travel literature and perform vacation counseling services.

TRANSPORTATION

Most visitors to New Mexico still drive their own cars or campers. But a fly-drive vacation may be your most convenient way to see the state. Car rental agencies are in all towns served by airlines. Albuquerque and also El Paso, Texas, serve as gateway cities to New Mexico. Other cities that currently have air service are: Alamogordo, Carlsbad, Clovis, Farmington, Gallup, Hobbs, Las Cruces, Los Alamos, Roswell, Santa Fe and Silver City.

Among the airlines that at present serve New Mexico are: Air Midwest, American, Aspen, Continental, Crown Air, Eastern, Frontier, Ross, Southwest, Texas International and TWA.

But there are other ways to come to the Land of Enchantment.

Rail passenger service by AMTRAK is furnished to Raton, Las Vegas, Lamy (Santa Fe), Albuquerque and Gallup in the north, and Deming and Lordsburg in the south.

Greyhound, Trailways, and New Mexico Transportation serve most towns in the state.

CIVILIZATIONS OF NEW MEXICO

THE FIRST NEW MEXICANS

Beginning about 20,000 or 25,000 years ago, squat, hairy-legged men dressed in animal skins followed mastodons, bison and saber-tooth tigers across the cold marshlands of the Southwest. They traveled in small family groups, the beginning of clans. They camped beside their kill until it was consumed, supplementing their meat diet with wild grains and grasses. Sometimes they sought shelter in caves and overhangs, and ceilings grew black with campfire smoke. Their weapons were stone spears, flaked to sharp points. They also made scrapers of stone, and left thousands of fragments and points where they fell for men to find millenia later and wonder whose hand had held it last.

As the climate warmed, lakes and swamps receded and rivers began to find channels. Before Christ was born, the Anasazi, the Ancient Ones, had a rudimentary knowledge of agriculture. They dug holes in the ground with their fingers or a sharp stick and dropped in seeds, gradually learning that when sufficient rain fell, crops grew. They began to assist nature by developing irrigation systems, and agriculture was born on this continent.

Now that they grew crops they didn't move so often; campsites became semipermanent homes. At first these were only what we call pit houses — shallow depressions in the ground covered with brush.

Another important development took place about the same time: They began to make baskets to store and carry grains. Basketry led to pottery (some think that baskets were first lined with clay to make them watertight). The people then began to weave sandals and cloth from yucca fibers, and ropes and nets of human hair. Life became easier and their numbers increased.

Changes and improvements escalated. Family groups merged into clans, governmental structures evolved, stories and legends became beliefs, dances became rituals — part of their religion. They began to build homes on top of the ground by putting layers of mud one on top of another until the wall reached the desired height, then they put poles and brush across the top. Or they built the walls out from caves. But they kept their pit houses as ceremonial chambers, a tie with the past that continues today in some Pueblo kivas — ceremonial chambers.

They found they could strengthen their houses by building rooms adjoining each other. Soon they were joining many small rooms together and stacking them like blocks.

Hunters found that if they took two spear shafts and joined them together in a V, that when they threw it by one end, it had much greater force — and the atlatl was born. It was only a matter of time until the bow and arrow evolved, which, with its many sizes, gave them great flexibility in weapons.

Women began to fire pottery to make it more durable. They found time to decorate and polish their pots. They learned to weave the fiber of wild cotton into cloth for garments, and turkey feathers and animal fur into blankets and robes. They cultivated wild beans, squash and corn and ground the corn between stones to make cornmeal, their staple food.

As life became more sedentary, regional differences began to evolve, especially in pottery and architecture, and probably in language. The Indians who lived in southern and western New Mexico have become identified as the Mogollon culture. Their pottery was a brown and red ware, while the Anasazi in northwestern New Mexico made a gray pottery. Both built pit houses, but the Mogollon people built larger communal ceremonial lodges as they developed. Trade and communication existed between the cultures and extended into Mexico. The Mimbres people, who are dated at roughly A.D. 950-1000, produced outstanding black on white pottery. By about A.D. 1000 the Anasazi influence with its remarkable architecture had spread over the entire Four Corners region — where today the four states of Utah, Arizona, Colorado and New Mexico come together.

By A.D. 1100 the Anasazi had entered the high point of their civilization, a golden age that lasted almost three centuries. Their homes grew to magnificent multistoried dwellings built of stone, quarried so well with stone tools that mortar was not always necessary. They fitted pieces together like tile mosaics, and the walls reached 40 and 50 feet high — though they knew nothing of the wheel, beasts of burden or metal tools. Some of those walls stand today at Chaco Canyon and Aztec National Monuments and Salmon Ruins.

Chaco Canyon probably flourished as a great trade center, supported by a vast network of roads and irrigation systems. Possibly 7,000 people lived there at one time.

But the great classic period of Pueblo Indian culture came to an end during the 13th century. Although the climate, it is now believed, was then much as it is now — dry — a prolonged drought may have been the cause of Chaco's decline. Whatever happened, the people began moving away from the great centers in the Four Corners country, migrating toward the Rio Grande and its tributaries. They wandered like the children of Israel, stopping in caves and on plateaus for generations, but irresistibly they were drawn toward the big river. They had established themselves on the Rio Grande when two other kinds of people entered their land.

From the north came a fierce, nomadic hunter, a red man like the Pueblos, but of a different disposition. These people came in small, furtive bands, stealing supplies of grain, taking women and children, killing the men.

From the south came a white man almost as frightening. He rode a strange beast, his head glittered in the sun and was so hard an arrow could not pierce it. Some of these strange men walked on the ground and carried two sticks, one crossed over the other, which seemed important to them. The Pueblo people, being peaceful by nature, soon learned that if they did as these men wished, they would not harm them and would even protect them from the marauding tribes of the north.

The Spaniards called the Indians Pueblos because they lived in villages. They called the nomadic Indians Apaches or Navajos del Apache.

THE SPANIARDS COME

The first men of European descent to see the Southwest were four members of a Spanish expedition which had shipwrecked on the gulf of Mexico in 1528. They made an incredible eight-year odyssey, subsisting on cacti, snakes or whatever the desert Indians gave them, and finally found Spanish soldiers on the western side of Mexico. They told the Viceroy in Mexico City about a rich civilization farther north on the big river. They hadn't gone far enough to see their wonderful homes, but they had heard many tales.

Another Peru! the Spaniards thought, and immediately plans were made to send an expedition north. The honor fell to Capitan-General Don Francisco Vasquez de Coronado. His army of 1,500 men reached the pueblos of Zuni in midsummer, 1540. After six months of exploring, the army moved on to the Rio Grande and established headquarters in December in the Tiguex province near present-day Bernalillo. For more than a year they explored in all directions, as far east as Kansas and as far west as the Grand Canyon, but they found no gold — only mud houses and souls to convert.

Spanish conquistador in pageant.

So great was the disappointment that for 40 years no more Spaniards came north. But then hope was reborn and four expeditions came between 1581 and 1598 when the first colonization expedition came to stay. They were soldiers, priests, adventurers, noblemen, farmers, men, women and children, and they established a colony where the Chama and Rio Grande met at the pueblo they called San Juan.

These tenacious people sank their roots deep into New Mexico's soil. Life wasn't easy, but no one expected it to be. They had their gardens, orchards, sheep, plenty of wood to burn, and earth to build adobe houses. Their foods added to the corn, squash and beans of the Indians, made a good diet. Besides new foods, the Spaniards introduced metal, the wheel, sheep, cattle, horses, beasts of burden, improved agricultural and construction methods. The Stone Age had ended in New Mexico.

Franciscan fathers directed the building of many mission churches throughout the province and forbade the Indians to practice their "pagan" religion. Civil authorities were determined to bend them to an alien form of government. Finally, in 1680, the patient Pueblo people united to drive out or kill every Spaniard in the province. The rebellion was a complete success, and for 12 years they held the land to themselves again. But after having lived a century with the Spaniards, they had come to depend on them for many things, especially protection against the nomadic Indians who now raided the Pueblos at will. In 1692, the Spaniards, led by Don Diego de Vargas, finally were able to reconquer the Indians. The Spaniards, however, had learned a valuable lesson: they would allow the Indians to perform their rituals if only they would accept Christianity, too.

For the next century New Mexicans lived in virtual isolation and neglect from the mother country whose role as a world power was on the wane. Spain did not have the resources or the energy to develop the province. The church concentrated on converting Indians, leaving Spanish settlers to fend for themselves.

During the century of isolation, customs, language, and social structure in New Mexico changed little. Old ways became so deeply ingrained that even today language and customs in some of the remote villages are still like Spain of

300 years ago. Two societies developed, Rio Arriba and Rio Abajo. Upriver, Rio Arriba, was mostly a land of small villages on community land grants given when as many as 30 families decided to break away from the feudal system and go out on their own. They shared water, farm and timber lands, and the land was theirs as long as they lived on it. When they moved, it reverted to the Crown. Santa Fe was the capital and only town of any size, and its inhabitants came and went with the whims of politics.

Downriver, Rio Abajo, with its milder climate and wider valleys, developed a more permanent agricultural society. Many individual land grants were made to men of station who could bring in colonists to till the fields and herd the sheep. The dividing line between the two New Mexicos was the volcanic escarpment between Santa Fe and Albuquerque called La Bajada.

Early in the 19th century, traumatic changes occurred. Beaver hats became the style, and French, English and American beaver trappers came down into the mountains of New Mexico, the first crack in the curtain of isolation that had shrouded the province for so many years.

Mexico was becoming impatient with the neglect of Spain, and in 1810 began a slow, painful revolution that lasted 12 years. With Mexico's independence in 1821, New Mexico became a department of that country, no longer tied to Spain except through blood and memory.

The Mexican government immediately opened the gates for trade with the United States, which had been strictly forbidden under Spanish rule. In 1821 the first pack train of goods came into Santa Fe. By the next year the Santa Fe Trail was established, bringing millions of dollars worth of goods into the area each year. New Mexicans were hungry for the manufactured goods from the east, and wagons returned home with hides, wool and some minerals. An extension of the trail went from Santa Fe down the old Camino Real to Chihuahua, Mexico.

The Missouri traders made a great impact on New Mexico. In the chaos of birthing pains, the struggling Republic of Mexico neglected New Mexico as much as Spain had, and New Mexico turned more and more toward the States. Inevitably New Mexico became part of that country's "Manifest Destiny."

AND THEN THE UNITED STATES . . .

On August 1, 1846, the American Army of the West under Colonel Stephen Watts Kearny camped on New Mexico soil near Bent's Fort on the Arkansas River. (The Louisiana Purchase had established the border between Spain and the United States at the Arkansas.) The flag was raised in the old plaza in Santa Fe on August 18, and the invasion of New Mexico was accomplished without firing a shot. There was sporadic resistance over the next few months, but most New Mexicans recognized the inevitable. They wept at the grave of their mother country, but accepted the reality of economic advantage.

The sweep of the New Mexico Territory by 1861 covered all of present-day New Mexico and Arizona, the southern triangle of Nevada, and Colorado south of the Arkansas and east of the Rio Grande — some 261,342 square miles. In 1863, Congress divided the land into the New Mexico and Arizona territories.

Rodeo — a Western tradition.

The Civil War in New Mexico lasted less than two months in 1862, but is important because the victor would control the West. The Confederates won the Battle of Val Verde south of Socorro, and took Albuquerque and Santa Fe, but a force from Fort Union met them at the Battle of Glorieta Pass east of Santa Fe, destroyed their supply train in Apache Canyon — and won the West for the Union.

After the war, the West opened as it never had before, and the era of the great ranches, the cowboy legend, the Indian wars, the gold rushes, the mining barons — the American Frontier — came into being.

The railroad arrived in 1879-1880 with fireworks, excitement, new residents, new ideas and fast communication with the rest of the world. It changed the landscape forever. Commerce on the Santa Fe Trail ended abruptly. New towns sprang to life.

By the beginning of the 20th century many changes had taken place in New Mexico: a more stable government evolved, forts with soldiers to protect travelers and residents, manufactured goods and implements, public education, communication through mails, telegraph and telephone, development of agriculture and the cattle and sheep industries, and the railroad that tied the continent together with ribbons of steel. Statehood was denied New Mexico until 1912, making it the last territory except Arizona to become one of the continental states.

The history of New Mexico during the 20th century has more or less paralleled that of other Western states with some major differences. In spite of scientific developments and installations that have made New Mexico a leader in the Space Age, it retains the exotic character of a foreign country within a country. In New Mexico, the Indian and Spanish civilizations each existed independently long enough that customs, attitudes and beliefs were never entirely overwhelmed by the newer society as it came in, and today New Mexico is a reasonably congenial blending of diverse people where each culture is respected for its contributions.

Herein lies the grace and charm of New Mexico — the Land of Enchantment.

Before the ethnically mixed New Mexico that we know today came into being, two older civilizations existed here, each one long enough and isolated enough that its imprint was left forever on the land. The United States occupied New Mexico in 1846, but for 306 years before that, Spaniards made this a province of Spain, and, for one generation, a part of Mexico. For thousands of years before that, Indians lived in New Mexico.

Descendants of two distinct groups of Indians still live in New Mexico, part of the mainstream, yet maintaining the customs, languages and beliefs of their ancestors, living on their own reservations. Each tribe has its own government, yet is subject to federal and some state laws. They have their own civil and criminal codes and police system. In many ways they are nations within a nation. Approximately 100,000 Native Americans now live in New Mexico.

Indian villages, homes and ways of life are of great interest to visitors, and in most cases visitors are permitted to watch ceremonial dances and other festivities on Indian reservations. Some tribes actively promote tourism. The work of Indian artists is available in shops and homes on the reservations, and in galleries, museums and stores all around the state.

Visitors who display courtesy and consideration will be treated the same way. Since each tribe has its own regulations, it is advisable for visitors to inquire at the tribal governor's office or tourism office for information concerning photography, taping, arts and crafts and events. Some tribes do not permit photography, taping or sketching under any circumstances; others occasionally permit it for a fee.

The Indians of New Mexico fall into two classifications: Pueblos and nomadic or Athabascan tribes. There are 19 pueblos (the Spanish word for village) today, occupied by descendants of the ancient farmers the Spaniards found in 1540. They are called Pueblo Indians and their villages are called pueblos. The land set aside for each Pueblo tribe is their reservation. Each of the 19 tribes is governed by its own governor and tribal council.

The other Indians in New Mexico are descended from Athabascan tribes who migrated slowly from the north around the 15th century. In New Mexico, these are the Navajos, whose reservation covers about 16 million acres (6,475,100 hectares) of New Mexico, Arizona and Utah; the Mescalero Apaches in the mountains of south-central New Mexico, and the Jicarilla Apaches in northwestern New Mexico. A small part of the Ute reservation, another Athabascan tribe, is in northwestern New Mexico but the area contains no towns.

Following is an alphabetical listing of, first, the Pueblo Indians, and then the Athabascan tribes, tourist facilities on the reservation, and major arts and crafts. Unscheduled dances occur at all pueblos throughout the year. Many are open to visitors, but, if not, signs will be posted. At the end of this chapter is a list of most commonly held Pueblo Indian feast days and dances. It is always wise to check first with tribal headquarters or the New Mexico Travel Division to verify the dates.

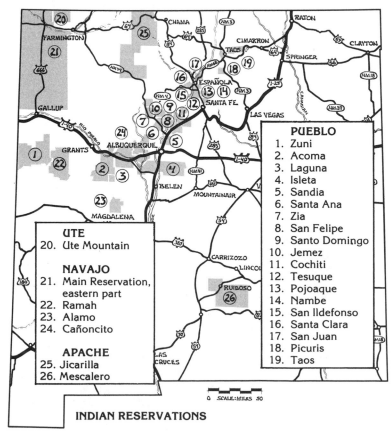

PUEBLO
1. Zuni
2. Acoma
3. Laguna
4. Isleta
5. Sandia
6. Santa Ana
7. Zia
8. San Felipe
9. Santo Domingo
10. Jemez
11. Cochiti
12. Tesuque
13. Pojoaque
14. Nambe
15. San Ildefonso
16. Santa Clara
17. San Juan
18. Picuris
19. Taos

UTE
20. Ute Mountain

NAVAJO
21. Main Reservation, eastern part
22. Ramah
23. Alamo
24. Cañoncito

APACHE
25. Jicarilla
26. Mescalero

0 SCALE:MILES 50

INDIAN RESERVATIONS

PUEBLO INDIANS

Acoma, 65 miles (105 kilometres) west of Albuquerque or 41 miles (66 kilometres) southeast of Grants.

Sky City has been the ancestral home of the Acoma Indians for about a thousand years. It rests like an eagle's aerie atop a sheer sandstone butte that rises nearly 400 feet above the surrounding plain. The Acomas speak the Keres language, and most of them live on farms and ranches and in two villages, Acomita and McCarty, but each year certain members of the tribe live on top of the rock to keep the houses and church in repair, operate the visitor center, guide visitors around the pueblo, collect fees, and keep everything in order for special feast days when the Acomas return to their city in the sky.

Visitors are required to report to the visitor center. From there a guide will take you through the narrow streets where centuries of moccasined feet have worn the rock smooth. Adobe and stone houses rise like stairsteps, two and three stories high, clustered together lest those on the outside tumble over the edge.

San Esteban mission church, 350 years old, stands as a reminder of the determination of the Franciscan priests who served here, and of the hard labor of the Indians who built it. Every timber had to be carried from a distant mountain, and water and dirt for mortar were carried up on their backs. The church was abandoned during the Indian rebellion of 1680, restored around 1700, and has been used continuously since then (see *Missions and Churches*).

Acoma pottery is thin, well-fired, and has distinctive black-on-white geometric designs. Some is all white with rows of "fingernail imprints" covering the entire piece. Many potters sell from their homes at Sky City or in the villages.

Acomita Lake on the reservation near I-40 has facilities for picnicking and fishing, but no overnight camping. A small store at the lake sells permits and supplies.

Cochiti, 36 miles (58 kilometres) southwest of Santa Fe or 45 miles (72 kilometres) north of Albuquerque.

Legend says that ancestors of the Cochiti Indians migrated to the present site along the Rio Grande about 600 years ago from the cliffs and caves of the Pajarito Plateau, part of the Jemez Mountains directly west of the pueblo. The area has been inhabited, however, since A.D. 1000. Today the Cochiti people farm the bottomlands of the river, and many work in nearby towns. They speak the Keres language.

The resort community of Cochiti Lake, a few miles north of the pueblo, is on reservation land and is one of the first such joint business ventures any of the Pueblo groups have entered into, to bring income and jobs to the reservation. Many people from Cochiti Pueblo work at the community. They sit on decision-making boards and operate a large campground at the lake.

Cochiti women make a good earth-tone pottery, decorated in black and red. Figures of frogs, fish, lizards and people are molded onto the pots. Their best-known pottery design is Old Woman Storyteller, a figure of a woman sitting flat on the ground with from two to a dozen children climbing over her. Small hunting fetishes made of clay are also sought by collectors. Excellent jewelry is made by several Cochiti craftsmen. Men of Cochiti are known for their fine double-headed drums made of hollowed-out aspen or cottonwood log sections, laced tightly over both ends with leather. The resonant beat of a Cochiti drum is a familiar part of most pueblo ceremonial dances.

Isleta, 13 miles (21 kilometres) south of Albuquerque. Shouldered against the suburbs of Albuquerque, the pueblo of Isleta retains its culture and customs well. Their Indian language is Tiwa. When most of the Pueblo Indians revolted against the Spaniards in 1680 and killed or drove out every Spaniard in the colony, most Isletas fled with the refugees to establish Ysleta del Sur in the Rio Grande Valley near El Paso. After the reconquest most of them returned to their ancestral home and rebuilt their mission church which had been partially burned and used as a sheep pen during the rebellion. Remodeled many times, this beautiful old church stands today as one of the most venerable in the United States (see *Missions and Churches*).

In recent years potters of Isleta have again begun producing a good grade of pottery. They also make woven belts, embroidered shirts and aprons, and their oven bread and pies are excellent. Most Isleta people work in Albuquerque, but several small industries lease land on the reservation, providing some employment there. Their reservation covers fine agricultural land along the river, and extends east to the top of the Manzano Mountains. About a mile north of the pueblo in a shady grove of trees near the river, they have built fishing lakes, a campground, picnic area and store as a tourist industry on the reservation. On the hills west of the pueblo, modern homes have been built, but the plaza area remains a traditional cluster of adobe homes.

Jemez, 48 miles (77 kilometres) northwest of Albuquerque. Set among the red and ochre cliffs of the Jemez Mountains, this is the only Towa-speaking pueblo, and, because of its western location, has had more contact with the Navajos than most other pueblos. At any feast or market day in Jemez, Navajos are always present. There is a craft center on the highway where Jemez pottery and other crafts can be bought. Until recently their pottery was a brightly colored tourist item, but they have revived ancient techniques and are producing many fine pots.

Most Jemez people work at jobs in nearby towns or at sawmills in the mountains, and they farm small fields along the Jemez River. The earth and canyon walls near the pueblo are blood red, making the fields of corn, chile, melons and orchards appear like emerald squares from the highway that winds along the canyon.

Acoma Pueblo.

When the Spaniards first explored New Mexico, there were several Jemez pueblos farther up the canyon and on top of the mesas above the canyon. Those have long since been abandoned, and all the Jemez people live in the present village. In 1838 they were joined by a few survivors from the pueblo of Pecos, to the east, the only other group that spoke the Towa language.

Jemez Pueblo offers two campgrounds 19 and 21 miles (31 and 34 kilometres) north of San Ysidro on a forest road to the right off NM 44. Inquire and pay fees at the San Ysidro store. There is fishing at both campgrounds.

Hunters may try for deer and elk in season. Tribal permits from the governor's office are required, as well as state licenses.

Laguna, 50 miles (80 kilometres) west of Albuquerque. Travelers on I-40 see the adobe homes of Laguna clustered around San Jose mission church on a sunny hillside near the highway. The timeless appearance of the old pueblo seems undisturbed by the proximity of a busy transcontinental highway.

A branch of Keres-speaking Indians from the Rio Grande Valley settled here around 1450 to farm small fields along San Jose Creek. When the Spaniards introduced cattle and sheep to New Mexico, the Lagunas became stockmen, still a basic industry. In recent years rich deposits of uranium ore have been found on the reservation, and the big open-pit Jackpile mine lies a few miles north of the highway at the very edge of the old Laguna village of Paguate, the oldest of the 10 Laguna communities. A good grade of marble is also mined on the reservation.

Some Laguna potters still produce high-quality traditional pottery. Laguna is one of the larger pueblos, both in size of reservation and in population. Brilliant shades of red, mauve and purple paint swaths of color on the cliffs and buttes that punctuate the land. Because of the interesting color and geological formations, several Hollywood companies have filmed at Laguna. Picnicking and fishing are permitted at Paguate Reservoir, with permits available at the Laguna post office.

Nambe, 21 miles (34 kilometres) north of Santa Fe. Using funds earned from the annual July 4th Waterfall Ceremonial at the Nambe Falls recreation area, the Nambe people collected enough money over 14 years to build a new church. Indian workmen from Northern Pueblos Enterprises finished it in 1975. A solar-assisted, pueblo-style tribal headquarters building is also noteworthy. A crafts center sells micaceous pottery, embroidery, and woven cotton belts, all traditional Nambe crafts. Crafts may also be purchased at individual homes, to which the visitor may be directed at the pueblo governor's office. Inquire there also for fishing permits at the recreation area. There is still some farming on the reservation, but most people are employed in nearby towns. Their Indian language is Tewa.

Picuris (San Lorenzo), 20 miles (32 kilometres) south of Taos. Tucked away in the mountains along the banks of the Rio Pueblo, Picuris today is a small pueblo. In the early days, Spaniards referred to Picuris as a major pueblo, and excavations have unearthed ruins of a much larger village. The people speak the same language (Tiwa) as those of Taos, and historians say this pueblo was founded between 1250 and 1300 by Indians who had lived in a large pueblo near Taos.

Women potters produce a well-fired utilitarian pottery that is used for cooking. Mica in the clay leaves little glittering flecks, giving a pleasing sheen to the reddish-brown surface.

There is a museum at the pueblo. Camping and picnicking are available nearby.

Pojoaque, 16 miles (26 kilometres) north of Santa Fe. Although Pojoaque Pueblo held on to its reservation lands, the population dwindled almost to extinction before the tribe reorganized a few years ago. They now have a tribal council and have recently reinstated the observance of their feast day. Their language is Tewa. The tribe has developed a small commercial/industrial complex near the junction of the Santa Fe-Los Alamos highway, revenue from which provides most of the tribal income. Most of the Pojoaque people work in nearby towns.

Sandia, 14 miles (23 kilometres) north of Albuquerque. This small Tiwa-speaking pueblo has survived as an entity even though its reservation boundaries abut suburban Albuquerque. Their land along the Rio Grande is fertile, and agriculture is one of their mainstays. However, they have capitalized on the metropolitan area by encouraging tourism as a major industry. Their land extends to the top of the Sandia Mountains east of the village, and they lease land to Sandia Peak Tramway, one of the major tourist attractions of Albuquerque.

The narrow plaza, worn concave by moccasined feet, with the rugged crags of the Sandias rising almost from the edge of it, provides a fitting stage for ceremonies they have been faithfully performing for hundreds of years.

San Felipe, 28 miles (45 kilometres) north of Albuquerque. Like other Keres-speaking tribes, the people of San Felipe migrated toward the Rio Grande from the Pajarito Plateau of the Jemez Mountains about 600 years ago. First they built a pueblo on a volcanic bluff overlooking the river, but in the early 1700s established themselves at the present site on the river, where they raise hay, corn, grain and fruits. The plaza has been worn several feet deep by dancing feet over more than 200 years.

San Felipe is one of the most conservative of pueblos, and does not permit photography of any kind at any time. The mission church may be seen only during services.

Pueblo Indian pottery.

San Ildefonso, 24 miles (39 kilometres) northwest of Santa Fe. This pueblo has won enduring fame through the work of the potter, Maria, and her husband, Julian. The tradition of making the matte-black and burnished ware that is simple and classic in form and design, as well as other fine pottery, continues at San Ildefonso.

Like all pueblos, it is basically an agricultural community, but since World War II, many have found work in the scientific community of Los Alamos as well as Santa Fe.

After the Pueblo Revolt of 1680, San Ildefonso was the last of the pueblos to submit to reconquest by the Spaniards. When the Spaniards marched on the pueblo, the people retreated to the top of Black Mesa. For four years they held out before they accepted the return of the Spaniards. Tewa is the Indian language spoken here.

San Juan, five miles (eight kilometres) north of Española or 29 miles (47 kilometres) north of Santa Fe.

In 1598, Don Juan de Oñate chose this large Tewa-speaking pueblo near the confluence of the Rio Grande and Chama rivers as the site of his colonial headquarters. This was the first capital established by Europeans in the continental United States, predating Jamestown by a decade. In 1610, one year after the English colonists arrived at Jamestown, the capital was moved to Santa Fe. Today, only a cross atop an unexcavated mound marks the original settlement. It is across the river from the present pueblo.

San Juan potters make good brown and red pottery with traditional symbols incised into the surface. In recent years, San Juan joined with other pueblos to form the Eight Northern Indian Pueblos Council (ENIPC), which promotes economic, educational and cultural advantages for its members. Each year an arts and crafts festival held at one of the member pueblos has brought recognition and rewards to their artists. ENIPC headquarters are at San Juan.

Santa Ana, 30 miles (48 kilometres) northwest of Albuquerque. Travelers on NM 44, 12 miles (19 kilometres) west of Bernalillo, can look across an often-dry stream bed and see the old pueblo of Santa Ana on a barren headland. The road leading to the pueblo is closed except on their feast day or other special days of celebration. Most of the people of Santa Ana live in farming communities along the river west of Bernalillo, but they return to the old pueblo for special events.

In the past Santa Ana was known for its traditional polychrome pottery, but it almost became a lost art. One remaining fine potter, however, taught the craft to a number of younger Santa Ana women, and a cooperative association was formed to market their work and that of other Santa Ana craftsmen.

Coronado State Monument (see *Monuments*), across the river from the farm lands of Santa Ana, preserves ruins of the ancient pueblo of Kuaua, said by the Santa Ana Indians to be their ancestral home. They speak the Keres language.

Santa Clara, two miles (three kilometres) south of Española. The people of Santa Clara migrated from the caves and cliffs of the Pajarito Plateau in the Jemez Mountains probably about the 13th century, to settle in the fertile valley of the Rio Grande. There they built a large and prosperous village, but each year on the last weekend in July, they return to the mesa top at Puye Cliffs where the tribe once lived. Cliff dwellings pock the face of the cliff, and ruins of an unexcavated pueblo are on top of the mesa. For two days, dance teams from Santa Clara and other pueblos perform dances and sell their crafts. The event is open to the public and photography is permitted for a moderate fee. The road to Puye follows Santa Clara Creek into the mountains, where the tribe operates four forest campgrounds and a fishing lake. A visitor center is open during the summer at the mouth of the canyon where fees are paid. Tewa is the tribe's Indian language.

Several outstanding potters belong to the Santa Clara tribe. The pottery is a polished red or black ware, often with intricately carved designs.

Santo Domingo, 31 miles (50 kilometres) southwest of Santa Fe or 39 miles (63 kilometres) north of Albuquerque.

During the early years of Spanish occupation in New Mexico, Santo Domingo was ecclesiastical headquarters of the province. From here Franciscan priests were sent out to serve the scattered pueblos, and during the Pueblo Revolt most of them were slain. Santo Domingo is a large Keresan pueblo and one of the most conservative, placing great emphasis on religious and ceremonial observances.

Santo Domingo craftsmen are most noted for their jewelry, particularly heishi — small, round-cut shells polished to a silky smoothness. They also love to trade, and among the sidewalk

merchants under the portal in Santa Fe and Old Town in Albuquerque are many Santo Domingo Indians.

Taos, two miles (three kilometres) north of Taos.
People in other states may not know where New Mexico is,
but they all know about Taos. This most photographed and visited of all pueblos offers visitors two large multistoried pueblos
facing each other across a large plaza bisected by a clear stream.
Modern plumbing and electricity are forbidden in the old part
of the pueblo, and any day Taos Indians can be seen going
toward the stream with a bucket or two. Rio Pueblo flows from
the high mountains east of the pueblo where the people of Taos
return each year to their sacred Blue Lake for special private
ceremonies. At a 7,000-foot (2,134-metre) elevation, the air is
always crisp and clear at Taos, and the sunlight is almost white
in its intensity. Blanket-draped Taos men, standing silently on
the rooftops of the pueblo, make a picture never forgotten. In
the past most Pueblo Indians built their communal villages four
and five stories high, but Taos is the only one remaining of that
height. The language of Taos is Tiwa.

During the days of Spanish and Mexican domination, Taos
marked the northern frontier of the province. Every year there
were one or two trade fairs where Spanish soldiers, settlers and
Pueblo Indians came to trade with the Plains Indians and American and French trappers. From that long contact with the Plains
Indians, the people of Taos adopted some of their characteristics and customs — long braids, beaded leather goods, and
blankets worn draped around their heads and shoulders. Potters
produce a good utilitarian red-brown micaceous pottery. Except
on certain feast days, photography is permitted. A visitor center
at the entrance to the plaza issues permits and collects fees.

Tesuque, 10 miles (16 kilometres) north of Santa Fe.
A mission church and adobe houses, some two stories high,
surround the plaza of this small Tewa-speaking pueblo. Tesuque
potters have produced a whimsical, brightly painted, unfired
pottery for the tourist trade for many years, but they also have
a few potters who make beautiful traditional pots in red and
gray-brown with figures of lizards, frogs and other animals
molded to them. The pots are decorated with traditional symbols. Tesuque is primarily an agricultural community, but many
of the people work in nearby towns. Near the Camel Rock landmark, on US 84/285 north of Santa Fe, Tesuque Pueblo operates

a public campground as a means of economic development in the tourist industry.

Zia, 36 miles (58 kilometres) northwest of Albuquerque. During Spanish colonial times, Zia was one of the largest and most important of the Keres-speaking Rio Grande pueblos. Today it is a small village situated on a volcanic mesa overlooking a few small orchards and farms. Most of their land is more suitable for grazing than for farming. From a few miles away, the mud-plastered houses hardly seem to be there, so well camouflaged are they atop the rocky bluff where the people settled about 650 years ago when they came down from the Jemez Mountains. Zia pottery is sought by collectors. It is usually earth tones, painted in stylized floral patterns, deer and birds, so distinctive it is always recognizable.

Pueblo Indian Cloud Dance.

Zuni, 39 miles (63 kilometres) south of Gallup. Separated by more than 100 miles (160 kilometres) from the pueblos of the Rio Grande, Zuni has the largest population of all and speaks a distinctly different language — Zunian. This was the first New Mexico pueblo seen by Coronado's expedition in 1540, when a brief battle subdued the pueblo. The pueblo people had killed one of the advance guard, and Coronado intended to establish his authority quickly.

Because of its isolated position, Zuni was one of the last pueblos converted to Catholicism by the Franciscans. Our Lady of Guadalupe mission church has been recently restored from almost total ruin to one of the most beautiful mission churches in New Mexico (see *Missions and Churches*). Large figures from Zuni religion are painted on the interior walls above the stations of the cross. Viga ceilings, brick floors, embroidered altar cloth, weaving, a mosaic of the saint, and buffalo heads are a strange but compatible combination of Indian and Spanish church decorations.

Zuni silversmiths are famous for their superb craftsmanship. Their jewelry is sold in several cooperatives on the reservation. Some traditional Zuni pottery is also available.

The Zunis have recently organized a tourist department to stimulate the industry on their reservation. Well-informed guides take visitors to see the newly restored church, the murals and the ruins of an older pueblo they hope to restore. This older pueblo is probably the one they were living in when Coronado came in 1540. The guides will also take interested persons to see outstanding examples of rock art, both petroglyphs and pictographs. There is no fee for this guide service, but contributions will greatly assist them in developing their tourist and restoration program.

The tribe also maintains a good campground with all facilities at Black Rock Lake near the junction of NM 32 and 53, about three miles (five kilometres) east of the pueblo.

PUEBLO INDIAN CALENDAR

Pueblo Indian dances are religious, performed usually for ceremonial purposes. Visitors are permitted to attend many of them, but in almost all cases photography, recording, taping and sketching are absolutely forbidden. The only safe thing to do is to inquire at the office of each pueblo governor. Even better, leave your camera at home, go with a smile on your face and a sincere interest in your mind, and you will have a rare experience. Some ceremonials are solemn occasions with deep religious significance, others are social, but even social dances benefit the performers and observers. Remember, these dances are not being presented for visitors. They are done for the benefit and pleasure of the Indians themselves, who are gracious enough to let outsiders attend.

Following is a calendar of fiestas and ceremonials performed by Pueblo Indians. Those indicated with an asterisk (*) are feast days, when the dance is almost sure to take place. Other dances may be changed without notice. On the other hand, you may visit a pueblo sometime and be surprised to find an unannounced dance taking place. If you arrive and are told the pueblo is closed to visitors, leave at once.

Buffalo dancer.

JANUARY

1	*Most pueblos:* New Year's Day. Various dances. Contact pueblo offices.
2	*Most pueblos:* Installation of pueblo governors. Various dances. Contact pueblo offices.
*22, 23	*San Ildefonso Pueblo:* Annual San Ildefonso Feast Day. Buffalo and Comanche dances. Vesper procession and Buffalo dance on 22nd.
25	*Picuris Pueblo:* St. Paul's Day. Dance announced near the date.

FEBRUARY

2	*San Felipe, Santo Domingo, Picuris pueblos:* Candelaria Day. Buffalo and various other dances.

MARCH

*19	*Laguna Pueblo:* St. Joseph's Day. Harvest and Social dances. Old Laguna village.

EASTER

San Ildefonso, San Felipe, Santa Ana, Santo Domingo, Santa Clara, Cochiti, others: Spring Corn, Basket, various dances.

MAY

* 1	*San Felipe Pueblo:* Annual San Felipe Feast Day. Green Corn dance.
3	*Taos Pueblo:* Santa Cruz Day. Green Corn dance and children's races.
3	*Cochiti Pueblo:* Coming of the Rivermen. Corn dance.

JUNE

*13	*Sandia Pueblo:* Annual San Antonio Feast Day. Corn dance. Other pueblos also observe San Antonio's Day, e.g.: San Ildefonso, San Juan, Taos, Picuris, Santa Clara: Corn dance.
*23, 24	*San Juan Pueblo:* Annual San Juan Feast Day. Vesper Buffalo dance on 23rd; Comanche dance on 24th.

24	*Taos Pueblo:* San Juan's Day. Corn dance.
24	*Cochiti Pueblo:* San Juan's Day. Grab Day.
29	*San Felipe, Santa Ana, Santo Domingo pueblos:* San Pedro's Day. Corn dance.

JULY

4	*Nambe Pueblo:* Waterfall Ceremonial. Various dances. Photography permitted. Fees charged.
*14	*Cochiti Pueblo:* Annual San Buenaventura Feast Day. Corn dance.
3rd Weekend	*A Northern Pueblo:* Eight Northern Pueblos Artists and Craftsmen Show. Dancers, food booths. Photography permitted for a fee.
25	*Acoma, Cochiti, Laguna, San Felipe, Santo Domingo pueblos:* Santiago's Day. Grab Day.
25	*Taos Pueblo:* Santiago's Day. Corn dance.
*26	*Santa Ana Pueblo:* Annual Santa Ana Feast Day. Corn dance.
26	*Taos Pueblo:* Santa Ana's Day. Corn dance.
Last Weekend	*Santa Clara Pueblo:* Puye Cliff Ceremonial. Various dances, food, arts and crafts. Photography permitted. Fees charged.

AUGUST

2	*Jemez Pueblo:* Old Pecos Bull dance. Morning. Celebration for those from former Pecos Pueblo.
*4	*Santo Domingo Pueblo:* Annual Santo Domingo Feast Day. Corn dance.
*9, 10	*Picuris Pueblo:* Annual San Lorenzo Feast Day. Sunset dance on 9th; dances and foot races on 10th.
2nd Weekend	*Gallup:* Intertribal Indian Ceremonial. Dances, arts and crafts exhibit, rodeo. Thurs.-Sun. Red Rock State Park.
10	*Acoma Pueblo:* San Lorenzo's Day. Corn dance. Acomita Village.
10	*Laguna Pueblo (all villages) & Cochiti Pueblo:* San Lorenzo's Day. Grab Day.
*12	*Santa Clara Pueblo:* Annual Santa Clara Feast Day. Corn, Harvest, Buffalo or Comanche dances.
*15	*Zia Pueblo:* Annual Our Lady of Assumption

	Feast Day. Corn dance.
15	*Laguna Pueblo:* San Antonio's Day. Harvest and Social dances. Mesita village.
3rd Weekend	*Santa Fe:* Indian Market. High-quality Indian arts and crafts for sale and show. Santa Fe Plaza.
4th Weekend	*Zuni Pueblo:* Zuni Tribal Fair. Parade, rodeo, dances. Thurs.-Sun.
28	*Isleta Pueblo:* San Agustin Fiesta. Spanish fiesta, carnival, concessions. No dances.

SEPTEMBER

* 2	*Acoma Pueblo:* Annual San Esteban Feast Day. Harvest dance.
* 4	*Isleta Pueblo:* Annual San Agustin Feast Day. Harvest dance.
8	*Laguna Pueblo:* Nativity of the Virgin Mary Day. Harvest and Social dances. Encinal Village.
8	*San Ildefonso Pueblo:* Harvest dance.
*19	*Laguna Pueblo:* Annual San Jose Feast Day. Eagle, Buffalo, Corn dances. Carnival. Old Laguna Village.
*25	*Laguna Pueblo:* Annual St. Elizabeth Feast Day. Harvest and Social dances. Paguate Village.
*29-30	*Taos Pueblo:* Annual San Geronimo Feast Day. Sundown dance on 29th; War and other dances, ceremonial races and pole climbing, trade fair on 30th.

OCTOBER

* 4	*Nambe Pueblo:* Annual San Francisco Feast Day. Elk or other dance.
17	*Laguna Pueblo:* St. Mary Margaret's Day. Harvest and Social dances. Paraje Village.

NOVEMBER

*12	*Jemez Pueblo:* Annual San Diego Feast Day. Corn dance.
*12	*Tesuque Pueblo:* Annual San Diego Feast Day. Buffalo, Deer, Flag or Comanche dance.
Late Nov. or early Dec.	*Zuni Pueblo:* Shalako ceremonial.

DECEMBER

*12   *Jemez Pueblo:* Our Lady of Guadalupe's Day. Matachines dance.

*12   *Pojoaque Pueblo:* Annual Our Lady of Guadalupe Feast Day. Comanche, Buffalo or Bow and Arrow dance.

25   *Various pueblos:* Christmas Celebration. Dances presented change from time to time. Possibilities are: *Picuris, San Ildefonso, San Juan, Santa Clara:* Matachines dance.
Taos: Matachines or Deer dance.
Cochiti and Jemez: Buffalo dance.
Santa Ana: Bow and Arrow — varies.
San Felipe, Santo Domingo: Wide variety of dances.

26   *San Juan Pueblo:* Turtle dance.

31   *Sandia Pueblo:* Deer dance.

Navajo weavers.

New Mexico Travel Division

APACHE AND NAVAJO INDIANS

Apache Indians

The Mescalero Apache Indians live on a reservation of 460,000 acres (186,159 hectares) in the Sacramento Mountains of south-central New Mexico. High mountain meadows and lush valleys offer fine grazing land for cattle and horses, which, with lumbering and tourism, are major industries on the reservation.

The Mescaleros have a federal charter, essentially the same as a federal corporation. They elect a council of men and women who operate under a constitution and by-laws.

Tourism flourishes on this reservation. Sierra Blanca Ski Area (see *Winter Sports*) is owned and operated by the Mescaleros, who also own a new luxury resort hotel three miles (five kilometres) south of Ruidoso. Shuttle buses carry guests to the Ruidoso Downs race track during the summer and to the ski slopes during the winter. The tribe also operates three campgrounds in its forest lands and offers fishing, boating, hiking trails and horseback riding.

Over the Fourth of July holiday each year Mescalero holds a four-day celebration at the rodeo grounds in the town of Mescalero where the dramatic Mountain Spirit Dance is performed at night around a large bonfire. Dancers' faces are covered with black masks, headdresses extend high above their heads. This is a puberty rite for young maidens, and non-Indians are not permitted to watch the entire ceremony. They can, however, attend the rodeo and watch the dance and a portion of the other ceremonies.

There is only one town on the reservation, the village of Mescalero, where tribal headquarters are located. The rest of the tribe lives in homes scattered through the mountains and valleys.

The Jicarilla Apache Indians live on a 750,000-acre (303,520-hectare) reservation in northwestern New Mexico, comprised mostly of high plateaus and mountains. Tribal headquarters are at the town of Dulce on US 64 between Chama and Farmington. Cattle and sheep ranching and oil leases are the major industries of the Jicarillas, but tourism is also important. A modern lodge at Stone Lake caters to guests who come to fish and boat at the lake, or to go on guided hunts for elk, deer, bear, wild turkey and waterfowl on the reservation.

The tribe operates campgrounds at Dulce and Mundo lakes, both good trout waters in scenic settings of rolling hills, piñon pine and spruce forests.

Stone Lake is the scene every September 14 and 15 of an annual celebration with races, dances and a rodeo. True to their nomadic ancestry, the Jicarillas camp in a large area on the grassy meadows surrounding the lake. Each family builds its own brush shelter or raises a tepee. Throughout the night, bonfires flicker from the hillsides and drums throb like the tribal heartbeat. Visitors are welcome, either to camp out or to stay at the lodge or one of the motels in Dulce. Dances, races and contests last most of the night and all the next day. A rodeo with all Indian contestants is held in the afternoon.

The old art of basketmaking is being revived (jicarilla means little basket) in the Dulce High School, and an arts and crafts museum in Dulce has encouraged renewed interest in traditional crafts of leather, beadwork and basketry.

The Jicarilla tribal government operates with an elected council of men and women. Profits from tribal leases for oil and mineral lands and income from other tribal enterprises are distributed on a dividend basis.

Navajo Indians

The Navajos, the largest Indian tribe in America, with more than 150,000 population, live on a reservation that sprawls over 16 million acres (6,475,100 hectares) of Arizona, New Mexico and Utah. The capital, Window Rock, is in Arizona just across the New Mexico border, 28 miles (45 kilometres) northwest of Gallup.

It is a lonely land of high plateaus, deserts, forests, mountains and canyons. Red sandstone pinnacles and buttes punctuate the landscape, sculptured by wind and sand to shapes of fantastic beauty. Most of the land is suited to grazing sheep, goats and a few cattle, an enterprise that fits well with the Navajos' nomadic heritage. Navajo shepherdesses in their bright velveteen blouses and gathered skirts make a dramatic picture against the unforgiving landscape. Irrigation projects now being developed may increase the limited tillable lands. Hogans, eight-sided dwellings of cedar logs mortared with mud, dot the reservation. Many Navajos now build conventional homes in scattered locations, yet there will often be a traditional hogan next to the new house, for ceremonial purposes.

Like the Apaches, the Navajos, who also speak an Athabascan language, migrated into the Southwest at about the same time the Spaniards came up from the south, or perhaps a century or two earlier. For many years these fierce nomads roamed the country, taking harvests and captives from Pueblo Indians and Spaniards. After the Civil War they were incarcerated at Bosque Redondo (see *Fort Sumner*).

The Navajo Nation holds democratic elections for judges and other tribal officers. They elect more than 70 men and women to represent the different areas of the reservation (called chapters) on the tribal council. Several Navajo men have served in the New Mexico Legislature since 1964.

Like other Indians, the Navajos want their children to be educated and want to bring economic development to the reservation. They have built sawmills, motels, restaurants, stores, shopping centers. Rich deposits of coal, gas, uranium, helium and oil have been discovered on their land, and they lease huge tracts to companies already engaged in those businesses. Income from these tribal enterprises provides money for education, and a Navajo Community College has been built at Tsaile.

Navajo rugs and silversmithing have been outstanding crafts for a hundred years. Fine rugs and jewelry are still made, but by fewer artists. They can make more money at other jobs. The Crownpoint Rug Weavers Guild holds periodic Navajo rug auctions at the Crownpoint Elementary School.

Navajo ceremonials are most often chants or curing ceremonies that may last several days and nights and are often in remote areas of the reservation. The Navajo Tribal Fair is usually in September at Window Rock. Several tribal parks, campgrounds and fishing lakes are owned and operated by the Navajos.

Three other small Navajo reservations are located in New Mexico. The Alamo Reservation is near Magdalena, Ramah near Zuni, and Cañoncito adjoins the Laguna Reservation west of Albuquerque .

SUMMER SPORTS

Rafting the Rio Grande.

In a land where the sun shines nearly every day, where white clouds sail in a turquoise sky, where clear streams cascade down mountainsides, where tall pines and aspens shade miles of trails — people spend a great deal of time outdoors. New Mexico is a land like that, and summer sports of all kinds await the visitor who enjoys them.

The national forests are prime areas for backpacking, camping and hiking (see *Forest Lands*). Visitors will find campsites and fishing on Indian reservations (see *Native Americans*) and state and national parks (see *Parks* and *Monuments*).

Lakes and streams have a large variety of fish, and are stocked with trout and salmon by the Department of Game and Fish (see *Fishing and Hunting*).

River running on the Rio Grande and Rio Chama can be a never-to-be forgotten thrill in spring and early summer when the water runs high. Sporting goods stores in Albuquerque, Santa Fe, Española and Taos can furnish information about river trips. And chambers of commerce in those towns usually can provide names of river-trip operators.

Mountain climbers can learn about places to climb from sporting goods stores and from local mountaineering clubs, Sierra Club offices, and the National Forest Service. There are peaks higher than 10,000 feet in all of New Mexico's mountain ranges.

Stables, guest ranches and working ranches that offer trail rides and horse rentals by the hour may be found in the telephone directory yellow pages.

Public facilities for swimming and playing golf and tennis are readily located through city recreation departments and chambers of commerce. Most resorts have fine swimming pools and tennis courts for guests, and a few racquet clubs admit temporary members, as do some golf and country clubs. A few resorts have golf courses.

Bicycling is prohibited on the interstate highways, but cyclists can find good wheeling on side roads, riding single file. Designated roads and trails in national forests, wildlife refuges and state parks are also possibilities. State and national monuments and national parks do not allow bicycling. Many towns have bicycle and roller skate rental shops.

New Mexico's people are sports minded, and most larger towns — and even some smaller ones — have good facilities.

WINTER SPORTS

It's the altitude that makes the difference. Although New Mexico is in the Sunbelt, the whole state is high country. The lowest point, south of Carlsbad, is about 3,000 feet (914 metres) in altitude. From there, the landscape goes up, up, up — to more than 13,000 feet (4,000 metres).

The mountainous areas give New Mexico the terrain for alpine and cross-country skiing, snowshoeing, snowmobiling, ice fishing and ice skating. Since New Mexico is at a southern latitude and has about as much winter sunshine as it is possible to have, winter sports areas have the unique advantage of dry powder snow and clear, crisp days when shirt-sleeve skiing is sometimes possible.

In New Mexico, the powder snow is the kind most places brag about — but don't really have. Here, too, the timberline is higher than in many other ski states — and the trails are protected by stands of fir, pine and aspen.

Outdoor ice skating rinks are to be found in Taos, Las Vegas, Los Alamos, Angel Fire and Red River.

Forest roads and trails, old logging roads and big open meadows provide hundreds of areas ideal for cross-country skiing and snowshoeing. Snowmobiling is great in many of these same areas. Every national forest has several district ranger stations open weekdays from 8:00 a.m. to 5:00 p.m. where rangers can tell you the best places in that area. There are 12 developed ski areas in New Mexico, with another in the planning stage. Following is a chart showing facilities available:

SKI AREAS

	Angel Fire near Eagle Nest 377-2301	Woodlands Ski Basin 754-2941	Red River Ski Area 754-2313	Eagle Creek Ski Area 336-4211	Sandia Peak, Albuquerque 296-9585	Val Verde near Eagle Nest 377-6011
Tram/Gondola					Tram	
Chair lifts	6	2	4	1	3	
T-bars/Pomas		3	2	2	3	2
Base elevation	8,500	8,600	8,750	7,400	8,500	8,300
Summit	10,680	8,750	10,280	7,900	10,360	8,700
Vertical rise	2,180	150	1,530	500	1,660	400
# trails	24	open	36	6	25	12
Beginner (%)	35	75	35	50	10	30
Intermediate (%)	50	25	45	35	80	60
Advanced (%)	15	—	20	15	10	10
Snowfall (inches)	120	145	145	85	130	120

	Santa Fe Ski Basin 983-9155	Sierra Blanca 257-9001 near Ruidoso	Sipapu near Taos 587-2240	Ski Cloudcroft 682-2587	Sugarite, near Raton 445-5000	Taos Ski Valley, 776-2266
Tram/Gondola		Gondola				
Chair lifts	2	6	—	—	1	6
T-bars/Pomas	3	—	3	3	1	1
Base elevation	10,400	9,700	8,200	8,550	8,000	9,207
Summit	12,000	11,400	9,000	9,050	8,800	11,819
Vertical rise	1,600	1,700	800	500	800	2,612
# trails	30	25	15	16	10	23
Beginner (%)	20	40	20	45	30	21
Intermediate (%)	40	40	60	25	50	56
Advanced (%)	40	20	20	30	20	62*
Snowfall (inches)	160	180	100	90	120	330

Area code for entire state is 505.
*Taos trails are both advanced and expert.

Note: Powder Puff Mountain's name has been changed to Woodlands Ski Basin.

Ruidoso Ski Area is now Eagle Creek Ski and Recreation Area.

FISHING

The New Mexico Department of Game and Fish, in co-operation with federal agencies, is responsible for managing the wildlife resources of the state for the propagation of the species, benefit of the natural environment, and for the pleasure of sportsmen and sportswomen.

In the mountain streams and rivers anglers catch rainbow, cutthroat, brown, eastern brook, Dolly Varden, grayling and golden trout and kokanee and coho salmon. In the warmer waters of reservoirs and ponds largemouth black bass, northern pike, white bass, walleye, crappie and catfish are taken. The varied terrain and elevations provide fishing waters for all kinds of fishermen — the purists who only dry fly, the bait fishermen or the worm dunkers. Some streams are deep in the wilderness, accessible only by horseback or foot. Many are reached by dirt or graveled forest and county roads, and some are along major highways.

In most cases the season begins April 1 and lasts through the entire year. The Department of Game and Fish sells resident and nonresident licenses for the season, the day, or for five days. The bag limit in most trout streams is eight with a possession limit of 16.

A few trout waters require a special trout stamp, and there are a few cases where the limit varies according to the place and time of year. For instance, there is a special kokanee salmon snagging season at Navajo and El Vado lakes where the bag limit is 24. The San Juan River for two miles (3.2 kilometres) below Navajo Dam is restricted to fly fishing with a limit of four fish 15 inches (37 centimetres) or more in length. Licenses can be purchased at sporting goods stores, concessionaires at lakes, stores near recreation areas, or from the New Mexico Department of Game and Fish (see *Information Sources*). The annual proclamation published by the department lists all special seasons, limits, stamp requirements and all other pertinent information for anglers. You will receive one wherever you buy your license.

Several Indian reservations have fishing streams and lakes within their boundaries, and, with the exception of the Mescalero Apache Reservation, a state license is required in addition to the Indian permit. Inquire at the tribal governor's office, or at the tribal office of tourism or recreation (see *Native Americans*).

HUNTING

There is as wide a choice in hunting as in fishing in New Mexico. Javelina inhabit the arid mountains and deserts of the southwestern part of the state; antelope are on the high plains; deer, bear and cougar are in the mountains and foothills in all parts of the state; elk live in the higher mountains; Barbary sheep are hunted in the colorful canyon country of the Canadian River; bighorn sheep in the Sangre de Cristo, Gila and San Andres mountains. Oryx and ibex are hunted in the deserts and mountains of south-central New Mexico under a special exotic game program of the Department of Game and Fish.

There are seasons on such game birds as wild turkey, dove, quail, pheasant, prairie chicken, and the many kinds of waterfowl that follow the Rio Grande Flyway and spend part of the year at the several wildlife refuges in the state.

Five Indian tribes permit hunting on their lands, but a special permit must be obtained. Deer, turkey, elk, bear, cougar and antelope are hunted on the Jicarilla Apache Reservation; deer, bear, cougar and turkey on the Navajo; deer, turkey and cougar on Zuni lands; deer and elk on the Jemez Reservation; and deer, turkey, elk, antelope and bear on the Mescalero Apache reservation. A state license is not needed for the Mescalero Reservation, but a tribal permit is required.

More than 300 vendors around the state sell licenses and have proclamations explaining all rules, regulations, maps, special seasons, fees and exceptions to general rules. The proclamations may also be obtained through the New Mexico Department of Game and Fish (see *Information Sources*).

All hunters under 18 years of age must take an approved hunter training course (New Mexico's or another state's), and must carry certification cards while hunting, even if accompanied by a parent or guardian.

ROCKHOUNDING

New Mexico is a rockhounder's heaven. The state has a larger variety — 440 — of minerals for collectors to look for than any other state except California, which has 520.

The visitor who wants to get a good perspective on rockhounding might start at the Mineralogical Museum at the New Mexico State Bureau of Mines and Mineral Resources in Socorro. The museum, on the New Mexico Institute of Mining & Technology campus, is open to everyone, free of charge, from 8:00 a.m. to 7:00 p.m., every Monday through Friday. More than 9,300 mineralogical specimens are on display, about a third of them from New Mexico.

There's a piece of smithsonite there that's 18 inches (one-half metre) across, from Kelly, a ghost town two miles (3.2 kilometres) south of Magdalena. It's blue-green from copper impurities in it and is probably the finest piece of smithsonite (a pale white zinc carbonate used in paints) in the world.

Kelly, which was famous for its zinc, lead and silver mines, is part of the Magdalena Mining District in west-central Socorro County.

For the most part, owners of the mines there don't allow collecting. The area is dangerous, with a lot of open shafts. But Bill Dobson, who owns a rock shop in Magdalena, owns a mine dump in Kelly, and sometimes he lets his customers collect there.

However, there are a couple of other areas in New Mexico that encourage collecting: the University of New Mexico's *Harding Pegmatite and Iceland Spar Mines.* Both are located in the Picuris district in southern Taos County. Permission must, of course, be first obtained.

Both mines are around four miles (6.4 kilometres) west of Picuris Pueblo. A half-mile (.8-kilometre) dirt road heads south of NM 75 to a small parking lot north of the Harding Pegmatite Mine. Visitors can then take a self-guided tour of its prospecting pits, quarry and dumps, and the open-pit Iceland Spar Mine, a hundred yards (91 metres) to the southwest.

Both mines were active during the first half of the century. The former had produced such rare minerals as lepidolite (a transparent lithium mica used in enamels, glazes and heat-resistant glass) and microlite (a radio-active calcium tantalite used in acid-resistant chemical equipment). During 1950-55, the mines also produced 20 percent of this country's beryl, a white beryllium silicate whose extreme hardness strengthened copper. The latter even distinguished itself, producing the second and third largest crystals of Iceland Spar (an optical-grade calcite) ever found. One crystal measured 720 cubic feet (22 cubic metres), the other, 616 (18 cubic metres).

Lepidolite, microlite and semiprecious aquamarine (a form of beryl) aren't the only minerals awaiting rockhounds here. There are some really good samples of rose muscovite (a pale red potassium lithium mica), the blue-green variety of fluorescent apatite (a calcium fluoride phosphate used in water softening) and two semiprecious minerals, feldspar (a predominantly white aluminum silicate) and spodumene (a pinkish-white lithium silicate).

Another rockhound area near this district is **Hondo Canyon.** Brown staurolite crystals can be found in the dirt and gravel, and on the slopes in schist (a coarse-grained metamorphic rock). Some of the crystals are an inch and a half in diameter.

The Petaca District in extreme eastern Rio Arriba County is another favorite locale in northern New Mexico. The district, a 10-square-mile (26-square-kilometre) area, starts 4½ miles (7 kilometres) due north of La Madera. Clustered among its ponderosa pine-covered canyons are more than 60 mines. NM 519, a nine-mile (14.5-kilometre) all-weather link to Petaca, leads to a half dozen forest roads climbing westward to the mines.

Just 3½ miles (5.6 kilometres) out of La Madera is the road to Cañon de Los Alamos. In Petaca itself is the road to Cañon de La Jarita. Two miles (3.2 kilometres) up the former are the Red and White Mines; seven miles (11 kilometres) up the latter is a place known as Big Rock (about a mile southwest of the promontory of the same name).

There are some very good samples of muscovite at the Red and White and some semiprecious red garnets (a brittle, almost transparent silicate), green fluorite (an eliminator of impurities in steel smelting), and a couple of radioactive minerals, black columbite (a platey iron-manganese oxide) and brownish-black samarskite (a rare-earth mineral).

Around Big Rock are blades of blue kyanite (an aluminum silicate used in ceramics and spark plug insulation) up to seven inches (16 centimetres) in length.

Other spots suggested by Robert North of the New Mexico

Bureau of Mines and Mineral Resources are:

Pueblo Creek Campground, 18 miles (29 kilometres) southwest of Reserve in Catron County, via NM 12, US 180 and a seven-mile (11-kilometre) forest road. Labradorite (a yellowish-tinged, almost transparent semiprecious feldspar) and white zeolites (a group of hydrous silicates used in water-softeners).

Mule Creek, 55 miles (88.5 kilometres) northwest of Silver City on US 180 and NM 78, in Grant County. Semiprecious obsidian (a lustrous, black volcanic glass often called Apache Tears). They're everywhere along the state highway in creek washes, within the right-of-way.

Red Rock Game Reserve, 26 miles (41.8 kilometres) north of Lordsburg on NM 464, also in Grant County. Green serpentine (a banded serpentine endemic to this particular location) is found on the game reserve two miles (3.2 kilometres) northeast of town. There's a chain across the road, and the walk is about two miles (3.2 kilometres). You have to ask the game warden there for permission. Serpentine samples are also found in creek washes just outside the reserve.

Round Mountain in the Black Range Primitive Area, about 10 aerial miles (16 kilometres) east-southeast of Wall Lake, and about five miles (8 kilometres) inside Sierra County. Black bixbyite (a shiny, cubed manganese oxide) and semiprecious topaz (a brownish-pink aluminum silicate of quartz). Difficult; it's only for the hard-core. It's about a 12-mile (19-kilometre) hike up the mountain from the nearest paved road. A permit from the (Beaverhead) ranger station seven miles (11 kilometres) north of Wall Lake is necessary.

Kilbourne Hole, an extinct volcano 18 miles (29 kilometres) west of La Union in Doña Ana County. Two semiprecious green minerals, augite (a pyroxene) and peridot (an iron-magnesium silicate). It's on BLM (Bureau of Land Management) land. There's a dirt road across the desert, but Kilbourne is not easy to find. Buy a county map first in Las Cruces.

The Pecos River Valley. From Fort Sumner in De Baca County, southward for 160 miles (257 kilometres) to Carlsbad in Eddy County, quartz crystals known as "Pecos Diamonds" lie among its river gravels.

Rock Hound State Park (see *Parks and Monuments*), south of Deming, is famous because this is one place where amateur rockhounds are permitted to pick up samples to take home.

Jasper and thundereggs are to be found.

Agate and petrified wood can be found all over the state, particularly along the western half. Good places to look are in the Carrizozo area, the Deming area, along the Rio Puerco north of Belen, and in the area between Santa Rosa and Fort Sumner.

Brown staurolite crystals — sometimes called fairy crosses — are often found in the gravel along the Rio Grande in Hondo Canyon, near Pilar.

For even more rewarding fun, there's always gold panning. Take a pan to the Rio Grande north of Embudo and maybe you, too, will hit paydirt. Others swear by the Pecos River near Terrero, and sections of Bear Creek near Pinos Altos, north of Silver City.

Maps of national forests and wildernesses may be bought from the National Forest Service. Other maps are available from the Bureau of Land Management. Information about Rock Hound State Park may be had from the New Mexico State Parks & Recreation Commission. For addresses, see *Information Sources.*

For permission to visit, and information about, the Harding Pegmatite and Iceland Spar Mines, write the Chairman, Department of Geology, University of New Mexico, Albuquerque 87131 (505) 277-4204. You'll get two copies of a liability release. Sign both, remit one by mail and retain the other on your person when you visit the mines. Children may visit when accompanied by an adult. But the shafts are forbidden to everyone.

For informat on about rockhounding in specific areas of New Mexico, contact any of the rockhound clubs. The chambers of commerce or rock shops usually have the names of local clubs.

But wherever you go in the state, and whatever you're looking for, do not go on private land without asking the owner's permission. Take nothing at all from state or national parks or monuments (with the notable exception of Rock Hound State Park), and be careful that you are not on someone's claim.

PARKS AND MONUMENTS

Chaco Canyon National Monument.

Within the boundaries of New Mexico are 38 state parks, nine state monuments, one national park and 10 national monuments.

State parks are primarily recreation sites with facilities for picnicking; most have campsites and hiking trails, some are lakes where fishing, boating and other water sports are available. Some park sites are chosen for their scenic beauty, some for historical or geological interest.

State monuments, which are managed by the Museum of New Mexico, are established to preserve historical or archeological points of interest. Most have museums.

National monuments designate sites of national importance in the history and prehistory of this country, or geological areas where nature's capricious hand has created wonderlands of surprising diversity.

National parks set aside natural landmarks that are unique areas of transcendent beauty and wonder.

Your travels in New Mexico will be enriched by visiting these places where you may enjoy strenuous or passive recreation, or where you can ponder man's development through the centuries.

In addition to parks and monuments, millions of acres of New Mexico's mountains are set aside in national forests where you may picnic, camp, hike, fish and hunt, and in wilderness areas where you may enter only on foot or horseback to experience the primeval beauty of land that has never known the destructive touch of the machine.

The camping fee in all state parks is $3.00 a night or $36.00 for an annual permit. Electrical and sewage hook-ups, where available, cost an additional $1.00 each. There is a 14-day camping limit at parks and monuments. For further details about each park, see the city or town it is near.

STATE PARKS

	Camping	Shelters	Electricity	Showers	Dump Station	Boating	Boat ramp	Boat marina	Boat rental	Fishing	Water skiing	Swimming	Playgrounds	Hotel/lodge	Restaurant	Airport
Belen Valley at Belen										•						
Bluewater Lake 28 mi. w/Grants	•	•		•	•	•	•	•	•	•	•	•	•		•	
Bottomless Lakes 16 mi. se/Roswell	•	•	•	•		•			•	•			•		•	•
Caballo Lake 18 mi. n/Hatch	•	•	•	•		•	•	•	•	•	•	•	•			
Chicosa Lake 9 mi. ne/Roy	•	•			•								•			
Cimarron Canyon 15 mi. w/Cimarron	•									•						
City of Rocks 28 mi. ne/Deming	•			•									•			
Clayton Lake 15 mi. n/Clayton	•	•		•		•	•			•			•			
Conchas Lake 34 mi. nw/Tucumcari	•	•	•		•	•	•	•	•	•	•	•	•	•	•	•
Coronado at Bernalillo	•	•	•	•	•					•						
Coyote Creek 14 mi. n/Mora	•	•		•						•			•			
Elephant Butte 7 mi. n/T or C	•	•	•	•		•	•	•	•	•	•	•	•	•	•	•
El Vado Lake 26 mi. sw/Chama	•	•				•	•	•		•	•	•		•	•	•
Heron Lake 15 mi. sw/Chama	•		•		•	•	•	•		•		•				
Hyde Park 12 mi. ne/Santa Fe	•	•	•		•								•			
Indian Petroglyph Albuquerque		•														
Kit Carson Taos		•											•			
Lea County 6 mi. nw/Hobbs	•	•	•	•	•											
Leasburg 15 mi. n/Las Cruces	•	•	•	•	•	•				•			•			
Living Desert Carlsbad																

All state parks have picnicking facilities, drinking water and hiking trails or nature walks; all but Santa Fe River have toilet facilities.

	Camping	Shelters	Electricity	Showers	Dump Station	Boating	Boat ramp	Boat marina	Boat rental	Fishing	Water skiing	Swimming	Playgrounds	Hotel/lodge	Restaurant	Airport
Manzano Mountains 13 mi.nw/Mountainair	●	●			●											
Morphy Lake 11 mi. sw/Mora	●					●				●						
Navajo Lake (Pine) 25 mi. e/Bloomfield	●	●	●	●	●	●	●	●	●	●	●		●			●
Navajo Lake (Sims) 25 mi. e/Bloomfield	●	●			●	●	●			●	●	●	●			
Oasis 18 mi. sw/Clovis	●	●	●	●	●					●			●			
Oliver Lee 10 mi. s/Alamogordo	●	●	●	●	●											
Pancho Villa 35 mi. s/Deming	●	●	●	●	●								●			
Percha 21 mi. s/T or C	●	●		●		●				●			●			
Red Rock 10 mi. e/Gallup	●	●	●	●	●								●		●	
Rio Grande 16 mi. sw/Taos	●	●				●				●						
Rock Hound 14 mi. se/Deming	●	●	●	●									●			
San Gabriel Albuquerque	●	●											●			
Santa Fe River Santa Fe										●				●	●	
Santa Rosa 7 mi. n/Santa Rosa	●	●		●	●	●	●			●	●					
Smokey Bear Capitan													●			
Storrie Lake 6 mi. n/Las Vegas	●	●	●	●		●	●			●	●	●	●			
Sumner Lake 16 mi.nw/Ft. Sumner	●	●	●	●	●	●	●			●	●	●				
Ute Lake 3 mi. w/Logan	●	●		●	●	●	●	●	●	●	●	●		●	●	●
Valley of Fires 1 mi. w/Carrizozo	●	●											●			
Villanueva 31 mi. sw/Las Vegas	●	●		●						●			●			

STATE MONUMENTS

Abo State Monument

The impressive ruins of San Gregorio Mission are preserved at Abo, 10 miles (16 kilometres) southwest of Mountainair, off US 60. It is one of the three large missions built by the Franciscan fathers between 1629 and 1675 to serve the Saline Pueblos (see *Gran Quivira*). Constructed sometime between 1629 and 1639, this church is said to have been one of the most beautiful in New Mexico. It is built of the same red sandstone as the church at Quarai (see below). As with Gran Quivira and Quarai, incessant attack by Indians hostile to those resident at Abo finally drove them to seek refuge with their relatives along the Rio Grande.

Coronado State Monument

About 16 miles (25.7 kilometres) north of Albuquerque near the town of Bernalillo, Coronado State Monument encompasses the ruins of a large Tiguex pueblo, possibly the one used by Coronado in 1540-41 as headquarters for his expedition. Two plazas, surrounded by the lower rooms of the pueblo, and several kivas lie on a sandy bluff offering a splendid view of the river and the Sandia Mountains. In one kiva the walls were painted with murals that were carefully removed during excavation. Replicas were painted on the present kiva walls for visitors to see. A museum and visitor center contain exhibits explaining the history of the ruins.

Abo State Monument.

Dorsey Mansion State Historical Monument
The monument is 23 miles (37 kilometres) east of Springer on US 56, then 12 miles (19.3 kilometres) north on a dirt road that is slick when wet. Sitting alone on the empty plains, awash in a sea of tawny grass, this two-story mansion made of stone and square logs is a monument to the fascinating era in New Mexico when the cattle industry came of age.

A military officer in the Civil War, president of both an Ohio tool company and an Arkansas railroad, and a senator from Arkansas — Stephen W. Dorsey came west in 1877 to go into the cattle business. This baronial mansion, with landscaped gardens and surrounded by dozens of stone buildings, served as headquarters for Dorsey's many-thousand-acre cattle ranch until economic conditions, drought and political scandal caught up with him. The mansion is occasionally open to the public during the summer, but it will be several more years before it is completely restored and refurnished. For some visitors an added attraction is the report that the mansion is haunted.

Fort Selden State Monument
Fort Selden, 18 miles (29 kilometres) north of Las Cruces by either I-25 or US 85, was built in 1865 to protect settlers and travelers on the Butterfield and Chihuahua trails, which intersected at La Mesilla, not far to the south. General Douglas MacArthur lived here when he was a child and his father the commanding officer. An excellent museum and an interpretive trail through the ruins make the exciting days of the frontier seem very real at this state monument. Along the Rio Grande less than a mile (1.6 kilometres) away is Leasburg State Park with camping and picnicking facilities.

Fort Sumner State Monument

In 1862, General James E. Carlton supervised the building of Fort Sumner, now a state monument, on the banks of the Pecos River about seven miles (11 kilometres) southeast of the present town. He named the fort in honor of General Edmond Vose Sumner. It was a pleasant location, shaded by big cotton-wood trees and surrounded by grassy, rolling hills. An unwalled fort with flat-roofed adobe buildings, the government built it not to defend against Indians, but to teach them civilized ways. These were the Civil War years, and the army rounded up Navajos and Mescalero Apaches and brought them to Fort Sumner, believing that it would require fewer soldiers to control them.

The attempt to teach these nomadic tribes the finer points of agriculture failed dismally. Poor soil, drought and insects defeated the Indians, who had always been warriors and had no taste for farming. Many Indians died before the experiment ended in 1868. The survivors were released to their newly established reservations in the mountains of south-central New Mexico (Mescaleros) and in the high plateau country of the Four Corners area (Navajos), where they still live.

The fort was abandoned in 1869, and the following year the land baron Lucien Maxwell bought it and lived there until his death. Billy the Kid met his death in the home of Maxwell's nephew, Pete.

A visitor center, museum and interpretive trail mark this very attractive site.

Fort Selden State Monument.

Jemez State Monument

Jemez State Monument preserves the red sandstone walls of San Diego Mission built around 1617, adjoining a convent and pueblo, only part of which has been excavated. The church was built like a fortress, with a tower and high firewall around the roof, giving the occupants a secure vantage point to watch for enemies approaching up the canyon. In the rebellion, the priest at Jemez was killed and the church abandoned. When the Spaniards attempted to reconquer them 12 years later, the Jemez Indians withdrew to the tops of the mesas above the old pueblo, where ruins today still show the sites. Jemez was one of the last pueblos to be reconquered, but the people never reoccupied the old pueblo or used the church again. They settled downstream about 10 miles (16 kilometres) where the canyon widens out into more farm land.

La Mesilla State Monument

Locally called Old Mesilla, this is a historic plaza in a village two miles (3.2 kilometres) south of Las Cruces. Most of the interesting shops and restaurants around the plaza are in buildings of historic significance. The Church of San Albino, built in 1906 to replace an earlier one that burned, dominates one side of the plaza.

The quiet shady plaza today belies its exciting and often violent past. A few miles to the south is the site of the only battle of the Mexican War fought on American soil. No sign of Brazito Battlefield remains, nor is there anything left of Fort Fillmore, built nearby a few years later.

During the 1870s and 1880s, La Mesilla saw more than its share of gunmen. The most famous was Billy the Kid (see *Lincoln*), a small, unimposing young man, captured finally by Sheriff Pat Garrett, a six-foot-four (1.95-metre) buffalo hunter from Las Cruces. Billy the Kid was tried for murder in La Mesilla on May 13, 1881, and sentenced to be hung. The old courthouse building where he was tried is on the corner of the plaza.

Across the street, in an old adobe building that was once an inn and stagecoach stop on the Butterfield Trail, is an interesting native food restaurant. Up the street, another old building houses a steakhouse decorated in elegant Victorian style.

Lincoln State Monument

Lincoln is a good place to get an idea what a real frontier town was like, minus the tall tales and larger-than-life images perpetuated by Western novels and motion pictures. The entire little town is a historic district, where about 50 people live. Visitors are advised to stop first at the Old Courthouse Museum to pick up a walking tour map of the stores and homes and Wortley Hotel where the Lincoln County War actually took place. It is a sleepy little town now, but it is still the same size as when Billy the Kid rode through its streets (see *Lincoln* for more details).

The Palace of the Governors

The Palace of the Governors is both the historical division of the Museum of New Mexico and a state monument. Built in 1610 by the founder of Santa Fe, the Spanish governor Pedro de Peralta, it is the oldest public building in the United States still in continuous use. Once the entire center of the Spanish command north of Mexico, it stretched for two blocks square and encompassed a parade ground.

The building that remains now dominates the north side of Santa Fe Plaza, where the old Santa Fe Trail ended. Inside, the museum maintains excellent exhibits pertaining to the history and culture of New Mexico. Outside, on the long portal that fronts the length of the building, Indian craftsmen sit on blankets selling jewelry and pottery, creating a picturesque scene.

The governments of Spain, a Pueblo Indian alliance, Mexico, the Confederacy and the United States have ruled from this building. Its venerable rooms have witnessed affairs of state conducted by men in ruffles and jewels, in moccasins and fringed leather. While Lew Wallace was governor of the New Mexico Territory, he wrote his famous novel, *Ben Hur,* within these walls.

Quarai State Monument

About nine miles (14.5 kilometres) north of Mountainair on NM 14, Quarai State Monument contains the ruins of magnificent La Purisima Concepcion, built between 1629 and 1639, the second mission church at this pueblo. The walls of the new church were 40 feet (12 metres) high and four and five feet (1.5 metres) thick. The church was 50 by 104 feet (15 by 32 metres) in cruciform. The adjoining convent and pueblo enclosed three plazas and several kivas.

But the strength of the people who built Quarai was nothing against the fierce nomads from the plains who overran them. During excavations, bodies were found in normal, everyday positions, indicating the village was taken by complete surprise and sacked.

Those who escaped over the mountains never came back after that dreadful day, but chose to live with their cousins in the Rio Grande Valley near Socorro. The great church was left to stare eternally heavenward through sightless eyes, its silent red walls and a tangle of wild roses of Castile touched by breezes that whisper of the Cities that Died of Fear (see also *Abo* and *Gran Quivira*).

Palace of the Governors, built 1610.

STATE MONUMENTS

	Picnicking	Toilets	Drinking water	Playgrounds
Abo 10 mi. sw/Mountainair		●		
Coronado Bernalillo	●	●	●	
Dorsey Mansion 35 mo. ne/Springer				
Fort Selden 15 mi. n/Las Cruces		●	●	
Fort Sumner 7 mi. se/Ft. Sumner		●	●	
Jemez 60 mi. nw/Albuquerque		●	●	
La Mesilla 1 mi. sw/Las Cruces			●	●
Lincoln Lincoln		●	●	
Palace of Governors Santa Fe		●	●	
Quarai 9 mi. n/Mountainair	●	●	●	

NATIONAL PARK

Carlsbad Caverns National Park

Carlsbad Caverns National Park, located 20 miles (32 kilometres) southwest of Carlsbad off US 180, contains the largest and most spectacular limestone caverns in the world.

The caverns are open every day of the year. The full, self-guided tour begins at the natural entrance. A comfortable trail — three miles (4.8 kilometres) long if the Big Room perimeter is included — leads past formations of iridescent beauty and subterranean lakes formed by water dripping through the strata of limestone.

Rangers no longer conduct tours through the caverns, and visitors may take the trail at their own pace with individual headphones that supply pertinent information. This system allows more privacy to enjoy the caverns and to comprehend the magnitude and beauty of the formations. The trail ends in the Big Room, a space as large as 14 football fields and as high as a 22-story-building. The Park Service suggests a time of two and one-half to three hours to walk the entire trail — a leisurely pace indeed.

Box lunches are on sale at the Big Room. Visitors may return to the surface on elevators. Those unable to walk the trail may take the elevators down to the Big Room, but unless there is a very limiting physical reason, the experience of walking through the whole underground fantasyland should not be missed.

The visitor center on the surface has dining rooms, shops, nursery and kennel. More than 800,000 people a year visit Carlsbad.

New Cave, a primitive cavern 11 miles (17.7 kilometres) from the main caverns, is open to visitors only on a limited basis. During the summer, the Park Service offers a lantern tour of New Cave, an experience in total darkness and silence seldom available to anyone other than spelunkers. The entrance is reached by steep hike of one mile (1.6 kilometres) up the side of Slaughter Canyon. Reservations must be made in advance at park headquarters, and tours are limited.

In some of the remote caves at Carlsbad, which scientists believe are about 25,500 years old, fossil remains of extinct species of bush oxen, antelope, a cheetah-like cat, mountain goat, dire wolf, shrew, marmot, horse and other animals of the Pleistocene Age have been discovered.

NATIONAL MONUMENTS

Aztec Ruins National Monument
Aztec Ruins National Monument, at Aztec, is one of the major
archeological sites in the Four Corners region, roughly contemporary with Chaco Canyon and Mesa Verde in Colorado.
By the early 1100s Anasazi Indians from scattered villages
along the Animas River began to come together into the great
communal dwellings.

One pueblo at Aztec, built between 1111 and 1115, covered
two acres (.8 hectares), was three stories high and had 500
rooms averaging 10 by 12 feet (3 by 3.6 metres) in size. The
U-shaped building is seven rooms wide at the base and four or
five rooms wide across the wings. During this same period
the early inhabitants began building and using the Great Kivas,
huge ceremonial chambers to accommodate an entire village.
Smaller ones were built for outlying pueblos or individual clans.

A system of irrigation canals, the use of banded masonry
walls, and the pleasing overall design of the large structures
indicate a high degree of engineering and artistic ability,
though they had no metal tools or beasts of burden, and didn't
know what a wheel was. Hardly had they finished these magnificent structures than they began to move away. By the
middle of the 1100s Aztec was abandoned, many of the people
moving east toward the Rio Grande.

Beginning around 1215, for about a century, there were
sharp fluctuations in rainfall west of the Continental Divide, but
around 1225 both Aztec and Chaco Canyon were reoccupied
for about 50 years by people who resembled the Mesa Verde
Indians. At Aztec they used part of the great pueblo and built a
new row of rooms across the plaza. By 1300, Aztec, Chaco
Canyon and Mesa Verde were permanently abandoned.

Aztec National Monument, mistakenly named for the Aztecs
by early settlers, is open all year. Self-guiding trails through
the impressive ruins, a visitor center, museum, films and
other exhibits describe the early people who lived here. Picnic
tables are in a shady park inside the monument and a city-
operated campground is nearby.

Bandelier National Monument

About 20 miles (32 kilometres) from Los Alamos on NM 4, Bandelier National Monument preserves cliff dwellings and the ruins of a large pueblo, both of which were inhabited between AD 1200 and 1500. The prehistoric Indians possibly came from such great centers as Chaco Canyon (see below) during the 1200s.

Here along a secluded mountain stream they found cliffs of soft volcanic ash eroded into hundreds of natural caves where they found shelter. Eventually they built rooms of volcanic rock along the base, and then the large pueblo in the valley. They tilled the meadows along the stream and found game plentiful in the mountains. Eventually they moved again, this time down to the valley of the Rio Grande, where they were when the Spaniards came, and where they are today.

Booklets describing the ruins, history, geology, flora and fauna are available for self-guided walks along the trails, or visitors may take hikes led by naturalists. The visitor center has exhibits, dioramas, films and books on the archeology of the area. Longer overnight trails that require good physical condition — backpacking or horseback packing — go to several major archeological sites in the monument. At head-quarters a shady picnic area is on both sides of the stream, and on the mesa above the cliff dwellings is a national forest campground. A snack bar near the visitor center is open in summer months. The monument is open all year.

Cliff dwellings, Bandelier

Capulin Mountain National Monument

Capulin Mountain National Monument is 38 miles (61 kilometres) northeast of Raton. It is an almost perfectly shaped
volcanic cinder cone. A visitor center and picnic tables are at
the base, and a road winds around the cone to the top where
trails lead around and down into the crater, now overgrown
with chokecherries and other plants and grasses. The cone
rises 1,000 feet (304.8 metres) above the surrounding plains,
and from the top a panoramic view sweeps across miles of
good range land and into Texas, Oklahoma, Kansas
and Colorado.

Chaco Canyon National Monument

Contemporary with Colorado's Mesa Verde, in many ways
rivaling and in some ways surpassing it, was Chaco Canyon,
now a national monument about 60 miles (96.5 kilometres)
south of Farmington (see *Civilizations of New Mexico*). All the
superlatives, "most beautiful masonry," "most beautiful pottery," "highest point of prehistoric culture," "largest single
ruin," "most impressive archeological site," do not exaggerate.

The first inhabitants were descended from Ice Age Man.

By about AD 200 the people had begun to cultivate wild
seeds and grasses to supplement their meat diet, and an agricultural civilization was born. Open campsites became pit
houses, which eventually became stone and adobe structures
above ground. The people learned how to weave baskets,
which led to pottery and the weaving of cloth from wild fibers
and fur. Spears became atlatls and eventually they had bows
and arrows.

As their numbers increased, so did the complexity of their
society. Clans grew from family units; beliefs and customs became religion; a sophisticated form of government evolved.

Most spectacular at Chaco was the flowering of architecture.
Pueblo Bonito, the largest single ruin, contained more than
800 rooms and 32 kivas. Walls were constructed of sandstone,
so finely worked and fitted together that mortar was not always
necessary. Parts of Pueblo Bonito were five stories high. Roof
timbers were cut and dragged from the mountains many miles
away, and raised to the height of the building. All this they did
without beasts of burden, metal tools or knowledge of
the wheel.

There are ruins of more than a dozen major sites, and more than 2,000 other archeological sites within the monument. Excavation and study have revealed ancient roads leading from Chaco like spokes from the hub of a wheel. Copper bells, macaw feathers and shells show they traded with other Indians as far away as central Mexico. Why did they leave such a place? No one knows for sure, but it may have been deforestation, overpopulation, disease, or superstition.

There are several ways to reach Chaco Canyon, all of them bad. It is the oldest national monument in the system (1907), but there is no paved access, which may be just as well. The fragile terrain and ruins could not cope with "Sunday diggers" and target shooters.

Probably the best way to reach Chaco from Farmington is to drive 41 well-paved miles (66 kilometres) on US 64 and NM 44 via Bloomfield to Blanco's Trading Post. Turn south and drive the unpaved 26 miles (41.8 kilometres) on NM 57 to the monument. This road is fairly wide and usually well maintained, but should not be attempted in bad weather.

Where the road drops down into the canyon where the visitor center, campground and most of the ruins are located, is a steep, hairpin turn that is difficult, if not impossible, for trailers longer than 17 feet (5.2 metres).

Another dirt road turns off NM 44 near Nageezi, which is not on the official map. It follows Escobado Wash to join NM 57. It is all right when dry, but has the same trailer problem at the end. The state map shows a dirt road turning off NM 44 at Nageezi, joining one that turns off at Counselors Trading Post. Avoid both of these.

For those approaching from Albuquerque, from the south or east, the best route is to turn off NM 44 just before reaching Cuba on to NM 197, which is paved all the way to the junction with NM 57, a distance of 100 miles (160.9 kilometres) from Cuba to Chaco, the last 20 of which are not paved.

Travelers on I-40 may turn north at Thoreau between Gallup and Grants and take NM 57 to Chaco, a total of 68 miles (109.4 kilometres), the last 20 (32 kilometres) unpaved.

The campground at Chaco has fireplaces, restrooms, running water and dump stations, but the nearest store or service station is at a Navajo trading post about five miles away.

El Morro National Monument

El Morro National Monument is about 40 miles (64.4 kilometres) southwest of Grants on NM 53. This sandstone mesa,
rising like the prow of a mighty ship surrounded by a sea of
grass and pine trees, was a landmark on early Indian trails and
on routes taken by Spanish conquistadores and padres, American pioneers and gold-seekers. The rock could be seen for
miles, and a large pool of fresh water fed by a permanent
spring at the base of the cliff was a godsend to weary travelers.

Into the soft sandstone of Inscription Rock, Indians carved
symbols and figures of animals and people, Spaniards recorded their discoveries and expeditions, American surveyors
and Civil War soldiers noted their passing. Hundred of inscrip-
tions are near the base of the cliff, and can be reached by a sur-
faced trail from the visitor center. Another trail climbs to the
top of the mesa where ruins of two abandoned pueblos remain,
probably ancestors of the Zunis, whose present pueblo is 25
miles (40.2 kilometres) west.

This monument, which records fleeting moments in history
for three races, is a setting of scenic beauty and is seldom
crowded.

A campground with tables, fireplaces and running water is a
mile (1.6 kilometres) from the visitor center, and during the
summer rangers conduct fireside programs at a small amphitheater near the campground.

Fort Union National Monument

Fort Union National Monument, for many years the most
important fort in the Southwest, is 29 miles (46.7 kilometres)
north of Las Vegas off I-25. It was active from 1851 to 1891
and many a stagecoach or wagon train thundered into its
welcome security, barely ahead of Comanches, Kiowas and
other Plains Indians.

At the base of the Sangre de Cristo Mountains, where plains
and mountains meet, this fort marked the end of the long trek
across the dangerous flat part of the Santa Fe Trail. An excellent exhibit at the visitor center and an interpretive trail
through the ruins, highlighted by dramatic recordings acti-
vated by pressing a button at each of the major points on the
trail, bring history alive. Reckless young soldiers discussing
adventures in the old stone guardhouse, or a young officer's

wife planning a supper of champagne and oysters seem as real as if they were happening before you.

Gila Cliff Dwellings National Monument

From Silver City, the road that goes to Pinos Altos (NM 15) continues through Gila National Forest to the Gila Cliff Dwellings National Monument. The narrow, scenic road curves through canyons and over rocky ridges, across meadows and beside small streams — beautiful and fairly wild terrain. Inviting picnic and camping areas are along the way. A monument to Ben Lilly, a legendary lion and bear hunter, is on the route.

The cliff dwellings were inhabited by a branch of the Mogollon Indians from early in the Christian Era until about 700 years ago. The trail from the visitor center goes along a stream where prehistoric men farmed small crops of beans, squash and corn, then up a steep talus slope about 180 feet (54.9 metres) to the small dwellings built in large natural caves of stone quarried from the soft volcanic cliffs.

The cliff dwellings are at the edge of the Gila Wilderness. Trails begin here leading into the wilderness where anglers can try the three forks of the Gila River. Campgrounds, both forest and commercial, are just outside the monument, and a commercial outfitter can arrange pack trips for fishing, hunting or sightseeing in the wilderness.

Inscription Rock.

New Mexico Travel Division

61

Gran Quivira National Monument

On the east side of the Manzano Mountains southeast of Albuquerque, salt beds on the floor of the Estancia Valley caused
early Spanish officials to name that province the Saline Province and the dozen or so Indian pueblos in that area the Saline
Pueblos. Between 1629 and 1673, the padres of the Franciscan Order built three great mission churches in the Saline
Pueblos — Abo and Quarai (see *State Monuments*) and
Gran Quivira.

The third large pueblo where the Franciscans built churches
was Tabira, known today as Gran Quivira National Monument
— though there was no connection with the legendary Quivira
sought by Coronado and other explorers.

High on a barren, windswept hill rising from the plains,
several miles from the protection of the Manzanos, the pueblo and churches were built of gray limestone. There is a
mystical, almost eerie, quality to the ruins at Gran Quivira.
One wonders why the fathers chose to build not just one, but
two churches in this isolated place without a nearby source of
water, and vulnerable to attacks from the plains.

The first church, dedicated to San Isidro, was built around
1629. A second, San Buenaventura, was begun around 1650
and never completed. Drought, famine and pestilence had
already reduced the population, and attacks by Indians hostile
to the resident Piro Indians finished the job.

In the early 1670s, like their cousins from Quarai and Abo,
the people left Tabira and took refuge with the other Piro
Indians near Socorro. During the Pueblo Revolt, the people of
these pueblos moved south with the retreating Spaniards and
established a new village near El Paso named Socorro. They
did not return after the reconquest, and the great pueblos between the Manzanos and the Estancia Valley were never reoccupied. They have become known as the Cities that Died
of Fear.

Pecos National Monument

On a rise near the village of Pecos, this monument has
marvelous views and is reached via I-25 and NM 223. In early
Spanish days, Pecos was the largest of the pueblos and had
two great communal dwellings, each four stories high with
more than a thousand rooms, and five plazas and 16 kivas.

The great mission church at Pecos Pueblo, Nuestra Señora de los Angeles de Porciuncula, was begun about 1617 and finished a few years later. The beams were of well-hewn timbers, and cornices and corbels were beautifully carved. During the Pueblo Revolt the church was burned and never re-built, but in the 1700s another smaller one of adobe was built within the foundations of the earlier stone church. Founda-tions of the earlier church, and ruins of the second one and of the pueblo are preserved in Pecos National Monument.

White Sands National Monument

White Sands National Monument, 14 miles (22.5 kilometres) west of Alamogordo on US 70, covers miles of a large white gypsum desert. Snowy, glistening "sands" are blown into dunes 30 to 40 feet (9 to 12 metres) high, a vast expanse of billowing waves reaching to blue mountains in the distance. Around the fringes of the constantly moving dunes a few species of plants adapt to the environment, but in the interior, the dunes area is a sea of uninterrupted white waves.

An exhibit at the visitor center explains geology, flora, fauna and history of the area. A drive of several miles takes you through the heart of the dunes, where there are picnic sites with tables, grills, water, restrooms and shelters. Photo-graphy on the dunes is best in early morning or late evening, when shadows define the ripples and contours. A gift shop and snack bar are at the visitor center.

Guadalupe Mountains National Park

Guadalupe Mountains National Park is a fairly new national park that is still being developed. Although it is actually in Texas, it is part of the same giant limestone reef that holds Carlsbad Caverns, and access to the park is by Carlsbad, New Mexico.

The park offers primitive camping and hiking over rugged mountain trails. Plants and trees grow in unusual juxtaposition in this wild, untouched park that also boasts the highest spot in Texas.

NATIONAL MONUMENTS

	Picnicking	Camping	Toilets	Drinking water	Hiking trails	Restaurant
Aztec Ruins Aztec	●		●	●		
Bandelier 12 mi. s/Los Alamos	●	●	●	●	●	
Capulin Mountain 38 mi. e/Raton	●		●	●	●	
Chaco Canyon 67 mi. s/Farmington	●	●	●	●	●	
El Morro 41 mi. sw/Grants	●	●	●	●	●	
Fort Union 29 mi. n/Las Vegas	●		●	●	●	
Gila Cliff Dwellings 44 mi. n/Silver City	●		●	●	●	
Gran Quivira 25 mi. se/Mountainair	●		●	●	●	
Pecos 25 mi. e/Santa Fe	●		●	●	●	
White Sands 14 mi.sw/Alamogordo	●		●	●	●	

NATIONAL PARK

	Picnicking	Camping	Toilets	Drinking water	Hiking trails	Restaurant
Carlsbad	●		●	●	●	●

WILDLIFE REFUGES

National wildlife refuges and state waterfowl areas are particularly fine for birdwatching, especially in November, December and January, when hundreds of thousands of sandhill cranes, Canada and snow geese and a variety of ducks distribute themselves upon the thousands of acres of water and fields of grain offered them by the refuges.

Shorebirds and songbirds begin to arrive in large numbers in April and May to take up residence for the summer. There are many other varieties of birds and native animals. In the Bosque del Apache, a small number of whooping cranes may be seen, with their adoptive parents, the sandhill cranes. In a big international project, whooping crane eggs were placed in sandhill crane nests, with the idea of encouraging a flock to take hold in the Central Flyway, with its shorter, less dangerous migration pattern.

Waterfowl areas are administered by the New Mexico Department of Game and Fish:

Artesia, two miles (3.2 kilometres) east of Artesia on US 82, then north two and one-half miles on access road; 800 acres (324 hectares).

Bernardo, 26 miles (42 kilometres) north of Socorro via the Bernardo exit off I-25; 1,500 acres (607 hectares). The rare whooping cranes enjoy the corn grown here.

La Joya, 20 miles (32 kilometres) north of Socorro off I-25; 3,550 acres (1,437 hectares).

The U.S. Fish and Wildlife Service refuges are:

Bitter Lake, 10 miles (16 kilometres) east of Roswell on US 380, south six miles (9.7 kilometres) on access road; 24,000 acres (9,713 hectares); fishing in season; toilets.

Bosque del Apache, 10 miles (16 kilometres) south of Socorro on I-25 to San Antonio, then seven miles (11 kilometres) south on US 85; 57,000 acres (23,068 hectares); fishing in season; toilets.

Grulla, 15 miles (24 kilometres) southeast of Portales on NM 88; 3,200 acres (1,295 hectares).

Las Vegas, two miles (3.2 kilometres) east of Las Vegas on NM 104, two miles (3.2 kilometres) south on NM 281; 8,000 acres (3,238 hectares); fishing in season; toilets.

Maxwell, two miles (3.2 kilometres) north of Maxwell; 3,000 acres (1,214 hectares); fishing in season.

FOREST LANDS

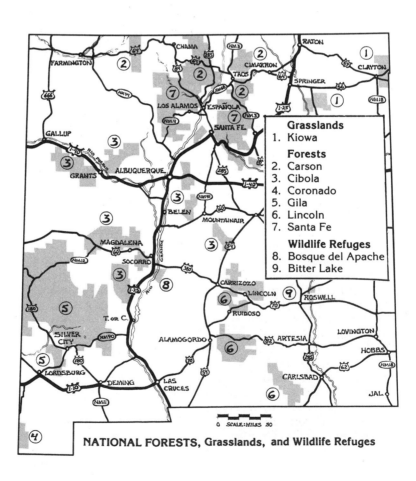

Grasslands
1. Kiowa

Forests
2. Carson
3. Cibola
4. Coronado
5. Gila
6. Lincoln
7. Santa Fe

Wildlife Refuges
8. Bosque del Apache
9. Bitter Lake

NATIONAL FORESTS, Grasslands, and Wildlife Refuges

NATIONAL FORESTS

New Mexico's 9,108,057 million acres (3,685,980 hectares) of national forests are a great natural resource for the timber and livestock industries, wildlife habitat, water and soil conservation, and recreation. Who is not refreshed, inspired, even re-created by a walk along a forest path? The timeless serenity of the mountains and trees lays a benediction on minds too often harried by noise, pollution, pressure. The Forest Service is custodian of this gift, attempting to strike a reasonable balance between recreational and other needs.

All national forests in New Mexico maintain recreational sites geared to the special qualities of that area. Some are near lakes and streams where fishing is available. Some are near unique geological phenomena. Others are in areas of special scenic beauty. Most have trails leading into the mountains, some especially planned for blind or otherwise physically handicapped persons.

User fees in National Forest campgrounds and picnic areas range from nothing to $3.00 a day. All developed sites have tables, firepits and toilets. If they have no drinking water or are not accessible to fairly good roads, they are classed as primitive, and there is usually no user fee.

Here are the National Forests in New Mexico:

Carson National Forest contains 1,392,253 acres (158,742 hectares) of land in three separate sections. The largest includes most of the mountainous area west of Taos in the Tres Piedras-Canjilon-Vallecitos area. Another portion includes the northern Sangre de Cristo Mountains east of Taos, and the other adjoins the Jicarilla Apache Reservation on the west. Elevations range from 6,000 feet (1,829 metres) to 13,161-foot (4,012-metre) Wheeler Peak, highest point in New Mexico. Many lakes and streams, scenic drives and picturesque Spanish villages are in the Sangre de Cristo Mountains. There are 37 campgrounds, picnic or recreation sites, ranging from primitive to fully developed.

Cibola National Forest contains 1,635,407 acres (661,840 hectares) in eight locations: the Sandia and Manzano mountains east of Albuquerque, an area southeast of Mountainair, the mountains north and south of Magdalena, the Mount Taylor area near Grants, and the Zuni Mountains southeast of Gallup. Elevations range from 5,000 feet (1,524 metres) to Mount Taylor at 11,301 feet (3,445 metres). Deer, elk, antelope and turkey hunting are good in some parts of the Cibola, as is fishing at Bluewater and McGaffey lakes. Twenty-nine campgrounds and picnic sites in the Cibola are developed.

Coronado National Forest in the bootheel of far southwestern New Mexico south of Lordsburg, laps over into Arizona. There are no developed recreation sites in these wild desert mountains of New Mexico, but one or two primitive forest roads and trails lead to canyons of unusual beauty. Javalina, deer and quail hunting are permitted in some areas.

Gila National Forest is the giant of New Mexico forests, containing 2,705,933 acres (1,095,076 hectares) ranging from 4,500 to 10,892 feet (1,372 to 3,320 metres) in elevation. In addition, there are 614,202 acres (248,564 hectares) of the Apache National Forest in New Mexico, which are administered by the Gila. The Gila extends from the rugged Mogollon Mountains between Silver City and Quemado, to the Arizona border, and includes the Black Range west of T or C. The Gila country seems hardly affected by civilization, much of it being set aside as a wilderness. The headwaters of the Gila, Mimbres and San Francisco rivers rise in these forests, and many beautiful mountain streams and lakes provide excellent fishing. Big game hunting, horseback riding and pack trips are popular. Twenty-eight developed recreation sites are in the Gila.

Lincoln National Forest includes the Capitan Mountains north of Ruidoso, the Sacramento Mountains south of Cloudcroft, and the Guadalupe Mountains west of Carlsbad, totaling 1,103,145 acres (446,437 hectares) ranging in elevation from 4,000 to 11,500 feet (1,219 to 3,505 metres). Sierra Blanca, at 12,003 feet (3,659 metres), is within the Mescalero Apache Reservation, which includes all the mountainous terrain between Ruidoso and Cloudcroft and is not part of the National Forest. Eighteen campgrounds and picnic sites are in Lincoln National Forest, and three on the Mescalero Reservation.

Santa Fe National Forest includes the southern Sangre de Cristo Mountains east of Santa Fe, and the Jemez Mountains to the west, an area of 1,585,007 acres (641,444 hectares), ranging from 6,000 to 13,000 feet (1,829 to 3,962 metres) in elevation. The highest is Truchas Peak, second highest peak in the state. The headwaters of the Pecos, Jemez and Gallinas rivers are in this forest, and the streams and lakes provide good trout fishing. Big game hunting and wilderness pack trips can be done in several areas. There are 45 developed recreation sites in the Santa Fe National Forest.

WILDERNESSES

Included within the national forests of New Mexico are 1,015,884 acres (411,123 hectares) of wilderness, pristine areas of beauty set aside so that generations to come may experience the same thrill as did the first man to tread the pine needle paths. No mechanized or wheeled vehicles of any kind may cross the border of a wilderness. Only on foot or on horseback may you enter the wilderness, and, even if you are not an experienced hiker, a short walk of a mile or two into a wilderness will be a sensation different from any other hiking.

For your own safety always check with a ranger at the nearest ranger station before entering a wilderness. A free permit is required in most areas for hiking or camping.

New Mexico's wilderness areas are:

Chama River Wilderness lies in Santa Fe National Forest along the ruggedly scenic Chama River south of El Vado Dam where it is joined by the Gallinas River.

Gila Wilderness in Gila National Forest in southwestern New Mexico is by far the largest wilderness in the state, and the oldest one in the United States. In 1924 almost a half million acres (202,347 hectares) were set aside of this wildly beautiful, rugged, unexplored mountainous country. A part of the Mogollon Plateau, the area is cut by deep canyons, streams and rivers, and was the last stronghold of the Apaches. Fishing, big game hunting, hiking and solitude are plentiful in this mountain fastness. This forest also includes two primitive areas, the Gila and the Black Range, which operate under the same rules as wildernesses.

Manzano Wilderness in Cibola National Forest, about 27 miles (43 kilometres) southeast of Albuquerque preserves some of these little explored upper areas of the Manzanos.

Pecos Wilderness in the Carson and Santa Fe National Forests in the majestic Sangre de Cristo Mountains is one of the most popular wildernesses in the state.

Sandia Wilderness in the Cibola National Forest includes most of the west escarpment of the Sandias overlooking the city, and the wild country on the east side of the mountains near Osha Springs and the east side of Sandia Peak.

San Pedro Parks Wilderness in the Jemez Mountains of Santa Fe National Forest east of Cuba has trails leading from San Gregorio Lake near the boundary through a high, moist plateau of rolling mountaintops and open meadows.

Wheeler Peak Wilderness in Carson National Forest northeast of Taos is the smallest wilderness in the West, but its trails lead to the alpine tundra of Wheeler and other nearby peaks. Plant and animal species here are unique in the Southwest.

White Mountain Wilderness in Lincoln National Forest south of Carrizozo rises from the surrounding desert abruptly to almost 12,000 feet (3,658 metres) with flora ranging from desert grassland to subalpine.

Brazos Peak

The Forest Service also administers **Kiowa National Grasslands** east of Clayton. Some 136,412 acres (55,205 hectares) of rolling plains country, covered with the rich grasses that led to the development of the cattle industry in the West, make up this federal reserve, which has one unimproved campground in Mills Canyon.

Not all forests in the state are part of the national forests. For example, the Vermejo Park country near Raton, and the mountainous areas of Indian reservations are private, and many pockets of private land, usually along streams, were homesteaded before the national forests were established. Most privately owned mountainous areas have tourist and recreation facilities.

Maps published by the Forest Service, available at district ranger stations, are extremely helpful to campers and hikers. Each forest is on a separate map, campgrounds and facilities are listed, and all trails and forest roads are marked.

WILD RIVER

The 48 miles (77 kilometres) of the Rio Grande south from the Colorado border, plus four miles (6.4 kilometres) of the tributary Red River are classed as Wild River, the first stretch of river in the nation to go wild. It flows through a gorge cut into a volcanic plateau, creating a chasm of sheer black and brown walls hundreds of feet deep. In some areas the canyon walls confine the water to a raging torrent of white water with boulders as big as houses, and drops of 10 to 15 feet (3 to 4.6 metres).

Unimproved trails on the east side reach several camp-grounds on the rim and at river level. The best trails into the gorge are from Cerro, and lead to Big Arsenic Springs Campground in the gorge. Poorly named, the crystal clear water from this cluster of springs is like champagne. The wild river is a challenge for rafters and kayakers, with whitewater runs graded from II (mild rapids) to VI (extremely difficult). No motor-powered machines are permitted below the rim of the wild river section. The Wild River, which is administered by the Bureau of Land Management, passes in some places through national forest land.

GHOST TOWNS

Loma Parda

They are ghost towns now. But in the late 1800s, each had a moment of glory that blazed and died like a sudden flame. Most were mining towns where men lusted after the earth's riches — gold, silver, turquoise, copper, lead and coal. A few were farming communities that flourished for a time and mysteriously fell silent. Literally hundreds of towns not only died, they vanished.

But traces of many linger on, haunting ties to days that used to be. They moulder into oblivion, their shells of buildings like spectres against the sky, these towns that witnessed some of America's most romantic and rapacious history.

And if you listen, you can hear the names of fabled mines whispered on the wind: Bridal Chamber, Confidence, Little Hell, Calamity Jane, Hardscrabble, Mystic Lode, North Homestake, Little Fanny, Spanish Bar. If you look, you can read the names of legendary people written in the dust: Johnny Ringo, Russian Bill, Toppy Johnson, Roy Bean, Butch Cassidy, Madame Varnish, Black Jack Ketchum, Mangas Coloradas, Billy the Kid, James Cooney.

More than a score of these towns have enough left in spite of the ravages of vandals and weather to be interesting to the special breed of human whose eyes light up at the mention of them.

Quite a few towns have a number of inhabitants. Please respect their privacy and do not enter private dwellings uninvited. And please do not remove remaining utensils or pieces of the buildings themselves, or in any other way diminish the remaining structures. Many of the towns are on private property. Approximately one-third of them are on dirt roads not to be attempted in wet weather.

CERRILLOS, MADRID
and GOLDEN *(About 24, 27 and 35 miles*
southwest of Santa Fe on NM 14)

The lore of the Cerrillos hills is rich with legends of mines being worked there for a thousand years. Turquoise has religious significance to many Indian peoples, nearby Mount Chalchihuitl is known to have contained a great lode of the precious gemstone, and stone tools found there seem to testify to the truth of the legends. Even by the late 1880s, Pueblo Indians — particularly those from Santo Domingo, who claim ownership of the mines — came to Cerrillos (little hills) asking to take out turquoise, and if refused were likely to fight for it.

Gold mining in the area surrounding Cerrillos is best described as hardscrabble until the big strike of 1879. Two genuine hard-rock miners from Leadville, Colorado, struck a big lode that year, and Cerrillos boomed. It became the center of the mining industry in the area that included Golden and Madrid, and encompassed gold, silver, copper, turquoise, lead and coal.

Along with prosperity came human predators like the outlaws Black Jack Ketchum and Texas Jack and a colorful malcontent named Choctaw Kelly. Cerrillos had its shootouts, one of them over a madam on whose charms two miners had staked claims at the same time. Eight newspapers burst into print — and failed.

The two leading hotels were the Harkness and the Palace. Ruins of the latter are still there. Prices were good: dinner, which might include steak, cost 35 cents, and a shot of whiskey could be had for three pinches of gold dust.

Cerrillos now is a charming, tree-shaded ghost of its former self, where movies and television series are sometimes filmed. It has a small but lively population and shops.

Although Madrid still likes to include itself among the ghost towns, it represents a unique example of resurrection. In the 1920s and '30s, Madrid was as famous for its Christmas lights as for its coal production, and airlines used to reroute traffic during the holidays to show passengers the sight. Coal became important in the 1880s and Madrid (pronounced MAD-rid locally) with it. After World War II, the demand for coal gradually diminished, and long forlorn rows of identical company houses stood empty and decaying.

In the 1950s, the then owner put the whole town up for sale. No one bought. Finally, in 1975, houses were sold to individual buyers — and the sound of hammers and nails could be heard throughout the town. But it will take a while for Madrid to rise from the dead, and several spectres from the past still remind the living of the way things used to be. The Old Coal Mine Museum is interesting, and there are enticing shops.

Placer gold was discovered on Tuerto Creek near Golden in 1839, but the big rush began in 1879. Formerly the site of a village named Real de San Francisco, it began to burgeon as Golden in 1880, became a post office, had a plethora of saloons, and even a stock exchange. Golden seems always to have had a housing shortage. In 1889, hundreds of campfires lit the surrounding hills, and even as late as 1900 several thousand never-say-die prospectors roamed the area, living where they could, some in unused coke ovens.

Long a trading post, Golden is still a popular stop on NM 14. A charming little Catholic church sits on a hill, and a garden of colored glass can be visited across the arroyo.

CHLORIDE

(4 miles west of Winston off NM 52)

The history of Chloride reads like the script for a bad Western — too much of everything happens. A silver strike, a population boom, many Apache raids, salvation by the militia, a continuing cattle versus sheep range war, tarring and feathering, attack by bears — and on and on.

The tarring and feathering occurred when the citizens of Chloride found out that shocking letters sent to some of the leading residents, both ladies and gentlemen, were written by none other than an elderly doctor who had been practicing there for five years. A group of men invited the doctor for a walk to the edge of town, coated him with tar and feathers, and told him to keep going.

The bear attack happened when a man called Love went out one day to check his claim. A grizzly bear caught him with his pants down. Love was in no position to engage in hand to paw combat, but he miraculously survived, and even shot the bear to death. Next day, badly mangled, he walked to town to a doctor.

Chloride had horse and burro races and balls to celebrate July and Christmas, and dreamed of becoming the county seat of Sierra County. Names of some of its mines, which yielded gold and copper as well as silver, were Silver Monument, Nana, Apache, U.S. Treasury, Unknown, Midnight, Wall Street and Mountain King. Chloride's dreams of glory failed, not so much because the silver supply waned, but because the price of silver dropped in the early 1900s. And some accounts say there was just too much strife with the constant unrest between cattle and sheep factions. Today Chloride has a few residents.

COLFAX
(About 15 miles northeast of Cimarron on US 64)

Colfax may be said to have ridden to prosperity on the coattails of Dawson in the late 1890s, when Dawson mushroomed as a coal boomtown. Dawson is gone, killed by diesel fuel, its remains hauled away by mining company salvage crews. But it once rivaled Raton — now the county seat.

Colfax, however, clings to mortality. Named for Schuyler Colfax, a vice president of the United States, it came into being on a spur of the Atchison, Topeka & Santa Fe Railway, and once had a hotel and a number of other buildings.

The decaying shell of the old hotel and a few other ruins still command the attention of travelers on the road between Cimarron and Raton. Even passersby who don't know about Colfax seem to sense that these old hulks are mourning a lively past, and they stop to wonder how it was then.

Chloride.

ELIZABETHTOWN
(5 miles north of Eagle Nest on NM 38)

Not much is left of Elizabethtown — just a few stone walls of the old Mutz Hotel crumbling in the beautiful broad Moreno Valley against the backdrop of snow-capped, 12,500-foot Baldy Peak. But in 1870, Elizabethtown became the first incorporated town in New Mexico and the county seat of a new county, Colfax.

The town's story began when Captain John William Moore of Fort Union rescued a badly wounded Indian and nursed him back to health. In gratitude, the Indian brought Captain Moore a gift of pretty rocks — in which Moore recognized copper. It was October 1866, and he sent three men to the place the Indian pointed out in the Moreno Valley to stake out claims before the first snow flew.

Just for fun, a man named Kelly began panning in Willow Creek — and found gold. The men swore silence, but by spring hundreds of miners swarmed over the area. Rich placers with romantic names — Mystic Lode, Humbug Gulch, Spanish Bar — sprang into being. The first newspaper, *The Lantern,* began in 1869, and the raucous gold camp had seven saloons, five stores, one drugstore, two hotels and three dance halls. Brawling lawless men became so numerous that the citizens decided to bring about law and order by forming a town. They named it Elizabethtown after Captain Moore's daughter, but it quickly became E-Town.

People poured in. Vigilante groups dispensed quick emotional judgments. The boom population is said to have been 3,000, 5,000, 7,000 — all on good authority. But whatever the head count may have been, E-Town lived up to the best traditions of American frontier towns — it was a rip-roarer.

Subsequently, the gold and the population dwindled, and in 1903 a catastrophic fire swept the business district, delivering the coup de grâce. Only one building was left.

KELLY

(2 miles southeast of Magdalena)

Lead, zinc, silver, copper and some gold were Kelly's reasons for being, and on that basis it lasted a long time for a mining town — 1866 to 1945.

Colonel J.S. (Old Hutch) Hutchason found the first rich lead ore. A second find went to his friend Andy Kelly, who worked it from time to time. Then that mine, too, showed signs of richness and Old Hutch showed signs of consternation. Fact is, he jumped the claim. This was the Graphic, one of the highest-yield lodes in the area. Kelly lost the mine, but gave his name to the town.

The Apaches, always intent on driving white intruders out of their territory, struck at Kelly fairly often. Kelly sat above the ranch town of Magdalena not far from Magdalena Peak, where a shale formation called Lady Magdalene lay. The Lady seemed to be sacred to the Apaches — at least they never came close to anyone who fled to the shale formation — and in short order the miners of Kelly became true believers.

The mountains around Kelly teemed with mines: Ambrosia, Vindicator, Young America, Hardscrabble, Mistletoe, Old Soldier and Legal Tender were a few of the names. In the beginning, the ores were smelted in an adobe furnace and shipped to Kansas City by ox team. When the town grew big — seven saloons and two each hotels, dance halls and churches — great ore wagons pulled by 16 horses or mules hauled the ore to Magdalena to be loaded on A.T. & S.F. cars for the smelter at Socorro.

Trouble was, the cowboys of Magdalena and the miners of Kelly lived in two different worlds, easily brought to blazing fury at the ends of guns. Cowboys would ride in to shoot up Kelly and the miners would retaliate in Magdalena.

Over its long history, Kelly produced more than $28.4 million worth of ore. It is deserted now — a few rock foundations, some walls, a mine superstructure, a tiny church — watched over by Lady Magdalene.

KINGSTON LAKE VALLEY

(17 miles south of Hillsboro on NM 27)

A rich lode of silver that became the Solitaire Mine sparked Kingston's existence in early August 1882. By August 26 a townsite had been surveyed, and by late fall 1,800 people lived there. Such was the pattern of a boomtown's growth when news of a gold or silver strike spread.

Kingston ranked near the top among the wildest of mining towns. It is said to have had 22 saloons, among which a hat was passed when the citizens decided they needed a church. Miners contributed a generous building fund of $1,500. The town celebrated its first Christmas by opening a new dance hall — free to all comers.

Like many other mining towns, Kingston was a tent city in the beginning, including some of its hotels and boarding houses. The story goes that lodgers competed for the lower bunks in preference to the upper ones in these tent hotels, because they were less likely to be caught by the bullets flying out of the saloons.

Kingston named its mines Calamity Jane, Caledonia, Black Colt and Little Jimmie, among others. The famous Apache war leader, Victorio, raided it, of course. But Kingston survived with a flourish — it even named its new three-story hotel Victorio. Kingston is set in the foothills of the Gila Country's beautiful rugged Black Range.

(On NM 90, 26 miles west of Caballo)

Two and one-half million ounces of silver came from Lake Valley's fabled Bridal Chamber mine. Silver lay only 40 feet from the surface, and tall tales of its purity abound. Lead and manganese were also found in abundance.

The first silver find occurred in 1878, but it was John Leavitt, a blacksmith, who found the Bridal Chamber on a claim leased from the Sierra Grande Company. (George Daly, the company's general manager, was killed by Apaches on the day of Leavitt's find.)

Lake Valley became an important railhead and prospered until the silver panic of 1893, when it began to fade away. Two or three houses and a few other buildings remain today. It is still a romantic place for a townsite, as newcomers said when they wrote home about it a hundred years ago.

LA BAJADA

(20 miles south of Santa Fe on I-25, turn west on Cochiti Lake Road, 3 miles to La Bajada Village sign, turn right.)

La Bajada (the descent) sits on the bank of a stream at the base of a black lava rock mesa at the end of what used to be one of the most treacherous pieces of road in New Mexico in bad weather. Originally called La Majada (sheepfold), this farming community was a stage stop on the Spanish El Camino Real (Royal Way). It had a peak population of around 300 people.

For 300 years the road — called *la bajada* — coiled down the mesa like an angry snake, striking fear into all who traveled it in icy or rainy weather. There was a saloon at the bottom. An inn used to stand about a quarter of a mile further on at the edge of the village.

Old-timers remember seeing prisoners from the state penitentiary — a chain gang — working on the road with hand tools. Ultimately, in the 1920s, the right-of-way was changed, and the highway passed straight down the hill on the other side of the mesa. La Bajada became almost deserted.

Part of the old adobe schoolhouse, walls of a few residences, and a beautifully weathered wooden corral still stand. San Miguel Church has been partly renovated — its original walls vary in thickness from two to three feet. There is an art gallery. The dozen or so people who live there have a splendid view of the Jemez Mountains — and so does the visitor.

La Bajada.

LA LIENDRE   TREMENTINA
(At the end of NM 67, off NM 104, about 25 miles south-east of Las Vegas)

Alone at the end of a dirt road on a bluff above the Gal-linas River, La Liendre lasted for almost a hundred years as the center of a Spanish stock-raising community. During the era of Vicente Silva, the notorious outlaw who operated in the Las Vegas country, the famous C de Baca family made the outlaw angry, and he cut many miles of their range fences between Las Vegas and La Liendre. What must have been two houses and the general store are still more or less standing. It is a pleasant drive to La Liendre over a ranch road where one must be sure to close the barbed wire gates as one passes through. In summer the road is lined with scarlet, blue, yellow and white wildflowers. The views from the bluff over the river val-ley toward bold blue mesas are lovely.

(About 46 miles east of Las Vegas on NM 104/65. Turn to the right just before the bridge)

Every once in a while an individual means the life and death of a town — so it was with Alice Blake and Trementina (turpentine). Before her advent as a missionary, the commu-nity consisted of a loose aggregation of Spanish families who earned a living selling pine oil and turpentine from the piñon trees that grew (and still grow) along the ridge beside the little stream on the edge of the *llano* (plain). Farming and stock raising were also main occupations.

Miss Blake arrived around 1900 and selected a site for her hospital and Protestant mission church. The hospital building also contained a gymnasium, a kitchen and Miss Blake's living quarters. At church services, hymns were sung in Spanish. The town grew up around the mission, and Miss Blake subse-quently became at different times principal of the mission school — there was also a public school — and postmistress. Trementina thrived. It had two saloons, a general store and a stage line.

Some sources say Miss Blake became ill and could no long-er continue her work. Others simply say she retired in 1930. In any case, severe drought crippled the community, and by 1950 Trementina was deserted.

The shells of many of its houses, though roofless, still stand among the piñons above the little stream on the edge of the *llano*. For this reason it ranks high as a true ghost town.

LOMA PARDA
(About 6 miles northwest of Watrous off NM 161)

In Spanish, *loma parda* means "gray hill." But Loma Parda was not gray. It flourished as a bawdy red silk petticoat of a town — for 40 years the sin city for Fort Union's soldiers. Loma Parda seems to have been inevitable.

After New Mexico became a United States territory in 1846, American troops were stationed in the capital city, the den of iniquity named Santa Fe (Holy Faith). When Lieutenant Colonel E.V. Sumner assumed command in 1850, he took one horrified look and ordered an isolated fort built on the other side of the Sangre de Cristo Mountains at the junction of the Santa Fe Trail and the Cimarron Cutoff. Only one short year later, his troops were quartered there, safe and far away from the vices of Santa Fe. The nearest town was the tiny farming community of Loma Parda, no threat to anyone.

But Colonel Sumner had not reckoned on the enterprise of farmers. Observing that soldiers will be soldiers, the farmers perceived the possibilities, and Loma Parda soon proliferated with dance halls, gambling places, saloons and brothels. Lonely Fort Union soldiers and officers — as well as wagon bosses and traders from the wagon trains — high-tailed it over the hill to join in the heartwarming, expensive and often dangerous democracy of Loma Parda.

The fort closed in 1891, having outlived its usefulness, and Loma Parda's gaudy trappings faded into oblivion. Today parts of buildings still stand, including most of a dance hall. The structure closest to being whole is the church. And over at Fort Union, now an impressive ruin watched over by the National Park Service, the best-preserved unit is the guardhouse, where many a man — civilian and soldier alike — once contemplated the consequences of an uninhibited night in bawdy Loma Parda.

MOGOLLON
(9 miles east of Alma on NM 78)

For nearly 60 years after the great gold strike of 1878, Mogollon (Mo-go-YONE) had a reputation as one of the most wide-open towns in the West. Butch Cassidy and his crowd once headquartered there, and gunmen, claim jumpers and gamblers kept things stepping lively. Not even the great Apache fighters, Victorio and Geronimo, nor troops sent in by the governor, could tame Mogollon — it just kept roaring along.

An estimated $19.5 million in gold, silver and copper came from Mogollon's mines. Little Fanny was the most famous mine, but some of the others were Deep Down, Maud S., Confidence, Last Chance, Leap Year and Bloomer Girl. Little Fanny and Confidence are said to have yielded $1.5 million apiece in gold, silver and other ores.

One of the saddest notes in Mogollon history is the death of James C. Cooney, the cavalry sergeant who started the rush in 1876. During an attack by Victorio in 1880, he sold his silver mine to go back east to marry his sweetheart, who had been waiting for him for years. Victorio's warriors caught him alone in the canyon that now bears his name and killed him. His brother came from New Orleans, carved him a tomb in the rock canyon wall and sealed it with ore from his mine.

Mogollon has survived its days of lust and lawlessness, has a few inhabitants, and mellows nicely with the years on the banks of Silver Creek — an aging roué remembering one helluva past.

PINOS ALTOS

(7 miles north of Silver City on NM 15)

Apache peoples divided — and rode patrol on — all the vast territory that stretches across what is now West Texas, the southern two-thirds of New Mexico and southeastern Arizona. When the white man invaded, the Apaches defended it all. But they bore down hardest on the Gila Country. Pinos Altos (tall pines) gold miners had a particularly tough time of it, and, although gold was mined there — very cautiously — from the spring of 1860, the Apaches made the enterprise so hazardous that the town never boomed the way Mogollon did.

Pinos Altos had to contend with Mangas Coloradas, possibly the greatest Apache war leader of them all. And if that were not enough, in September 1861, Mangas Coloradas joined forces with Cochise in one major sweep with 500 warriors.

The mines were pretty quiet for a while. The government built Fort West to help protect the gold interests, and it was there that Mangas Coloradas met his death. Fort Bayard replaced Fort West, but the Navajos joined the raids and things were still very risky by 1868, five years after Mangas Coloradas' death. Finally the settlers made an agreement with the Indians that included placing a large cross on a hill north of town and, as long as the cross stayed there, there were no killings.

Samuel G. Bean lived in Pinos Altos and had a general store with his brother Roy — who later moved to Texas and became the "law west of the Pecos." After the Indian threat finally diminished, silver, copper, lead and zinc also figured in the mining history of Pinos Altos until the 1920s. Shops occupy the old stores now, and some of the mine superstructures can be seen in the nearby mountains — a very pleasant spot on the edge of the Gila National Forest.

SHAKESPEARE
(2½ miles south of Lordsburg)

Now off the beaten track and privately owned, Shakespeare had a tenuous beginning in the 1850s as a stop called Mexican Springs on the Butterfield Overland Stage line. As Ralston, it played a peculiar role in the life of William C. Ralston, founder of the Bank of California — resulting in the ruin of both the bank and Ralston.

Silver that assayed 12,000 ounces per ton was found by a man named W.D. Brown, who took it to Ralston in San Francisco. Not much silver of any kind — certainly no rich lode — was located at Shakespeare, and Ralston's New Mexico Mining Company went broke.

Diamonds planted by two prospectors and appraised for Ralston by Tiffany's at $150,000 resulted in Ralston's forming a new company that attracted stockholders like Horace Greeley and Baron Rothschild. It was a hoax, of course — and Ralston paid off the stockholders out of his own pocket. The 1875 depression struck while he was down, and his bank failed. One day he went for a swim in San Francisco Bay from which he never returned.

The town changed its name to Shakespeare in 1879 — and also changed its luck. It went on to prosperity — in a silver boom. A building frame with walls of unbleached muslin served as the Stratford Hotel, and the main street was Avon Avenue. The red light district was Poverty Flat.

One fine night, Sandy King and Russian Bill, two desperadoes who took up residence, got themselves hanged from the rafters of the Grant Hotel dining room by a vigilante group. It is said that stagecoach passengers found them the next morning, cut them down, buried them, and then had breakfast. The graves are in Shakespeare's Boot Hill.

The first silver boom died in the 1890s, and another one flourished for a while from about 1907 until the 1930s. Then Shakespeare became a ghost town and part of the Frank Hill ranch. The Hill family still owns it, and it is open to visitors at specified times. Inquire at the Lordsburg Chamber of Commerce for details.

STEINS
(17 miles west of Lordsburg on I-10)

Doubtful Canyon, Steins Pass and Steins (pronounced Steens) are names associated with events that occurred at or near this spot.

The name Doubtful Canyon came from settlers on their way westward, who doubted that they would make it through the canyon without being attacked by Apaches. They were right. Later, Doubtful Canyon became a stop on the Butterfield Overland Stage route in the late 1850s, still a favorite Apache target. A Captain Steins died defending it, and grateful survivors called it Steins Pass.

In 1888, the present site of Steins became a post office for gold camps in the Peloncillo Mountains and a stop on the Southern Pacific Railroad. Black Jack Ketchum and his gang held up the Southern Pacific Sunset Limited at Steins in December 1897. They killed a trainman, but the good guys won, and Black Jack and his boys rode off without a penny. A few gaunt adobe walls stood baking in the sun for many years, but a restoration began in 1977.

Pinos Altos.

WATROUS
(20 miles northeast of Las Vegas on I-25)

Before the days of Fort Union, Watrous was the first New Mexico settlement reached by wagon trains on their way west over the Santa Fe Trail. Watrous was to the western end of the trail what Independence, Missouri, was to the eastern end. Here the wagons rendezvoused to form new caravans before venturing out on the last perilous segment of the trail to Santa Fe. Before them lay predatory Kiowa and Comanche Indians and the high barrier of the Sangre de Cristo Mountains, and a man needed all the friends he could find. The trail ruts of the wagon trains are still visible on the nearby bluffs that border the Mora River.

Settled in 1843, the town's first name, La Junta de los Rios Mora y Sapello, meant The Meeting of the Rivers Mora and Sapello. In 1879, Samuel B. Watrous gave the town his name. His store and ranch house date from 1849 and are now beautifully restored as a private home.

An old livery stable, a blacksmith shop, the Schmidt & Reinkens store and the old hotel are readily pointed out by residents. The old Presbyterian church building may be the oldest Protestant church structure in the state, and the Masonic temple is believed to be the oldest or second oldest in New Mexico. Fine big cottonwood trees shelter the quiet village today, where about a dozen families still live.

WINSTON
(35 miles northwest of Truth or Consequences on NM 52)

Fairview they called it in its heyday. Along with Phillips-
burg, Grafton, Robinson, Roundyville and Flourine, it became
one of Chloride's neighbors at the peak of the silver boom.
Fairview began officially in 1881, settled by folks who liked its
lower altitude better than Chloride. Frank Winston moved
there in 1882 and became a leading citizen as miner, owner of
a general store and a cattle company and, by 1915, a garage.
His house in Fairview had the first bay window in town —
noted in the *Black Range* newspaper, a gossipy sheet that
commented in a hapless citizen's obituary, "He came of a bad
family and he himself was the worst of the lot."

The town's literary society put on amateur theatricals and
literary recitals and strove to form a little center of culture on
the frontier. Fairview's horse races, however, were far more
popular. But the town never really got off the ground. It fell on
very hard times when silver failed, and Frank Winston carried
the whole town on credit with little expectation of ever being
paid back. His customers were so grateful they renamed the
town after him. Winston has a small population today, but a
few of the old silver-boom structures still stand precariously.

White Oaks.

WHITE OAKS

(11 miles northeast of Carrizozo on NM 349)

They say that George Wilson, probably a fugitive from the law, discovered the North Homestake lode in 1879 and sold it to a buddy named Jack Winters for $40, a pony and a bottle of whiskey. In due course, the North Homestake gave up half a million dollars in gold.

Be that as it may, White Oaks had a sudden violent birth, got christened for the trees around two nearby springs, and 25 years later had mined $3 million worth of gold and silver. In addition to the North and South Homestakes, other well-known mines were Old Abe, Little Mack, Rip Van Winkle, Large Hopes and Little Hell.

White Oaks' population grew to 4,000. Famous cattle rustlers and outlaws like Billy the Kid, Toppy Johnson and Jim Greathouse hung out there. It had four or five weekly newspapers that did not hesitate to take verbal potshots at each other. It also had hotels, churches and saloons — one saloon sold three grades of whiskey at different prices from the same barrel. A faro dealer named Madame Varnish ran the biggest casino in the best crooked tradition of Western boomtowns.

One of White Oaks' finest homes was Hoyle's Castle, a brick Victorian structure that still stands in faded grandeur today. It had imported woodwork, stained-glass windows, a fancy fireplace and, it is said, a real bathtub. The town even had the Starr-Opera House, which was also a saloon that featured traveling entertainers. Emerson Hough used White Oaks as the background for his novel *Heart's Desire,* published in 1903.

The town produced New Mexico's first governor, W.C. McDonald, and the state's first United States Marshal, Judge Andrew Hudspeth. It had dreams of glory and planned long and enthusiastically for the advent of the El Paso and White Oaks Railroad, even to the point of forming a brass band to celebrate. But the railroad went to Capitan, and White Oaks died of disappointment.

These aren't New Mexico's only ghost towns, of course. On every lonely mountain road, on every dusty track, in every remote corner of the state, you can come across an unexpected sign of vanished life — a crumbling wall, a jagged chimney pointing to the sky, a vacant house staring with dead eyes across a lonely stretch of range that once was someone's garden ringed with roses and hope. Perhaps there's a tiny village where once a city thrived. Or perhaps there's no sign at all that here, not so very long ago, people worked and wept, laughed and loved, where today there are only wildflowers and grass bending in the wind.

We chose these ghost towns as representative of a booming era and because they may readily be seen by travelers. (Some other ghost towns are on private land whose owners do not countenance trespassers.)

The empty cities of Chaco Canyon, the silent rooms of the Gila Cliff Dwellings are also ghost towns, from a different era, as are the diminished farm towns of the eastern plains. But we think our selection will give visitors a taste of those riproaring days of yesteryear when the cry across the land was "Gold! Gold! Gold!"

More About Ghost Towns

Jenkinson, Michael, **Ghost Towns of New Mexico: Playthings of the Wind,** University of New Mexico Press, 1967. 156 pp. Photographs by Karl Kernberger.

Looney, Ralph, **Haunted Highways: The Ghost Towns of New Mexico,** University of New Mexico Press, 1969. 220 pp. Photographs by the author.

Meleski, Patricia, **Echoes of the Past: New Mexico's Ghost Towns,** University of New Mexico Press, 1972. 254 pp. Photographs by R.P. Meleski.

Sherman, James E., and Barbara, **Ghost Towns and Mining Camps of New Mexico,** University of Oklahoma Press, 1974. 270 pp. Historic photographs from many sources.

THE ARTS

Yoshimi Takeda conducting New Mexico Symphony Orchestra.

Perhaps it is the vibrant colors in the landscape, or the sky, or the almost-white sunlight that casts lavender shadows. Perhaps it is the interplay of different cultures, one stimulating the other. Whatever its source, there is a creative environment in New Mexico that cannot be denied. It produces artists of every calling.

Thousands of years ago art became part of the prehistoric Indian world when they began to decorate their pottery and to make ornaments to adorn their bodies. They painted, scratched or chipped pictures on the walls of caves and cliffs as part of their religion. Their civilization had reached the point where they could think beyond the next kill.

The modern world began to take note of New Mexico's artistic environment in 1912 when a group of artists came together to form the Taos Society of Artists: Blumenschein, Phillips, Ufer, Higgins, Dunton, Berninghaus, Sharp and Couse. Today hundreds of regionally and nationally known artists live and work in New Mexico. They may exhibit and sell in Manhattan, but they draw their inspiration from roots deep in the soil of this contradictory geography.

Music, literature, sculpture, drama, dance, lithography, and all other forms of creative expression have their place. The paintings, pottery, jewelry and weaving of Indian artists are a major facet — and influence — of New Mexico art. Religious folk art is a contribution of the Spanish colonial period. Churches, museums and private collections cherish many pieces of this strangely moving, primitive art form. Some of the old methods and materials are still used by producing artists today. The state's Museum of International Folk Art in Santa Fe has a collection that is outstanding and world-renowned.

Taos is synonymous with art. In proportion to the number of people living there, there are probably more galleries and studios than in any other town in the country. Not all artists who exhibit and sell in Taos live there. Mabel Dodge Luhan came to Taos in 1917, recognized its special qualities, and was responsible for bringing many other creative people there, among them D.H. Lawrence. The ranch Mabel gave the Lawrences in the mountains north of Taos is now owned by the University of New Mexico, and is sometimes used for seminars in the humanities. The shrine Lawrence's widow, Frieda, built for his ashes is open to the public.

The major branches of the Museum of New Mexico are located in Santa Fe, including the Fine Arts Museum and the Museum of International Folk Art. Privately owned galleries are concentrated in the Santa Fe Plaza and Canyon Road areas, though studios are in all parts of the city.

At the University of New Mexico in Albuquerque are the Fine Arts Museum, Jonson Gallery and the Tamarind Institute, where fine lithography is done. Galleries are in the Old Town area and several other parts of the city, and many of the state's professional artists live in Albuquerque. Alamogordo, Roswell, Lincoln, Silver City, Las Cruces, Raton, and many other towns in New Mexico have their resident artists and studios. Whether it is the stark simplicity of Georgia O'Keeffe from Abiquiu, the lonely windmills of Peter Hurd from San Patricio, or the mystical women of R.C. Gorman, the Navajo painter, their work evokes the elemental qualities of this land. And art buyers come from all over the world to look — and to buy.

Sculptors have excellent art foundries within easy reach within the state. And photographers from Edward Weston, Laura Gilpin and Ansel Adams to today's innovators have roamed the state for creative images for the past 100 years.

New Mexico is home to writers, too — poets, novelists, travel writers, philosophers, historians, mystery writers, science fiction writers and writers of everything on the best-seller lists from cookbooks to juveniles.

Little theater groups abound in the state, as do university theater groups, and children's theater flourishes in several towns. One has only to check the local newspapers for performances.

Several cities have opera and light opera associations, not to mention resident choruses of high caliber.

Music festivals such as the June Music Festival in Albuquerque and the Santa Fe Chamber Music Festival bring in world-famous talent. And who can overlook the remarkable and exciting Santa Fe Opera, which every summer draws the best singers and directors of the world to the mountains outside of Santa Fe for outstanding productions.

The New Mexico Symphony, under the direction of Yoshimi Takeda, is based in Albuquerque but plays throughout the state. Other notable orchestras are the Albuquerque Chamber

Orchestra, the Roswell Symphony, the Orchestra of Santa Fe, and the various university orchestras.

As you travel New Mexico take time to visit the galleries and museums, attend the opera and plays, browse the arts and crafts shows and open air art markets, check out the book stores. You will soon see what the French writer, Michel Butor, meant when he said, "In New Mexico the works of man fit in magnificently with the works of nature. All of New Mexico is a museum."

Some of the museums in New Mexico are listed below.

Abiquiu — Ghost Ranch Museum.

Alamogordo — International Space Hall of Fame; Otero County Historical Society Museum.

Albuquerque — Art Museum, UNM; Ernie Pyle Memorial Branch Library; Geology Museum, UNM; Indian Pueblo Cultural Center; Jonson Gallery, UNM; Lovelace Foundation - Albert K. Mitchell Collection of Western Art; Maxwell Museum of Anthropology, UNM; Museum of Albuquerque; National Atomic Museum; Rio Grande Zoological Park; Sandia Laboratories Exhibit Center; Telephone Pioneer Museum.

Artesia — Artesia Historical Museum and Art Center.

Capitan — Smokey Bear Museum & State Park.

Carlsbad — Carlsbad Municipal Museum; Living Desert State Park.

Cimarron — Ernest Thompson Seton Memorial Library and Museum, Philmont Scout Ranch; Kit Carson Museum, Philmont Scout Ranch; Old Mill Museum; St. James Hotel Museum.

Cloudcroft — Cloudcroft Museum.

Columbus — Pancho Villa Museum.

Deming — Deming CC Museum; Luna County Museum.

Farmington — Farmington Historical Museum; Salmon Ruins Museum.

Folsom — Folsom Museum.

Fort Sumner — Billy the Kid Museum; Old Fort Sumner Museum.

Galisteo — Galisteo Historical Museum.

Gallup — Museum of Indian Arts & Crafts.

Grants — Chamber of Commerce Museum.

Hobbs — Confederate Air Force Museum.

La Cienega — Old Cienega Village Museum.

Las Cruces — Museum of Old Dolls & Toys; New Mexico State University Museum.

Las Vegas — Rough Riders Memorial & City Museum.

Lincoln — Lincoln County Courthouse Museum.

Los Alamos — Bradbury Science Hall & Museum; Los Alamos

County Historical Museum.
Lovington — Lea County Museum.
Madrid — Old Coal Mine Museum.
Magdalena — Magdalena Museum.
Mesilla — American Desert Museum; Gadsden Museum.
Moriarty — Longhorn Ranch & Museum of the Old West; Moriarty Chamber of Commerce Museum.
Mountainair — Old Southwest Museum.
Picuris Pueblo — Picuris Pueblo Museum.
Portales — Blackwater Draw Museum; Miles Museum; Natural History Museum, ENMU; Paleo-Indian Museum; Roosevelt County Museum.
Ranchos de Taos — Fort Burgwin Research Center.
Raton — Raton Museum.

Museum of Fine Arts, Santa Fe.

Roswell — Chaves County Museum; Roswell Museum and Art Center; Spring River Park and Zoo.

San Jon — Pioneers' Dugout.

Santa Fe — Chapel of San Miguel; Museum of Fine Arts; Institute of American Indian Arts; International Institute of Iberian Colonial Art (College of Santa Fe); Laboratory of Anthropology; Museum of International Folk Art; Palace of the Governors; Santuario de Guadalupe; Wheelwright Museum.

Silver City — Silver City Museum; Western New Mexico University Museum.

Socorro — Bureau of Mines & Mineral Resources Mineral Museum.

Springer — Santa Fe Trail Museum & Historical Society.

Taos — Governor Bent Museum; The Harwood Foundation; Kit Carson Home & Museum; The Leon Gaspard House; Millicent A. Rogers Foundation; Stables Gallery of the Taos Art Association.

Tome — Tome Parish Museum.

Truth or Consequences — Geronimo Springs Museum.

Tucumcari — Tucumcari Historical Museum.

Other museums located at most state monuments, national parks and monuments.

Santuario de Chimayo.

No one can understand New Mexico without understanding her churches. There are churches still in use today that were built 150 years before the missions of California, Texas and Arizona.

These New Mexico missions were massive, majestic architectural wonders, almost brutal in their strength, with little ornamentation. They were built by Indian labor in a unique style that combined classic pueblo construction with Spanish architecture.

Other churches have been built since then, almost as impressive, sometimes more beautiful. Some were built in remote valleys to serve a single family or farming community, and they still stand, tended carefully by loving hands. Some are slowly returning to the earth from whence they came. They are the heart of New Mexico in tangible form for all the world to see.

We have singled out only a few. There are many more, just as historic, scattered through the villages, pueblos, towns and cities of New Mexico. They are monuments in stone, mud and wood to the early Franciscans, who were determined to bring their faith to this "pagan" land, and to the settlers who followed them.

Even before Oñate, the colonizer, established a civil capital, he established an ecclesiastical headquarters and assigned missionaries to the various tribes. This he did in July 1598 at Santo Domingo Pueblo. He continued north to San Juan Pueblo, which he chose for his capital, and the first building erected was a small chapel. From then until the great Pueblo Revolt of 1680, Franciscan missionaries directed the construction of about 80 churches. The rebellion was a convulsion of resentment by the Indians against an alien government and religion. They killed or drove out every Spaniard in the province. Churches were desecrated or destroyed, but, when the Spaniards returned 12 years later, they began rebuilding them.

Of the mission.churches built before 1680, seven remain today. Two are still used by the Indians as a regular place of worship. Ruins of the other five are preserved as state or national monuments (see *Parks and Monuments*).

The first mission church at Isleta Pueblo, dedicated to San Antonio, was built between 1613 and 1630, and early records say reading, writing, singing and playing musical instruments were taught here, making it one of the earliest seats of Indian education in America. It was a thick-walled, heavily buttressed church more than 100 feet (30.5 metres) long, dominating one entire side of the plaza. During the rebellion many Isleta Indians went south with the Spanish refugees and established Ysleta del Sur near El Paso. After the rebellion, the returning Isletas found their church a burned-out shell, but they rebuilt, using the same walls, and dedicated the new church to San Agustin. It has been remodeled several times, but the exterior walls are original.

San Esteban mission church at Acoma was built around 1629 under the direction of Father Juan Ramirez. The rocky island mesa on which the pueblo and church are built is devoid of vegetation and soil, so that all building material for the church, as well as dirt for mortar and for the cemetery, had to to be carried up a steep trail on the backs of Indians. Tree trunks 40 feet (12 metres) long to use as roof beams were carried from mountains 30 miles (48 kilometres) away. Beautifully carved corbels, beams and reredos decorated the interior. In the courtyard Father Ramirez planted grapevines and peach trees to remind him of his home in Spain.

The church was abandoned and desecrated during the revolt, but not destroyed. It was restored and has been used continuously since then. The location, massive walls and history of San Esteban defy comparison.

The churches of Isleta and Acoma are the two oldest in the United States.

San Jose Mission at Laguna Pueblo is one of the most pleasant to visit of the Indian pueblo churches. Stark white on a hill that marks the high point of Old Laguna Pueblo, bright against the dark blue backdrop of Mount Taylor, it commands the attention of motorists on I-40. Built in 1699, it is decorated inside with Indian motifs around the walls. One of its altar decorations is an oil painting on buffalo hide of St. Joseph. It is the original church, since it was built after the Pueblo Revolt and therefore not destroyed and restored, as were those at Isleta and Acoma.

During the 18th and 19th centuries, many churches were built in New Mexico, an important and cherished part of New Mexico's heritage. Some of them will be mentioned in the section on towns, but we would like to call attention to a few that deserve special attention.

Santa Cruz, a village near Española, became an official settlement in 1695, although Spanish farmers lived there for a number of years. A small chapel served the community until the present Holy Cross Church was finished in the 1740s. It is possibly the biggest of the old adobe Spanish mission churches — bigger even than Acoma — and is constructed in the shape of a cross with a chapel on each side and a convent attached. Its buttressed walls are three feet thick, vigas are corbeled, and it contains several altarpieces that are excellent

San Jose Mission, Laguna Pueblo.

Lee Marmon

101

specimens of New Mexico's Spanish colonial art. The screen behind the main altar has been restored to its original state, and it alone is worth stopping to see.

When Albuquerque was founded in 1706, the first building erected by the colonists was a small chapel dedicated to San Felipe de Neri. A few poor adobe huts outlined a plaza, and farms spread out in the fertile valley of the Rio Grande. The church has been remodeled and enlarged many times, encompassing the original chapel. The first baptism at San Felipe was recorded in 1706, and services have been held without interruption since that time. During the Victorian period, ornate wooden towers and trim were added, and still remain, testimony to the adaptability of adobe architecture.

St. Francis of Assisi Mission at Ranchos de Taos is considered one of the most beautiful in the Southwest and is surely one of the most photographed and painted. The rear, which faces the highway, with its massive buttresses and gently undulating lines from years of replastering, is better known than the front view. It was built sometime after 1776 to serve a Spanish farming community a few miles south of the village of Taos. On either side of the plaza was a long row of two-story homes, a few of which remain. Inside the church are priceless old santos and religious paintings, the most famous of which is the luminous painting of Christ done by Henry Ault in 1896. In the dark a cross that cannot be seen in daylight glows from the painting.

The village of Santo Tomas de Las Trampas was founded around 1750 in the hills east of Santa Cruz to protect the people of Santa Cruz Valley from Comanche raids. In 1760 permission was granted to build a church and save the villagers a nine-mile walk through dangerous Indian territory to the church at Picuris Pueblo. The church was dedicated to the Twelve Apostles, and legend says only 12 men were permitted to work on it, which is why it took 20 years to complete, the villagers paying for it by giving one-sixth of their crops each year. Two bells of silver and gold were hung in the towers. The deep-toned one, Refugio, was rung for solemn occasions such as deaths and funerals. The other, Gracia, which had a gentler tone, was rung for happier events, but it was stolen. The church, now named San Jose de Gracia, and the village of Trampas were declared a Historic Landmark recently as one of the best examples of Spanish colonial mission architecture.

Thousands of pilgrims make their way annually, especially during Holy Week, to the Santuario de Chimayo, hoping for a miraculous cure of their ills. In a small room to the left of the altar transept, a hole in the dirt floor extends down about two feet deep. Here pilgrims kneel and get a few pinches of the holy healing earth to rub on their bodies. Walls of the adjoining room are hung solidly with braces, crutches and canes, discarded by people who no longer needed them. An aura of faith and hope emanates from this modest church, whose out-of-plumb walls attest to the inexpert but faithful adobe masons who built it.

Tewa Indians are said to have used the waters of a spring here for its healing powers. As the spring slowly dried up, both Spanish and Indian used the healing mud on their ailing bodies. The santuario was built by Don Bernardo Abeyta in 1816 after a vision telling him to dig in his field for earth endowed with healing powers. Another legend says he uncovered a cross and pieces of clothing belonging to two priests who were martyred on this spot.

Several churches in Santa Fe are noteworthy. San Miguel Mission in downtown Santa Fe is built over the foundations of an earlier mission church that was built before 1626 for the Mexican-Indian laborers and servants of the prominent citizens of Santa Fe who attended a church on the plaza. The original chapel was destroyed during the Pueblo Revolt, and the present church was built anew in 1710. The exterior has undergone several restorations, and many 18th-century religious artifacts are housed inside.

St. Francis Cathedral, a block off the plaza, was built in 1869 to 1884 under the direction of Archbishop Lamy, whose life was fictionalized in Willa Cather's *Death Comes to the Archbishop*. Lamy brought masons from Europe to build the cathedral in the Romanesque style of his native France.

Between 1873 and 1878 the Sisters of Loretto built a stone chapel on Old Santa Fe Trail containing the lovely "miraculous staircase," constructed entirely without nails, screws or center post, and built by a mysterious itinerant carpenter sometimes said to be an incarnation of St. Joseph. Stained glass windows cast exquisite patterns of light in the interior. Open to the public, it is no longer used as a church.

A more recent church of classic mission architecture is El Cristo Rey on upper Canyon Road, largest building of its kind ever built of adobe. The altar piece, or reredos, 40 feet high and 18 feet wide, was carved of stone in 1761 for an earlier military chapel near the plaza. When the chapel was demolished the altar piece was kept in storage for almost 100 years until El Cristo Rey was built. The carved stone altar piece is considered one of the most extraordinary examples of Spanish colonial religious art in existence in the United States.

The Santuario of Our Lady of Guadalupe on Agua Fria Street, about two blocks west of the plaza, restored during the Bicentennial Year, also contains beautiful 18th-century reredos and hand-carved vigas and corbels in the choir loft.

First Presbyterian Church on Grant Avenue is said to be the

San Felipe de Neri Church, Old Town.

first Protestant church built in the mission style. It is a lovely example of the work of the famous architect, John Gaw Meem.

The San Miguel Mission in Socorro has undergone many changes. It probably was built around 1626 and ruined in the Pueblo Revolt. It was rebuilt, however, and in 1853 a new wing was added. It has two-tiered bell towers, red trim, and although it is the same age as some of the northern New Mexico Indian mission churches, it looks quite different. The contrast is interesting.

St. Francis de Paula Catholic Church, on the main thoroughfare in Tularosa, is the pride and joy of its parishioners and is lovingly tended. It is a simple, New Mexico-style church, built in 1869, and in modern times has been given a California-style tile roof. The St. Francis de Paula Fiesta is held the weekend following the city's Rose Festival (see *Tularosa*).

The stone St. Joseph's Mission church on the Mescalero Reservation is noteworthy because of its beauty and because of the love that went into its building. The Apaches did most of the work on it themselves.

New or old, large or small, Protestant or Catholic, the churches of New Mexico are a legacy of great beauty.

COLLEGES AND UNIVERSITIES

Institutions of higher learning throughout New Mexico not only add to the cultural, academic and recreational opportunities for the residents of those communities, but offer a great variety of programs of interest to visitors. Campus museums with exhibits on history, art, anthropology, geology, biology, astronomy and many other subjects are as available to travelers as they are to the local citizenry and students.

Musical programs including symphony, concerts and student recitals; theatrical productions staged by professional, semiprofessional and student organizations;interesting architecture and restorations of historic buildings; displays in special fields such as engineering, medicine, and architecture; films on wildlife, archeology and art; literary and poetry readings; lectures; athletic events of all kinds and sizes; golf courses, tennis courts, pools, rodeos and fiestas. . . these make up some of the offerings by the colleges and universities to the enrichment of their communities.

Some universities or colleges have housing facilities that may be rented by travelers for a nominal fee during off seasons. Some have tour and camping programs open to the public. Some offer workshops and seminars of special interest in unique locations, such as activities at the D.H. Lawrence Ranch at Taos, owned by the University of New Mexico.

When visiting any town or city in the state where there is an institution of higher learning, take time to call their information or activities office to find out what's happening on campus. You will probably find some surprisingly good entertainment and recreation. Following is an alphabetical list of New Mexico's public and private institutions of higher education. All are coeducational.

Artesia Christian College, Artesia. Enrollment, 140.
College of Santa Fe, Santa Fe. (Formerly St. Michael's College.) Enrollment, 1,179. Accredited by North Central Association.
College of the Southwest, Hobbs. Enrollment, 150. Candidate for accreditation by North Central Association.
Eastern New Mexico University, Portales (main campus). Enrollment, 3,698. Accredited by North Central Association. Branches: Roswell; enrollment, 1,009. Clovis; enrollment, 811.
New Mexico Highlands University, Las Vegas. Enrollment, 2,219. Accredited by North Central Association. Professional accreditation in chemistry.
New Mexico Institute of Mining and Technology, Socorro. Enrollment, 1,204. Accredited by North Central Association.
New Mexico Junior College, Hobbs. Enrollment, 1,459. Accredited by North Central Association.
New Mexico Military Institute, Roswell. Enrollment, 467. Accredited by North Central Association.
New Mexico State University, Las Cruces (main campus). Enrollment, 11,864. Accredited by North Central Association, and by numerous professional agencies in specialized fields. Branches: Alamogordo; enrollment, 1,222. Carlsbad; enrollment, 559. Doña Ana (Las Cruces); enrollment, 455. Grants; enrollment, 287. San Juan (Farmington); enrollment, 1,198.
Northern New Mexico Community College, El Rito. Enrollment, 892.
St. John's College, Santa Fe. (Other campus: Annapolis, Maryland.) Enrollment, 284. Accredited by North Central Association. Curriculum based on Great Books Program.
University of Albuquerque, Albuquerque. (Formerly St. Joseph's.) Enrollment, 1,253. Accredited by North Central Association.
University of New Mexico, Albuquerque (main campus). Enrollment, 22,033. Accredited by North Central Association, and by numerous professional agencies in specialized fields. Branch: Gallup; enrollment, 500.
Western New Mexico University, Silver City. Enrollment, 1,515. Accredited by North Central Association and by the National Council for Accreditation of Teacher Education.

Enrollment figures: N.M. Board of Educational Finance.

Albuquerque — New Mexico's big city.

CITIES AND TOWNS

New Mexico cities and towns can't be categorized. The variety is too big, too wide, too mind-boggling. There are large modern bustling cities, throbbing with activity and lusty life. And tiny mountain villages where archaic Spanish is still spoken, and the seasons are more important than digital clocks. Old towns, where painters, sculptors and musicians relax in mellow surroundings. New towns, crackling with the activities of oilmen, cattlemen, miners, atomic scientists.

There are towns that came slowly into being, hundreds of years ago, and towns that were thrust onto the map overnight by the steel-driving impact of the railroad or by the necessities of war.

There are Indian towns, Spanish towns, Anglo pioneer towns. Big towns spread across the desert and basking in the sun. Little towns huddled in the deep snows of the high country.

The only thing they all have in common is that they all have stories to tell — something to give the visitor. We've selected 63 New Mexico communities for you to visit — most of the bigger cities and a number of the smaller towns. If you can't find the town that interests you, look in the index. It may be grouped with a nearby larger town.

The numbers in parentheses refer to the coordinates on the official New Mexico road map, a copy of which will help you find your way around the state. (Get your copy from the New Mexico Travel Division.)

We only wish we had room to write about every single community, large and small, in the state. They are all fascinating in some way. They all deserve mention. But one town will lead an interested traveler to another. And we hope this book will be just the beginning of your travels in New Mexico.

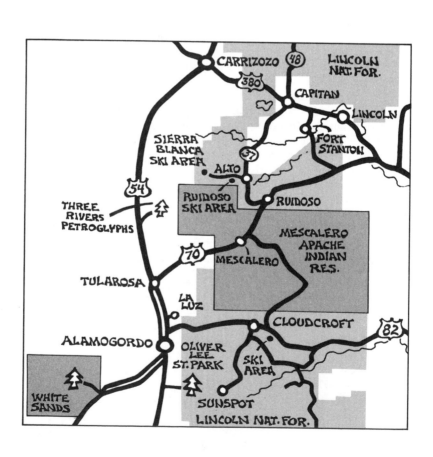

ALAMOGORDO (I-6)

Population, 29,215   *Elevation, 4,350*

Just before the turn of the century Alamogordo began as a trade center for ranchers, farmers and the lumber industry. Cattle grazed the sparse desert lands to the south and west, farms flourished in the fertile valley a few miles north, and the Sacramento Mountains, nudging the east edge of the village, were blue-black with timber. Since World War II, Alamogordo has become a scientific and defense-oriented city. Guided missiles, target drones and jets streak above the desert, once crossed on foot by padres and Spanish settlers.

Near Alamogordo is Holloman Air Force Base. Major facilities include a high-speed test track and central inertial guidance laboratory.

With White Sands National Monument on one side and the mountains on the other, tourism has become a major industry. Alamogordo has a pleasant year-round climate, practically pollution free, and good hotels, motels, restaurants, campgrounds and all service facilities for travelers.

The new International Space Hall of Fame is a giant cube of golden glass set in concrete pillars. Individuals from many countries, who have made major contributions to knowledge of space, have been inducted into its honored halls. New members are added annually. Each person is depicted by a marble tablet with a brief biography and some of the artifacts associated with his work. The exhibits also contain equipment used in space research, models, historical information and films. The building is open every day except Christmas, and has a small admission charge. Also in Alamogordo are the Tularosa Basin Historical Museum, a branch of New Mexico State University, and the New Mexico School for the Visually Handicapped.

White Sands National Monument, 14 miles (22 kilometres) southwest of town on US 70, covers miles of big, glistening, white gypsum dunes (see *Parks and Monuments*).

Trinity Site, toward the north end of White Sands Missile Range, marks ground zero where the first atomic bomb was detonated at 5:30 a.m. on July 16, 1945, ushering in the atomic age. The site is off-limits except for one day a year, usually the first Sunday in October, when the Army conducts visitors in for a brief visit. For the date, rendezvous point and other details, contact the Alamogordo Chamber of Commerce.

La Luz, four miles (six kilometres) northeast of Alamogordo, is the oldest settlement in the Tularosa Basin. Founded in 1705 by Spaniards, it is now a quiet plaza surrounded by a few old adobe buildings, homes and artists' studios. One folktale says that in the early Spanish colonial days, when men of the village went to the mountains to gather wood, their wives built a big bonfire every night in the plaza so their men would know all was well and there was no threat of attack by the Apaches. Thus the name *La Luz* — the light — came to be the name of the· settlement.

Oliver Lee State Park, in the foothills of the Sacramentos 10 miles (16 kilometres) south of Alamogordo, has a visitor center, trails, campground, rest rooms and picnic facilities. It marks the site of a spring that was used, and often fought over, by early cattlemen and Indians.

At the end of the first week of September, the Otero County Fair is held at the fairgrounds in Alamogordo. A rodeo, parade, contests, livestock exhibits, and agricultural exhibits from the rich Tularosa Basin farms highlight the event.

The Sacramento Mountains rise abruptly from the eastern edge of Alamogordo and provide a year-round playground. A 20-mile (32 kilometre) drive goes from the desert through rolling foothills, valleys filled to overflowing with apple orchards, to the high mountain meadows and peaks. At Mountain Park and High Rolls you can buy excellent cider and nuts.

During the last week in September and the first week in October, depending on the year, it is a popular pastime to drive through the Sacramentos to Cloudcroft and Ruidoso on an "aspencade" to see the glorious golden color of the changing aspens.

ALBUQUERQUE (E-5)

Population, 317,000 (city limits)   *Elevation, 5,312*
435,000 (metropolitan area)

Albuquerque, named for the Duke of Albuquerque, was founded in 1706 by a few Spanish families who built a small chapel and adobe homes around a plaza close to the Rio Grande. It was fertile farmland, and their crops grew well. Several Indian pueblos were close by. Oxcart caravans on El Camino Real (Royal Highway) passed through the plaza on their way to Santa Fe from Mexico.

When the Santa Fe Trail opened trade between the United States and Mexico in 1821, an extension went south from Santa Fe to Chihuahua, and traffic increased greatly through the plaza. In 1846, when the United States took the land from Mexico, Albuquerque saw a great increase in travelers. Forts were built in the southwest to protect pioneers and forty-niners, and ranches, villages and Indian pueblos from nomadic Indian tribes, and Albuquerque became a transportation and military supply center.

The greatest change came to Albuquerque in 1880 when the railroad came through, missing Old Town plaza by two miles (3.2 kilometres). A new town grew up along the railroad tracks, and a horse-drawn streetcar connected the two Albuquerques. For many years Old Town dozed in the sun, gradually being engulfed by the growing city, but it never lost its historic character. It remains an island of yesterday surrounded by a modern city.

During World War II, Albuquerque became an important military base and a liaison with the highly secret activity at Los Alamos. Albuquerque has evolved into a multifaceted city of scientific research and development, military bases, thousands of federal and state offices, a trade center for the state, a center for retirement and recreation, and a hub of transportation and communication. The city spreads over miles of valley and mesa land, crowding against the Sandia Mountains on the east and the volcanic escarpment of the west. In spite of its size, it is still a friendly, comfortable place to visit, and a good place to headquarter for interesting trips in all directions.

Old Town is still the city's historic heart. Shops of local and imported crafts, art galleries and restaurants surround three sides of the plaza, and venerable old San Felipe de Neri Church occupies the fourth. The church has been enlarged and remodeled many times. The once-dusty plaza is now a grassy park where benches invite leisurely sitting. In the summer

impromptu shows and musical offerings often take place. At
Christmas, luminarias (candle and paper bag lanterns) glow
from every walk and wall.

Albuquerque Museum, a block off Old Town Plaza, presents
exhibits of art, history and science pertinent to the area.

The University of New Mexico, founded in 1889 two miles
east of New Town, offers events of interest to visitors the year
around. Popejoy Hall presents concerts, lectures, light opera,
drama and road shows. It is the home base of the New Mexico
Symphony Orchestra. The Fine Arts Gallery and the Maxwell
Museum of Anthropology have outstanding exhibits. Jonson
(art) Gallery and museums of geology, astronomy, meteor-
itics and the Tamarind Institute of Lithography are all open to
the public. All buildings on the campus are variations of

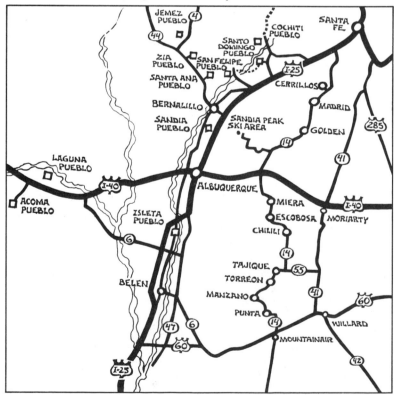

pueblo architecture, an interesting study in how the style has evolved from traditional to modern concepts without losing its integrity. The Sports Complex, two miles (3.2 kilometres) south of the main campus, on the corner of Stadium and University Boulevards, includes UNM Lobo Football Stadium, UNM Lobo Basketball Arena, and the Albuquerque Dukes Baseball Stadium.

The University of Albuquerque on the west side of town began as a teaching school for Catholic nuns, and is now a four-year general college. Drama, art shows, lectures and musical programs are open to the public.

New Mexico State Fairgrounds on East Central Avenue is the scene of intense activity for three weeks in September and October during the State Fair, one of the largest state fairs in the nation. Visitors take in horse racing with parimutuel betting, livestock shows, home, school and industrial exhibits of every kind. During the rest of the year, major events of many kinds are staged at Tingley Coliseum and other permanent buildings at the fairgrounds.

The New Mexico Arts and Crafts Fair, usually held in June at the State Fairgrounds, brings together 200 of the Southwest's leading artisans. Booths line the shady streets of the fairgrounds, offering browsers and buyers a remarkable selection. Many artists who started showing here have gone on to great fame and fortune.

The National Atomic Museum at Kirtland Air Force Base-East traces the development of nuclear weaponry since 1945 and has exhibits dealing with different forms of energy research. It is open to the public.

Several hundred kinds of animals and birds are displayed at the Rio Grande Zoo on Tenth Street, SW, including a special petting zoo for children. The zoo is surrounded by acres of shady, grassy park where visitors may picnic. Public tennis courts and a swimming pool are in the same park.

The International Balloon Fiesta in October is unadulterated fun for everyone. These giant balls of brilliant crazy-quilt colors float over the city, making people smile just to see them. Competitions are held during the fiesta with a mass ascension on the first and final days, when up to 400 balloons rise at the same time.

The Indian Pueblo Cultural Center on 12th Street, NW is a

joint effort of the 19 Indian Pueblo tribes in New Mexico. Each tribe displays its crafts and art in a separate gallery, and a sales room handles authentic Indian jewelry, paintings, pottery and other crafts. A restaurant serves delicious Pueblo Indian food. In the enclosed patio of the D-shaped building, different tribes perform dances Thursday through Sunday during the summer. On the walls of this courtyard several famous Pueblo Indian artists have painted giant murals. The center is open every day and has no admission fee, but contributions are appreciated.

More than 100 parks, four public golf courses, 22 tennis complexes and 10 public swimming pools round out the public recreation facilities in Albuquerque.

Indian Petroglyph State Park on the western edge of the city off Coors Boulevard, NW preserves carvings made by prehistoric Indians on the volcanic escarpment.

Sandia Peak Aerial Tramway glides up the steep west face of the Sandia Mountains in a 2.7-mile ride (4.3 kilometres), longest in the United States. At the summit is a U.S. Forest Service Visitor Center and a glass-enclosed restaurant with an incomparable view of thousands of square miles of mountains, valleys and plateaus. Trails lead along the crest through Cibola National Forest and down the gentler slopes of the east side. Skiers and hikers can take the tram to the crest in 15 minutes, or drive around the mountain to the base of the ski run and the trails and picnic sites in 45 minutes. Ski season at Sandia Peak Ski Area usually lasts from December through March (see *Winter Sports*).

Cibola National Forest includes most of the Sandia and Manzano mountains east of Albuquerque. No overnight camping is allowed in the Sandias, but it is permitted in the Manzanos (see *Forest Lands*).

A scenic-historic trip out of Albuquerque, often called the Mission Trail, circles the Manzano Mountains to the magnificent ruins of Quarai, Abo and Gran Quivira (see *Parks and Monuments*). The route goes past the old villages of Cedro, Escabosa, Chilili, Tajique, Torreon, Manzano, Punta, and joins US 60 at Mountainair. Most of these villages were founded on small community land grants during the first half of the 1800s. Weathered wood and rusty tin roofs, adobe and stone walls dot the green foothills. A road turns west at Tajique to a beautiful grove of maples in Fourth of July

Canyon where there are camping and picnicking facilities. In October the maples are a blaze of red, one of the few places in the state where sugar maples grow. The road loops around to rejoin NM 14 at Torreon, a distance of about 20 miles (32 kilometres). It is unpaved and rough, but not usually dangerous.

Indian Pueblos near Albuquerque are Isleta, Sandia, Santa Ana, Zia, San Felipe, Santo Domingo, Cochiti, Jemez and Acoma. Beautiful ceremonial dances take place at all of them (see *Native Americans*).

The Turquoise Trail out of Albuquerque, sometimes called the back road to Santa Fe, goes east on I-40 and north on NM 14 along the east side of the Sandias through Golden and Madrid. Though these are sometimes referred to as ghost towns, people live there, so the ghosts are pretty lively.

International Balloon Fiesta.

Golden is the site of the first gold strike west of the Mississippi in 1826. A few piles of stones remain from some of the early buildings. A small church sits on a hill, well cared for, and visited regularly by a priest to serve the residents. Madrid, 11 miles (18 kilometres) north of Golden, began as a coal mining town in 1835, but it wasn't until the railroad came in 1880 that mining became a big operation. When railroads switched to diesel fuel, the town almost breathed its last. Some of the "company houses" have been bought and restored, and the company store, machine shop and part of the mine are an interesting museum.

A 200-mile (322-kilometre) circle trip out of Albuquerque leaves I-25 at Bernalillo, 18 miles (29 kilometres) north. Take NM 44 to NM 4 to make the circle trip through the Jemez Mountains, past Jemez Pueblo, then through the bright red-earth canyons, the scientific city of Los Alamos, the cliff dwellings at Bandelier National Monument, and historic Santa Fe, founded in 1610 (see *Bernalillo*; *Jemez Pueblo*; *Los Alamos*; *Bandelier National Monument*; *Santa Fe*).

Sandia Peak Tramway.

ANTHONY   (K-5)

Population, 2,000   *Elevation, 3,825*

See *Las Cruces* map

About 20 miles (32 kilometres) north of El Paso, Texas, Anthony is the gateway to New Mexico from the south. A Tourist Welcome Center off Interstate 10 has maps and brochures about the state.

Anthony was founded when the Santa Fe Railway came through in 1881. A station was built on the Texas side of the state line and named La Tuna. A small chapel dedicated to St. Anthony was built on the New Mexico side, and the town grew around it, the people preferring the name Anthony to La Tuna.

As an alternate to the interstate, NM 28, three miles (4.8 kilometres) west of Anthony, goes up the Rio Grande Valley, almost paralleling the old Camino Real, the path followed by Spaniards 400 years ago. Later this route became known as the Chihuahua Trail, an extension of the Santa Fe Trail. Because of Apache attacks, no permanent Spanish settlements were made in this area until around 1850. Several old Spanish or Mexican villages remain on NM 28 between Anthony and Las Cruces: Chamberino, La Mesa, San Miguel and La Mesilla. After the Mexican War this area remained in Mexico until the Gadsden Purchase of 1853. No trace of El Camino Real remains. The ground has long since been planted to pecans, cotton, fruit and other crops in the rich Mesilla Valley of the Rio Grande, but there is a sense of history here, nevertheless.

119

ARTESIA (I-8)

Population, 13,700

Elevation, 3,380
See *Carlsbad* map

This city was named for water because artesian wells were discovered in the early days. But oil took over as the most important liquid when it was discovered in 1923. Artesia is a clean, modern city with wide business and residential streets. The huge landmark Navajo Oil Refinery defines the skyline.

The town's earliest roots go back to 1866 when John Chisum, Oliver Loving and Charles Goodnight began driving longhorns up the Horsehead Route. Goodnight and Loving came first, followed the same year by Chisum. There were no settlements along the entire 400-mile (644-kilometre) route, which began on the lower Pecos River above Big Bend, Texas, and followed the Pecos northwest.

The Chisum branch of the Horsehead Route turned near where Artesia is now and went northwest to Lincoln and on to the Rio Grande. Chisum bought land and established a ranch at the junction of the trail. Other settlers followed, a stage route took over the cattle trail, then a railroad. And finally a town was born.

Farming (along the Pecos), ranching and oil are the basic industries of the town today. In mid-August the town holds its annual Pioneer Days and Junior Livestock Fair, and in mid-October the annual Arts in the Park Show. Painters, potters, quilters and others exhibit their crafts. Bands, folk singing and other entertainment are offered in Central Park.

The Artesia Waterfowl Area, four miles (6.4 kilometres) northeast of town, provides resting and feeding grounds for migratory birds. No hunting is allowed, but it is a good place for bird watchers to see sandhill crane and other waterfowl from late November through January. Pronghorn antelope and upland game bird hunting are good farther east on the Llano Estacado (Staked Plains).

Hagerman, about 20 miles (32 kilometres) north of Artesia, is a farming and ranching town named for J.J. Hagerman, president of a small railroad, who spent most of his mining fortune developing irrigation near here. The town was named for him in 1906 while his son, Herbert, was governor of New Mexico.

Motels, restaurants and other tourist facilities are available in Artesia.

AZTEC

Population, 7,200

(A-3)

Elevation, 5,650

See *Farmington* map

Aztec is on the Animas River a few miles above its con-fluence with the San Juan. Irrigated valleys are fragrant with orchards, and the rivers, lakes and reservoirs of this high pla-teau country provide excellent outdoor recreation. The city was founded in 1890 and named for the then unexcavated pre-historic Indian ruin nearby, which turned out to have no con-nection with the Aztec Indians. But the name stuck — to the ruins and to the town.

The Aztec Museum in the old City Hall on Main Street has a Pioneer Room and the Lobato Collection of rocks and miner-als. The first weekend in July each year, Aztec Fiesta Days features mariachi bands, a parade, sidewalk sales, a carnival and fun for the whole family.

Aztec Ruins National Monument (see *Parks and Monu-ments*), one of the major archeological sites of the Four Cor-ners region, just on the edge of town, is an outstanding attrac-tion, and is open year round.

Motels, restaurants and other travelers' needs can be found in Aztec, and others are in Farmington, 28 miles (45 kilo-metres) away.

Aztec Ruins National Monument.

121

BELEN   (F-4)
Population, 8,200   *Elevation, 4,800*

In spite of its big neighbor to the north (Albuquerque),
Belen retains a distinctive character. A Spanish land grant,
Nuestra Señora de Belen (Our Lady of Bethlehem), was made
in 1740 to a group of Spanish settlers. The grant extended
from near the present site of Belen to about 15 miles (24 kilometres) south on both sides of the river. Soon two villages
were established, one for Spanish colonists and one for
genizaros, Indians of mixed blood or who had been captured
by Plains Indians and ransomed or recaptured and Christianized by Spaniards.

Rich agricultural land along the river has always made Belen
a center for farming and cattle ranching. After the railroad
reached Belen in 1880 it became a division point where east-
west and north-south lines cross.

A few interesting old adobe buildings remain, such as the Don Felipe Chavez house, restored by the Western artist Gordon Snidow, and the church, built around 1860. (The earlier one was destroyed by fire in 1855.) A partly abandoned business district near the depot reflects brick architecture from the turn of the century, and shaded residential areas show the influence of early-day Midwestern settlers, many of them originally from Germany. A new residential development across the river has many contemporary style houses and a golf course.

In early September each year, the Valencia County Fair is held at the Sheriff's Posse Arena in Belen. It features a parade, arts and crafts exhibit, rodeo, horse show and Western dances. The New Mexico Boys Ranch Rodeo usually takes place the second week in July, and in mid-August is the annual Our Lady of Belen Fiesta, with masses, burning of the devil, parade, carnival, dances, crafts exhibits and barbecues.

Between Belen and Albuquerque on NM 47, which follows the route of the old supply wagons to Mexico, El Camino Real, and later the Chihuahua Trail, are several old Spanish villages of interest.

Peralta, named for the Spanish family who first settled there, was the home of Henry Connelly, governor of New Mexico during the Civil War. Invading Confederate soldiers occupied his hacienda for a short time as they made their brief foray into New Mexico. The last battle of the New Mexico campaign was fought here on April 15, 1862, ending in defeat for the Confederates.

Two miles (3.2 kilometres) south of Peralta is Valencia, originally the county seat of Valencia County. Captain Francisco de Valencia established a hacienda here before the Pueblo Revolt of 1680. The Catholic church, remodeled several times, was built around 1750, and the original walls still stand.

Tome, six miles (9.7 kilometres) farther south, was settled before the Pueblo Revolt by Tome Dominguez de Mendoza. He did not return after the reconquest, and the area was not settled again until 1739, when a group of colonists from Albuquerque applied for the Tome Land Grant. Tome was harassed by raiding Comanches and Apaches, but the settlers held on to their lands. A small sign on the highway indicates the Tome plaza and an old church a block away where an outdoor museum of religious folk art and history is enclosed in a glass-fronted building. The grassy plaza is shaded by giant cotton-woods. On one side are the remains of the jail built around the time of the Civil War. During Holy Week the Passion Play is presented.

Los Lunas, on US 85, 13 miles (21 kilometres) north of Belen, is the present county seat of Valencia County. It was settled by the family of Don Diego Luna, who received the San Clemente Land Grant early in the 1700s. This was an illustrious family through the years, its members holding many public offices. The Luna mansion on US 85 and NM 6 is now a fine restaurant, preserving much of the history of the family through photographs and other memorabilia.

Limited motel and restaurant facilities are available in Belen, but a wide selection is available in Albuquerque, 35 miles (56 kilometres) north.

Near Belen.

BERNALILLO

(D-5)

Population, 2,600   *Elevation, 5,050*

Bernalillo was founded shortly after the reconquest and was probably named for one of the Bernal family who had owned a hacienda there before the Pueblo Revolt of 1680. Today it is the county seat of Sandoval County and a trading center for several Indian pueblos in the vicinity.

When the Coronado Expedition came to New Mexico in 1540, they were said to have had their headquarters at one of the prehistoric pueblos across the river. However, some think the expedition may have made its base at what is now Coronado Monument, next to Bernalillo. At that time there were a dozen pueblos along the Rio Grande between Bernalillo and Isleta, about 30 miles (48 kilometres) to the south.

In 1704, Governor Diego de Vargas, who had reconquered New Mexico in 1692-1694, died in Bernalillo, possibly of food

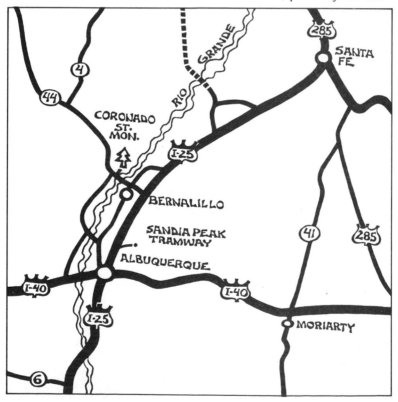

poisoning, after a campaign against the Apaches in the Sandia Mountains. A block west of the main street, a few traces of the old village's adobe walls remain.

On August 10 each year, the people of Bernalillo stage a beautiful version of the Matachines Dance in honor of their patron saint, San Lorenzo. This dance, with versions still found throughout Europe and Britain, was brought by the Moors to Spain, and then to the New World, where it was performed as a morality play of the forces of good and evil in combat. The dance was adopted by both Spaniards and Indians, and several versions are still performed in villages and pueblos.

Coronado State Monument is one mile (1.6 kilometres) west of Bernalillo (see *Parks and Monuments*).

Adjacent to the monument is Coronado State Park with pueblo-style shelters, camping and picnicking facilities. During construction of the shelters, bulldozers uncovered foundations of a hacienda that was burned during the Pueblo Revolt, and beneath that, fire pits believed to have been used by migrating bands of Indians as early as three or four thousand years before Christ. After recording the site it was covered over again, but visitors to this beautiful setting today can relish the knowledge that this spot has been inhabited by man for thousands of years.

Motel and other facilities are available in Albuquerque, 18 miles (29 kilometres) south.

BLOOMFIELD   (B-3)
Population, 4,500   *Elevation, 5,395*

See *Farmington* map

Bloomfield, in the northwestern part of the state at the intersection of US 64 and NM 44, is a farming and ranching community on the San Juan River.

Just west of Bloomfield on US 64 is the Salmon Ruins archeological site and museum. The people of San Juan County own the site and the museum-research center that houses artifacts unearthed in the excavation project. All artifacts remain here. During the summer, students from around the country, led by professional anthropologists, excavate the ruin, and visitors are invited to watch. Roughly contemporary with the larger Anasazi sites at Aztec, Mesa Verde and Chaco Canyon (see *Parks and Monuments*), Salmon Ruins contains more than 700 rooms, and may have been as much as four stories high. The San Juan County Historical Society is also restoring the cabin of George Salmon, who homesteaded the property before the turn of the century.

Angel Peak, south of town on the Nacimiento Badlands, is a wonderland of grotesquely shaped mesas, cliffs and canyons in a land where no sign of human habitation can be seen in any direction. Subtle shades of gray, blue, lavender, pink and buff band the formations. Millions of years ago this was an inland sea. In its own good time it dried up, leaving the earth to be played with by wind and water. This is a barren, eerie place, but like so much of New Mexico, impossible to look at without reacting to it. The BLM maintains two picnic areas and one campground where there are restrooms, shelters and tables, but no other facilities. The Badlands are located 13 miles (21 kilometres) south of Bloomfield on NM 44, and five miles (eight kilometres) east of the highway on a graded and graveled road.

Motels and additional travelers' facilities are available in Farmington and Aztec.

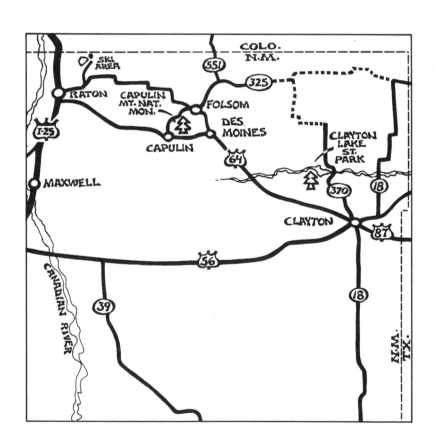

CAPULIN, DES MOINES,   (B-9) FOLSOM

Only a few houses and stores remain of Capulin in northeast New Mexico, but it was a busy trading center when that area was opened to homesteading in the early part of this century. It was first named Dedman in 1909 for a superintendent on the Santa Fe Railway, but in 1914 the name was changed because of nearby Capulin Mountain. The word means wild cherry, or chokecherry, which grows in the area. The land that was plowed by homesteaders became the fringes of the dust bowl in the 1930s, and has since reverted to cattle range land.

Capulin Mountain National Monument (see *Parks and Monuments*), an almost perfectly shaped volcanic cinder cone, is several miles north of town.

Des Moines, nine miles (14.5 kilometres) east of Capulin on the Colorado & Southern Railroad, is a cattle ranching center.

Folsom, nine miles (14.5 kilometres) northeast of Capulin, another old ranching and railroad town, is the site of the first discovery of prehistoric spear points that gave the name to Folsom Man, one of New Mexico's prehistoric hunting-gathering cultures dating back to 10 or 15,000 years ago. A good regional museum is in an old mercantile building, and if it is locked, a sign on the door will tell you where to get the key. An abandoned stone hotel and other buildings will remind you that once Folsom was the boisterous, booming shipping center of northeastern New Mexico.

There is a wide choice of motels and restaurants in Raton, 30 miles (48 kilometres) west.

Capulin Mountain National Monument.

129

CARLSBAD

Population, 28,980

(J-8)

Elevation, 3,110

This clean, modern city in far southeastern New Mexico at the junction of US 285 and US 180 traces its beginnings back to the days when large herds of longhorn cattle were trailed from Texas to stock the ranges of New Mexico, Colorado, Wyoming and Montana. The pioneer cattleman Charles Goodnight started a new trail in 1866, following the east side of the Pecos River from near San Angelo, Texas, to approximately the site of Carlsbad, where he crossed the Pecos and continued north up the west side. That same year he met Oliver Loving, another Texas cattleman, they joined forces, and the route became established as the Goodnight-Loving Trail. Hundreds of thousands of cattle were driven over this trail until the railroads came west and made long cattle drives unnecessary.

By 1888 a town had formed at the river crossing, named

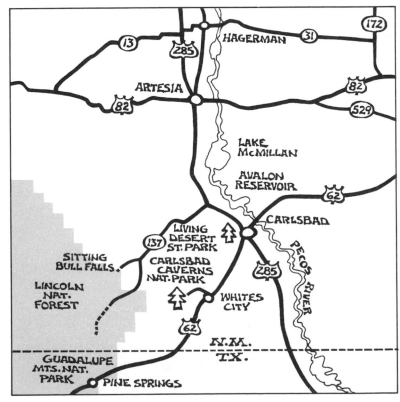

after the Eddy brothers, who held large ranching interests in the area and were promoting a railroad and townsites. In 1899 the name was changed to Carlsbad because waters in a spring near the town were believed to be similar to those at the famous Bohemian spa, Carlsbad.

Cattle ranching is rivaled now by potash mining and farming in the fertile Pecos Valley. Because of Carlsbad Caverns National Park, tourism is also a major industry. A dam on the Pecos forms Lake Carlsbad in the city, and Presidents' Park, a small but delightful privately owned amusement park, has been developed on the east bank. Here there is an old-fashioned Western railroad station, and a narrow-gauge steam train of 1880s vintage takes passengers on a two-mile (3.2 kilometre) trip along the lake shore. Elegant old private railroad cars are on exhibit. An authentic small paddlewheel boat, driven by an 1858 steam engine, takes visitors for rides on the lake. One of the most popular attractions at the park is a 1903 carousel, completely restored and in operation.

Water-skiing, swimming, boating and fishing can all be enjoyed on Lake Carlsbad, and dozens of picnic tables and a nine-hole golf course make it a complete family fun area.

Living Desert State Park on Ocotillo Heights at the northern edge of the city is very attractive and contains dozens of kinds of plant and animal life indigenous to the area, including bear, deer, otter, raccoon, bison, birds and reptiles, and thousands of species of cacti.

The Tri-State Arts and Crafts Exhibit is held each year in mid-July at the Carlsbad Fine Arts Museum, a new addition to the library complex, where sculpture, painting, photography and crafts by artists from New Mexico, Texas and Arizona are exhibited and sold.

The most famous attraction in the area is Carlsbad Caverns National Park, the largest and most spectacular limestone caverns in the world, located 20 miles (32 kilometres) southwest of town off US 180 (see *Parks and Monuments*).

The highway to El Paso (US 180) continues past the park along the rugged Guadalupe Mountains and across the border into Texas and Guadalupe Mountains National Park. The escarpment is part of the Capitan Reef, containing extensive fossil beds. The park is undeveloped, but a dirt road leads to beautiful McKittrick Canyon, and at Pine Springs, entrance to the Park, are the ruins of a Butterfield Trail stage station.

Ten miles (16 kilometres) north of Carlsbad on US 285, NM 137 leads 40 miles (64 kilometres) to another portion of the Guadalupe Mountains. Sitting Bull Falls is a sylvan delight of rainbow mists, grass and flowers hidden within the craggy folds of the desert mountains. Camping and picnicking facilities are at the falls.

The small town of Loving, eight miles (13 kilometres) southwest of Carlsbad on US 285 was named for pioneer cattleman, Oliver Loving, who was fatally wounded by Indians on a cattle drive on the Goodnight-Loving Trail. Eighteen miles (29 kilometres) north of Carlsbad on the same highway is Seven Rivers, another watering place on the old cattle trail. Several old timers who wrote their names in the dusty trails of the early cattle days are buried in a cemetery here.

Motels, restaurants, campgrounds and all tourist facilities are in Carlsbad, plus a few more at Whites City near the entrance to Carlsbad Caverns National Park.

Carlsbad Caverns National Park.

CARRIZOZO   (H-6)
Population, 1,300   *Elevation, 5,425*

Like many other towns in New Mexico, Carrizozo began when a railroad line came through the area. Usually towns developed where work crews were quartered in temporary shacks. In 1899, the El Paso & Northeastern reached here, and within a few years a handsome depot and business buildings were erected. Most of these are now abandoned, but the buildings facing the depot still have examples of the ornate woodwork and pressed tin facades that recall turn-of-the-century architecture.

Business has moved a few blocks west along US 54, but the town still has much of the look of the early days. It is still a trade center for large ranches in the area, and the railroad, now the Southern Pacific, goes through. Carrizozo is the county seat of historic Lincoln County.

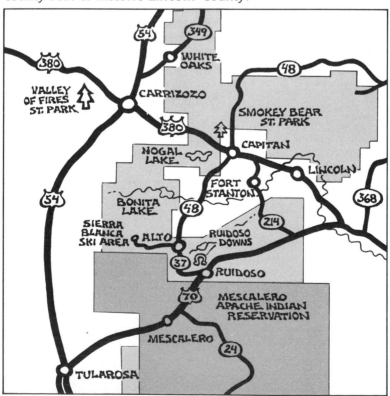

Valley of Fires State Park, a mile (1.6 kilometres) west of Carrizozo on US 380, has camping and picnicking facilities on an island of volcanic rock in one of the youngest lava fields in the United States. A river of basalt flowed 44 miles (71 kilometres) down the Tularosa Basin from a small peak near the northern end of the *malpais* (badlands), solidifying for eternity into a black, tormented mass covering 127 square miles of valley floor. In some places the ribbon of lava is only a half mile wide, in others it spreads out over five miles (6.4 kilometres). Trails from the campground lead down into the buckled, twisted, grotesque formations.

Windblown dirt has collected in holes and crevices of the lava, affording fertile bases for many types of growth that defy nature and thrive in the unlikely environment. These in turn attract small animals, so the forbidding landscape is not as devoid of life as it seems at first glance.

The malpais comes to an end where White Sands begins — an unlikely combination of stark black and white that readily identifies southern New Mexico from far-distant satellites. Some species of mice have adapted themselves to be black in the malpais, while their cousins are white in White Sands.

Prehistoric man also inhabited the area, as petroglyphs and occasional bits of pottery testify. Indians of the Jornada Branch of the Mogollon Culture passed through the malpais on migrations up to about A.D. 1400. Later it became part of the Mescalero Apache domain.

At Three Rivers, about 28 miles (45 kilometres) south of Carrizozo, the BLM manages a magnificent area that has miles of petroglyphs that date back hundreds to possibly thousands of years.

Three miles (4.8 kilometres) north of Carrizozo, a paved road goes nine miles (14.5 kilometres) into the foothills of the Jicarilla Mountains to the ghost town of White Oaks, where gold was discovered in 1879. More than $2 million in gold was mined here, but by the 1890s it had played out, and the town died when it asked too high a price for railroad right-of-way, thus losing the railroad to Carrizozo in 1899. A few families still live in this quiet setting, neighbors to crumbling adobe walls filled with memories of the past. One fine home still stands, Hoyle's Castle, a two-story brick and woodwork home of the Victorian period, built for a bride who never came.

134

CHAMA

(A-5)

Population, 2,200   *Elevation, 7,860*

Chama is located on US 84 at the foot of Cumbres Pass in the scenic northland. With snow-tipped peaks of the Sangre de Cristo Mountains to the north, wind-sculptured pinnacles to the south, and the Carson National Forest all around, Chama is a vacationland all seasons of the year.

Lumber and mining drew the first settlers to the area as early as 1865 when a few stores, saloons and a tent hotel made up the town. Five years later a sawmill was built, and for a while the community was called Slabtown. Today, many log buildings are still in use.

In 1880, the Denver & Rio Grande Railroad built a narrow-gauge line from Walsenberg, Colorado, through the San Luis Valley and west to the Four Corners country and north to the mines at Silverton, Colorado. The line crossed and recrossed

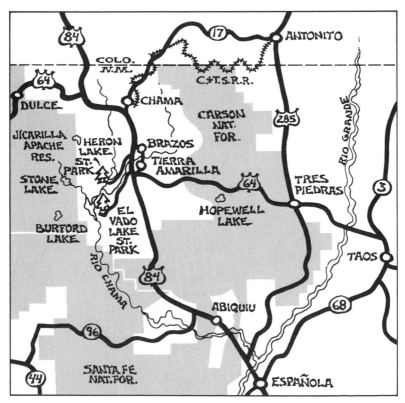

the boundary between New Mexico and Colorado, going through Chama, which became the leading town in Rio Arriba County. With the opening of passenger service the following year, Chama was well established and had a population about the same as today.

Passenger service was discontinued in 1951, and in 1969 the entire line was abandoned. The portion from Durango to Silverton had already been preserved as a scenic and historic attraction for tourists, and in 1974 New Mexico and Colorado pooled resources and bought the 64 miles (103 kilometres) of line between Antonito, Colorado, and Chama. The line is almost equally divided between the two states. The route crosses 10,015-foot (3,053-metre) Cumbres Pass, goes over trestles, crosses deep canyons and winds through awesome Toltec Gorge, a dramatic and thrilling experience for riders.

Known now as the Cumbres & Toltec Scenic Railroad, restored rolling stock carries delighted tourists on a spectacular ride. Depots and terminal facilities are in both Chama and Antonito.

The C & TSRR operates from June through early October with each month offering different scenes and experiences.

Cumbres & Toltec Scenic Railroad.

June is least crowded, and there will still be patches of snow in places. July and August bring out a profusion of wildflowers in the alpine meadows, and dramatic thunderheads over the mountains. In late September aspen leaves begin to turn, and golden cataracts tumble down the mountainsides. Reservations are always advisable but are necessary during aspen time. Tickets may be ordered from C & TSRR, Box 78, Chama, NM 87520.

Fishing for rainbow and German brown trout in the Chama River for about four miles (6.4 kilometres) south of town often yields limit catches. Picnic tables and camper turnout areas are provided. Twenty-eight miles (45 kilometres) downstream from Chama are Heron and El Vado lakes, where trout fishing is often the best in the state. A recreation area and boat-launching facility are at El Vado State Park, and two smaller camping areas are upstream along the Chama (see *Parks and Monuments*).

Parkview Trout Hatchery near the village of Los Ojos produces around seven million rainbow trout eggs a year, as well as most of the state's supply of kokanee and coho salmon, and about a third of the brown trout. Visitors may take a tour of the hatchery.

Hopwell Lake on US 64 about 40 miles (64 kilometres) southeast of Chama is a blue jewel lying in a meadow surrounded by evergreens high in the mountains. It is stocked with rainbow and brook trout, and camping and picnicking sites are available.

Good elk and deer hunting is in the Chama area, both on state lands and at private hunting preserves. Heavy snows fall in Chama, which calls itself the snowmobile capital of New Mexico. Old logging roads and big open meadows covered with deep snow provide miles of trails for snowmobiling. Chama is also the cross-country skiing capital, and lures thousands every winter to enjoy the silent wonder of the white hills and to join in races.

Tierra Amarilla, county seat of Rio Arriba County, is an interesting old Hispanic village about 15 miles (24 kilometres) south of Chama, just off US 84. It came into being after the Tierra Amarilla Land Grant was made in 1832.

Several lodges, motels, restaurants and resorts are in the Chama area.

HIGH ROAD TO TAOS — (C-6) CHIMAYO AND THE MOUNTAIN VILLAGES

About 16 miles (26 kilometres) north of Santa Fe, just beyond the turnoff to Los Alamos, NM 4 turns east. This and NM 76, 75 and 3 have come to be called the High Road to Taos (see map).

None of the villages on this road is large enough to be called a city, but they are of such singular charm and historic interest that they deserve to be treated as a special group. Most were founded in the 17th and 18th centuries on communal land grants. They developed in almost complete isolation during the Spanish colonial period, when New Mexico was a neglected province of Spain and such out-of-the-way settlements were left to their own devices. The people of these mountain villages clung to their old ways and beliefs. Customs became deeply ingrained, creating a pocket of Spanish provin-

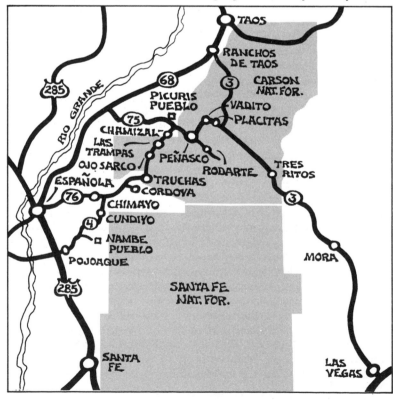

cial life that still exists, reminiscent of a way of life that existed 300 years ago. This route takes you through the heart of the Rio Arriba or Upriver culture of old New Mexico.

Cundiyo, 20 miles (32 kilometres) northeast of Santa Fe, was a settlement of the Cundiyo Grant made in 1743 near the site of an ancient Tewa Indian pueblo. A cluster of adobe houses, a church, and small fields along the stream look much as they have for two-and-a-half centuries.

Four miles (6.4 kilometres) farther is Chimayo, originally Plaza del Cerro, a square of contiguous adobe houses around a fortified plaza — customary in colonial times. This old part of Chimayo is off the highway near Ortega Weavers. The settlement was near a Tewa Indian pueblo on a community land grant possibly dating as far back as 1695. Newer parts of the village extend two or three miles (three to five kilometres) along NM 76 and 4, which meet here.

Just off NM 4 is the famous and beloved Santuario de Chimayo (see *Missions and Churches*), built between 1813 and 1816 by Don Bernardo de Abeyta as a private family chapel. In the 1920s this "Lourdes of America" was given to the Catholic Archdiocese of Santa Fe.

On Good Friday, thousands of pilgrims walk to the chapel, some hiking from as far away as Las Cruces, 300 miles (485 kilometres) in fulfillment of a vow.

Another private chapel was built near the Santuario in the 1860s, and legend says that a small papier-mâché statue of the infant Jesus enshrined in this chapel walks the Chimayo Valley every night to protect His children.

In July the people of the valley re-enact a vivid drama on horseback of the Christians and the Moors, an old Moorish-Spanish morality play, to which visitors are invited. Chimayo is a special place to visit at any time of year, but is particularly lovely in the fall when open stands along the highways are ablaze with baskets of red and yellow apples, green and red chile, pumpkins and flowers.

About three miles (4.8 kilometres) east of Chimayo on NM 76, a dirt road circles down the hillside to the village of Cordova, made famous by the George Lopez family and other woodcarvers, whose New Mexico folk art, both religious and whimsical, can still be bought in the village. Originally called Pueblo Quemado (Burned Pueblo), the name was changed to honor the Cordova family who settled in Santa Cruz after the reconquest of 1692, and whose descendants later moved farther up Santa Cruz Creek.

Truchas, the next village, sits high on a bench of the Sangre de Cristos looking across steep canyons and hills to Truchas Peak, 13,102 feet (3,993 metres) high, second highest in the state. It's a vision from Spain or even Switzerland. The gray walls, rusty red corrugated tin roofs, and emerald fields set against the backdrop of dark or snowy mountains make a scene that has been recreated more than once by New Mexico artists.

The highway drops down through the forest to Ojo Sarco, a cluster of farms along a tiny stream by the same name, and a couple of miles beyond is the village of Las Trampas. Founded about 1750 as a typical adobe-walled colonial village, this is the site of one of the most beautiful mission churches in New Mexico (see *Missions and Churches*). This was good beaver-trapping country, which gave the village its name — *trampas* is Spanish for traps.

The route continues through the villages of Chamizal, Rio Lucio, Llano, Rodarte, Peñasco, Vadito, Placitas — names that flow from the tongue like poetry. Most are no more than a few adobe houses set in tiny fields of corn and chile or old apple orchards. They seem undisturbed by the fact that the scientific world of Los Alamos is only one mountain away. To travel this High Road to Taos defies time and space. Your mind is deftly drawn through a curtain separating two worlds, letting you relive a few hours of 18th century New Mexico, when time stood still.

There are no motels in the mountain villages, but at Chimayo is an outstanding restaurant in an old hacienda.

CIMARRON   (B-7)
Population, 1,000   *Elevation, 6,500*

The living legend of Cimarron is intertwined with the Maxwell Land Grant given to Charles Beaubien and Guadalupe Miranda in 1841. Lucien Maxwell, scout, buffalo hunter, beaver trapper, merchant on the Santa Fe Trail, Indian agent and cattle baron, married Beaubien's daughter and eventually inherited and bought the entire 1.74 million-acre grant. It contained gold, silver and coal deposits, timber and farm and grazing lands.

There were no permanent settlements until after the American occupation in 1846. Soon a station and trading post on the Santa Fe Trail were built on the Cimarron River, where a trail branched to Taos. Maxwell had first settled on the Rayado about nine miles (14.5 kilometres) south of the stage station, but decided the Cimarron location was better, so built a home

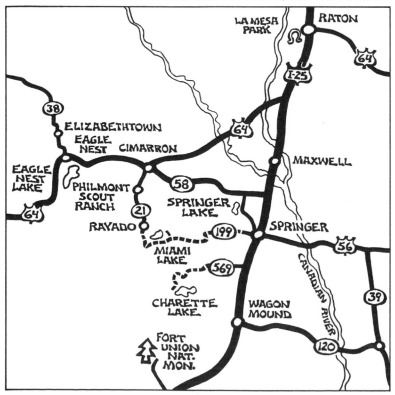

across the road from the station. The town of Cimarron grew up around him. Maxwell's mansion became famous for his flamboyant hospitality to travelers. When gold was discovered in the mountains, Virginia City and Elizabethtown were started, but Cimarron remained the most important town on the grant for many years.

Maxwell sold the grant to a British syndicate and moved to Fort Sumner in 1869.

Cimarron became the scene of the Colfax County War, a culmination of several years of dispute over ownership of the grant, which had seemingly nebulous or stretchable boundaries. This bloody confrontation brought outlaws to Cimarron, and for several years it had the well-deserved reputation of being one of the wildest places in the West. With the coming of the railroad in 1879, the cattle industry boomed, and many large corporate ranches were formed on the Maxwell Land Grant. This area of New Mexico, with its rich grasslands, sheltered canyons and mountain meadows, was a leader in the development of the cattle industry in the entire Southwest.

The Old Mill Museum is in the four-story grist mill built by Maxwell in 1864 when he was Indian Agent to the Utes and Apaches. It contains hundreds of photographs, farm and ranch tools, books, furniture, costumes and memorabilia from Cimarron's exciting past. It is owned by the CS Cattle Company and operated as a regional museum.

The St. James Hotel was built by Henri Lambert in the 1870s. A French immigrant, he had been field chef for General Ulysses S. Grant and in Lincoln's White House, but came West to the gold mines on the Maxwell Grant. The hotel was the vortex of Cimarron's hectic life, and 29 bullet holes still show in the pressed tin ceiling of the room that used to be the saloon. Rooms have been carefully restored, and notes and photographs list dozens of famous and infamous people who stayed there. The hotel is operated as a museum, and a newer motel has been built close by.

A stone jail, Wells Fargo station and old brewery date back to the 1870s and 1880s, and a little cemetery on a hill above town contains graves of people who helped write the history of New Mexico.

Four miles (6.4 kilometres) south of Cimarron on NM 21 is Philmont Scout Ranch, once part of the Maxwell Land Grant.

In 1941 the Oklahoma oilman, Waite Phillips, and his wife gave 137,493 acres (55,643 hectares) to the Boy Scouts. Every year thousands of scouts from all over the world have a week's experience camping, hiking and exploring in the mountains. It is still an operating cattle ranch, and the Phillips mansion at headquarters is used for conferences. The public may tour the grounds, administrative buildings and mansion. About six miles (9.7 kilometres) farther south on the same road, at the site of the old town of Rayado, Maxwell's first house has been completely rebuilt and restored by the scouts and is used as a leaders' training center. Next door is a restoration of a hacienda-style adobe house built by Kit Carson, who was a great friend of Maxwell's, and across the road is the Ernest Thompson Seton Museum and Library. The library and the Carson house are open to the public.

The main branch of the Santa Fe Trail came from Bent's Fort on the Arkansas River near present-day La Junta, Colorado, over Raton Pass, down through Cimarron and almost straight south to Fort Union. NM 21 from Cimarron to Rayado follows approximately the same route.

US 64 east from Cimarron to Eagle Nest (see *Eagle Nest*) goes through the canyon of the Cimarron River, in some places between palisades several hundred feet high. At either end of the canyon is a campground operated by the New Mexico Game and Fish Department, but in order to camp you must have a fishing license. The Cimarron is a good stream for German brown trout. This is in the Colin Neblett Wildlife Area. Old lumber roads make good hiking trails into the mountains (no off-road vehicles).

There are two private campgrounds in Cimarron and good motels, restaurants and other tourist accommodations. Since 1923 Cimarron has staged a celebration on the Fourth of July with parade, rodeo and dancing, showing that in Cimarron, the spirit of the Old West lives on.

CLAYTON

Population, 3,900

(B-10)

Elevation, 5,050

See *Capulin* map

Nine miles (14.5 kilometres) from the border of the Texas-Oklahoma panhandles, Clayton, in the northeastern corner, is the first New Mexico city visitors from those areas encounter. High, rolling grasslands, punctuated by volcanic cones and mesas, make a panorama of immense solitude and beauty. One portion of the Kiowa National Grasslands extends from the state line almost to the edge of Clayton, and it was this rich nutritious grass that led to Clayton's founding in 1887. A vast area of this corner of the territory made up the range of the Dorsey Cattle Ranch — the town was named for his son, Clayton Dorsey (see *Springer*). A few years later when the railroad came through, Clayton became a cattle shipping center. Livestock growing, feeding and shipping are still major industries in Clayton.

The Cimarron Cut-off of the Santa Fe Trail, which avoided Cimarron and shortened the journey — but at some risk of attack by Plains Indians — ran a few miles north of Clayton, where ruts are still clearly visible. Half a dozen famous landmarks and watering holes on the Trail are within an hour's drive of Clayton.

In downtown Clayton several old buildings remain from the turn of the century. The dining room of the old Eklund Hotel has been restored to all its Victorian elegance. In 1900 Clayton was the scene of the hanging of the notorious train robber, Black Jack Ketchum.

Clayton Lake State Park lies 12 miles (19 kilometres) north on NM 370 (see *Parks and Monuments*). The drive goes over rolling green farmland and drops into canyons where lava escarpments contrast with the pastoral ranch scenes in the valleys. Rabbit Ear Mountain, a landmark on the Santa Fe Trail, is a mile or two south of the lake. It was named for a big-eared Indian chief, not for an animal. A dam on Seneca Creek backs up the irregularly shaped lake that has rocky sandstone ledges rising from the shoreline. The park has a campground, shelters, showers, electricity, dump, boat ramp and permits "no wake" boating. Trout, wall-eye pike, channel cat and bass are taken here.

CLOUDCROFT

Population, 700

As the lovely name suggests, this year-round resort area rests in the clouds and tall pines of the Sacramento Mountains of south-central New Mexico. A 25-mile (40 kilometre) drive from Alamogordo leads a vertical four-fifths of a mile (1.3 kilometres) up to Cloudcroft. From the heights of the mountains you look down on the mysterious snowy dunes of White Sands, an eerie contrast.

In 1898-1899 the El Paso & Northeastern Railroad ran a narrow-gauge line into the Sacramentos to get timber to make ties. Next they built an exclusive resort and named it Cloudcroft. El Pasoans seeking the mountain coolness made up the majority of guests. On weekends the little train carried vacationers; on weekdays it hauled logs. Part of a high trestle still standing along the highway is a reminder of those early days.

The lovely old lodge is still in operation, and summer homes, lodges, motels, restaurants and campgrounds, both private and in Lincoln National Forest, offer a wide choice in accommodations. The golf course at Cloud Country Lodge is open to the public, and at more than 9,000 feet (2,743 metres) elevation, is the highest in the country.

Cloudcroft ski area, two-and-a-half miles (4 kilometres) east of town (see *Winter Sports*) is the most southerly ski area in the state. Cloudcroft is also a winter snowmobiling center.

To reach Sunspot, a giant solar observatory, take NM 24 south two miles (3.2 kilometres) from Cloudcroft to Forest Road 64, paved, which goes 18 miles (29 kilometres) to the observatory. Two large white buildings, one shaped like a bowl, the other like a needle, house the telescope and other equipment that monitors activity on the sun at all times. Self-guiding tours go daily through the installation, and on weekends guided tours are conducted. Families of scientists live in attractive rows of houses on this high mountain retreat, where the clean air is one of the reasons for the observatory's location.

In the fall, aspens light up the mountainsides with living gold, and several forest roads out of Cloudcroft take you to them. NM 24 from Cloudcroft to Ruidoso goes across the Mescalero Apache Reservation, mountainous country where fat cattle graze the valleys. The road is paved, and two camping and picnicking areas are along the way.

CLOVIS
Population, 34,428

(F-10)
Elevation, 4,280

In 1907 it was called Riley's Switch, simply a place on the new railroad that was reaching across the plains of eastern New Mexico. A siding and a few rough shacks were all that were there, but when railroad officials decided that this was the proper spot to make the division point for the Belen cut-off, they decided to establish a proper town with a proper name. They chose Clovis, King of the Franks, whose conversion to Christianity in 496 changed the course of the Christian religion.

The railroad yards at Clovis are busy. This is the largest city in the area and has a stable economy based on farming, livestock, the railroad and a military base. Mile after mile of grain, alfalfa, sugar beet and wheat fields stretch to the horizon. Some of the largest feed lots in the Southwest fatten

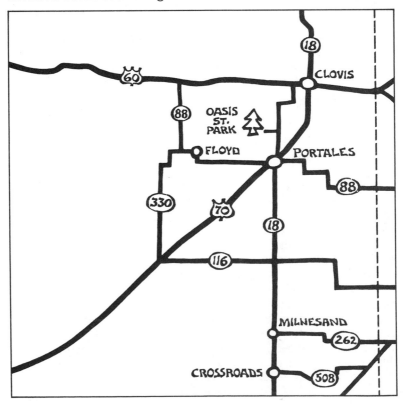

thousands of cattle each year before shipping. Livestock auctions held weekly in Clovis are interesting to watch, even if you don't know the difference between a Hereford and a Charolais. Cannon Air Force Base near Clovis is part of the tactical air command and is important to the life of the community.

Clovis Pioneer Days, the second week in June each year, recall days when homesteaders and ranchers were sinking roots into the fertile soil of Curry County. A parade, rodeo, pageants and exhibits take place at the fairgrounds. Curry County Fair is held in early September with large agricultural exhibits, rodeo and parade.

The Llano Estacado — Staked Plains — stretch to infinity, it seems, east of Clovis. The Spaniards found grass here belly-high to their horses, and encountered a few bands of roving Indians. Within a few years fearless warriors moved in from the north, and, once introduced to the Spanish mustang, became the scourge of the West, raiding Spanish villages and Indian pueblos at will.

Thousands of years earlier prehistoric man tracked mastodons, bison and saber-toothed tigers from waterhole to waterhole across this country. Near Clovis prehistoric spear points have been found that have been dated to several thousand years before Christ, and are identified as Clovis points.

Blackwater Draw Museum, exhibiting archeological material and information about the area, is ten miles (16 kilometres) south of Clovis. Museums on the campus at Eastern New Mexico University have exhibits on geology, history and natural history. Clovis has good accommodations for travelers.

COCHITI LAKE   (D-5)
Population, 300   *Elevation 5,500*
                                              See *Bernalillo* map

This new resort community between Santa Fe and Albuquerque was created when a dam on the Rio Grande backed up waters about eight miles into the volcanic canyons of the Pajarito Plateau. Located on NM 22 about 15 miles (24 kilometres) northwest of I-25, the lakeside community is on land leased from Cochiti Pueblo (see *Native Americans*), and Indians of the pueblo participate in recreational activities at the lake. They also operate an attractive campground with all facilities on the west side of the lake. Boat ramps and marina provide facilities for owners of sail and small motor boats. Only wakeless boating is permitted.

Sailing up the canyon of the Rio Grande between steep walls of dark lava rocks induces a sense of remoteness and silence, broken only by the occasional song of a bird or perhaps the yowl of a coyote.

NM 22 continues as a dirt road past Cochiti Lake over the Jemez Mountains to join NM 4 between Jemez Springs and Los Alamos. A rough road vehicle is needed for this drive and the route should not be attempted in bad weather. Geologically and historically the Pajarito Plateau is one of the most interesting areas in the state, and approaching it from this direction gives a good look at some of the canyons and mountains where so many prehistoric Indians lived. One canyon contains cone-shaped formations, a cluster of cream-colored tent rocks not far from Cochiti Pueblo. Turn west at the pueblo on a dirt road for about five miles (6.4 kilometres) until you see the tent rocks on the right. It is a good place to hike, picnic, or pick up Apache tears, those smooth bits of obsidian.

Except for the campground, there are no overnight accommodations at the lake.

CUBA (C-4)

Population, 2,000

Elevation, 6,905

See *Los Alamos* map

First called Nacimiento after the mountains to the east, the name was later changed to Cuba. It is a lumbering town as well as a trade center for ranchers and for Navajos and Jicarilla Apaches, whose reservations are not far away. This is in the Checkerboard area of northwest New Mexico where every other square mile is Indian land, and where groups or families of Navajos live apart from the main reservation or, as they call it, the Big Navajo.

About three miles (4.8 kilometres) east of Cuba, NM 126 enters Santa Fe National Forest with its abundant opportunities for camping, fishing, hiking and hunting. Two forest campgrounds are about a dozen miles (19 kilometres) from Cuba. At Clear Creek Campground a dirt road goes two miles (3.2 kilometres) north to the boundary of San Pedro Parks Wilderness. There cars and other wheeled vehicles must stop, and foot power takes over to reach the trout fishing at San Gregorio Lake, one mile (1.6 kilometres) farther. From around the edge of this high meadow lake (elevation 9,400 feet — 2,865 metres), several trails lead into the wilderness for hikers and backpackers. Anyone planning to hike or camp in the wilderness should stop at the ranger station in Cuba to register.

NM 126 continues east through the forest to Fenton Lake, considerably larger than San Gregorio, and joins NM 4 to go to Jemez Springs. The road goes through 49 miles (79 kilometres) of beautiful forest, but it is unpaved and slick when wet. If thunderclouds hang over the mountains, make local inquiry. There are more camping facilities near Fenton Lake and Jemez Springs (see *Jemez Springs*).

There are limited motel and restaurant facilities in Cuba.

DATIL   (G-3)
Population, 300   *Elevation, 7,500*

See *Socorro* map

US 60 runs west from Magdalena across a wide sea of grass
encircled by mountains. At the western edge of the plains is
Datil, the only town on the San Agustin Plains. This great
basin, once an inland sea, is 20 miles (32 kilometres) wide and
60 miles (96.6 kilometres) long. The lowest point on the
plains is 6,775 feet (2,065 metres), with the surrounding
mountains rising to more than 9,000 feet (2,743 metres).

As early as 4000 B.C. ancient man raised corn around the
edges of the receding lake. Spaniards crossed the plains but
made no permanent settlement. In the 1870s and 1880s
cattlemen began to take up land, homesteading where there
was water, and running their cattle on the open range.

The San Agustin is still a land of big cattle ranches, of
remoteness and a sense of mystery. Snows sweep the plains by
winter, and, after summer showers, wildflowers explode from
the earth. Two good New Mexico books have been set in this
area: Conrad Richter's *Sea of Grass* and Agnes Morley
Cleaveland's *No Life For a Lady*.

Datil grew as a trade center for ranchers and homesteaders,
and later as a supply station along the Magdalena Cattle Drive
Trail that went from St. Johns, Arizona, to the railhead at
Magdalena on the eastern edge of the plains. US 60 parallels
parts of the historic trail, and a few wooden windmills that
were placed about every ten miles (16 kilometres) along the
trail still stand as skeletal monuments to those days roman-
ticized as no other in American folklore.

For almost 30 years Datil has held a rodeo in mid-August,
and those days of long ago are revived with junior and regular
rodeo, wild cow milking and other events.

NM 12 begins at Datil and runs southwest along the edge of
the plains, following a branch of the Magdalena Trail that
began at Old Horse Springs. Only a few old wooden buildings
remain of that once lively town. The highway leaves the plains
and rises into the Gila National Forest, follows the pastoral
valley of the Tularosa River for a while, and continues to
Reserve. It is a paved, two-lane scenic route to the southwestern part of the state. Occasional winter storms can be
severe at this elevation.

In the triangle formed by the junction of NM 12 and US 60 at
Datil, the BLM maintains Datil Well Campground, a large area
on a piñon-covered hill. The campground has tables, benches,

fireplaces and restrooms. The excellent drinking water comes from Datil Well, one of the watering places on the Magdalena Trail.

Datil is at the edge of a portion of Cibola National Forest, and US 60 goes through the forest for almost 20 miles (32 kilometres). There are no developed campsites in the forest, but a few dirt roads lead to areas of great quiet and solitude. These roads are often impassable when wet, and there is practically no traffic — so be warned.

Except for a restaurant and limited motel accommodations in Datil, the nearest are in Socorro, 62 miles (100 kilometres) east, or Quemado, 78 miles (126 kilometres) west.

Rodeo in cattle country.

DEMING   (J-3)
Population, 12,500   *Elevation, 4,331*

See *Silver City* map

In 1881 when the Santa Fe and Southern Pacific railroads met at Deming, both companies had depots at opposite ends of the same building, with a Harvey House between. The time of day depended on where the passenger lived, since the Southern Pacific used Pacific Time, and the Santa Fe, Mountain Time. This route completed the second transcontinental rail line across the United States.

Deming continues to be an important railroad town, but cattle ranching and irrigated farming play major roles too. The desert blooms with fields of lettuce, cotton and grains. Beyond the fields, the desert glows with magnificent sunrises and sunsets, silhouetting jagged peaks and creamy yucca blooms in this Kingdom of the Sun.

Cooke's Peak, a landmark on the Butterfield Trail, is a few miles north of Deming. Near the base of the peak was Fort Cummings, now only a few crumbling walls. It is on private property and not generally open to the public. US 180 goes northwest from Deming past Cooke's Peak to Silver City. Twenty-three miles (37 kilometres) from town, take NM 61 to City of Rocks State Park, a grotesque cluster of rock formations rising from the desert like a long-forgotten city.

City of Rocks State Park.

New Mexico Travel Division

Hot rock flowed from the lips of volcanoes a million years ago, solidifying into a form called welded tuff. Wind and water have scaled off particles to leave rounded, monumental forms, a fantasy playground for children of any age. Campsites are built in sheltered coves between the rocks, shaded by alligator juniper trees. Nature trails lead through the streets and alleys of the rock city, and a sharp eye can find smooth places on the surface, which Apaches used for grinding bowls — perhaps as they sat there they watched for stagecoaches on the Butterfield Trail. A desert arboretum adjacent to the campground has ocotillo, yucca and many other plants native to the Southwest.

Twelve miles (19 kilometres) southeast of Deming is probably the only park in the country where visitors are encouraged to take part of it home with them. At Rockhound State Park visitors may take up to 15 pounds (6 kilos) of jasper, agate, quartz crystal, flow-banded rhyolite and other rocks found in the park. The park is at the base of the rugged Florida Mountains where trails lead across ravines and cactus-studded foothills. From the campground is an unsurpassed view of desert mountains reaching into Mexico. In early March each year Deming holds a Rock Hound Roundup where collectors can swap and sell rocks and take field trips to some of the surrounding rockhound areas.

The border of Mexico is 32 miles (51.5 kilometres) south on NM 11. At Columbus, New Mexico's border town, is Pancho Villa State Park, set aside not to honor a revolutionary, but to commemorate the last time American soil was invaded by foreign armed forces, and the first time air power and mechanized equipment were used for military purposes. Here at Camp Furlong on the night of March 9, 1916, shots rang out, killing a sentry. Before the soldiers could get themselves dressed and their weapons out of a locked storehouse, the raiders had swept through the fort and town, killing eight soldiers and nine civilians. Six hundred Villistas had cut the international boundary fence near Columbus, and moved quietly in small groups to surround the town and camp. The raid ended as quickly as it had started, with the Villistas fleeing back across the border. No reason was ever established for the attack. The two countries were not at war. On March 15, a punitive expedition under General John J. "Black Jack" Pershing marched into Mexico in what turned out to be a fruitless chase. On March 19, eight little single engine planes based at Fort Sam Houston, Texas, took off from Camp Furlong to provide air support for Pershing's troops.

Pancho Villa State Park preserves the few ruins of Camp Furlong (it was a tent fort except for two or three adobe buildings), including a cement-lined ditch into which trucks backed for easy loading, another sign of the beginning of mechanized warfare. A botanical garden, modern shelters and facilities are at the campground. Across the border from Columbus is Las Palomas, a small village built around a plaza.

Columbus has several old buildings that go back to its founding as a railroad town, including the Southern Pacific depot. The southern few miles of New Mexico were not part of the United States according to the original boundary agreement after the Mexican War (1846-1848), but in order to assure an easy route for a southern railroad line, the Gadsden Purchase was made separately, adding this strip of land to the country.

Deming is on I-10, and has a number of motels and restaurants.

Pancho Villa State Park at Columbus.

DULCE
Population, 2,257

(A-4)
Elevation 7,000
See *Chama* map

Jicarilla Apache tribal headquarters are at Dulce, the only town on the reservation. Located near the Colorado border on US 64, Dulce has tribal offices, homes, medical facilities, schools and churches to serve the Jicarillas, and motels, restaurants, stores and service stations to serve travelers. Information about recreational facilities and services on the reservation may be obtained at the Department of Tourism at tribal headquarters (505) 759-3442 (see *Native Americans*).

Little Beaver Roundup in mid-July and Stone Lake Fiesta in mid-September are the two major events sponsored by the tribe. Terrain on the reservation is generally mountainous, with plateaus and scattered timber lands. The reservation has abundant outdoor recreational resources.

Little Beaver Roundup.

EAGLE NEST
Population, 200

(B-7)
Elevation, 8,320
See *Cimarron* map

This resort community in the Moreno Valley of the Sangre de Cristo Mountains came into being one year after completion of Eagle Nest Dam in 1919. The dam was designed and built by Charles Springer, a pioneer cattleman, engineer, banker and merchant, to irrigate part of the Maxwell Land Grant where he owned the CS Ranch. The dam is at the head of Cimarron Canyon, midway between Taos and Cimarron, and backs up a lake five miles (8 kilometres) long and two miles (3.2 kilometres) wide. Lodgings, restaurants, stores, fishing and boating facilities are on the west side of the lake on US 64.

A newer resort community 12 miles (19 kilometres) south on NM 38 is Angel Fire, with a country club, golf course, public dining room, beautiful homes and a ski area (see *Winter Sports*).

Fishing at Eagle Nest.

On a low hill along US 64 about six miles (9.7 kilometres) south of Eagle Nest, a small chapel sweeps like an arrow toward the sky. This was built by the Westphall family to honor their son and all soldiers killed in the Viet Nam war. It is open to the public. Val Verde Ski Area, a small family-oriented winter sports area, is also here on the Westphall property (see *Winter Sports*).

North from Eagle Nest, NM 38 continues up the Moreno Valley about six miles (9.7 kilometres) to all that remains of Elizabethtown (E-town), where gold was discovered in 1866 on the Maxwell Land Grant. Only a few scraps of stone walls and weathered wood mark what was once the rip-roaringest mining town in the Territory. Within two years of the strike, more than a hundred buildings and 3,000 persons were in E-town, and gold and silver claims dotted the hillsides. By 1870 it had doubled in size and become the first incorporated town in the New Mexico Territory as well as the county seat of the new county of Colfax. Hotels, churches and two newspapers brought civilization to E-town, and outlaws and bad men took it away. By 1871 the richest deposits had begun to play out, and the attempt to bring water for hydraulic mining over the mountains from Red River had failed. By 1875 E-town was a ghost. Two or three times over the next 30 years attempts were made to revive mining in the district, but it never lasted long, and E-town was left slumbering on the hillside.

Carson National Forest covers most of the mountains between Eagle Nest and Taos, offering a wealth of summer and winter recreation. Angel Fire holds a hot air balloon festival the third week in August. At Eagle Nest a high-altitude glider and soaring festival takes place on Thanksgiving weekend; the Moreno Valley Fish Fry and Square Dance is the third weekend in May; and the Fourth of July sees a traditional celebration of dances, contests and fireworks.

Eagle Nest has several small motels and restaurants.

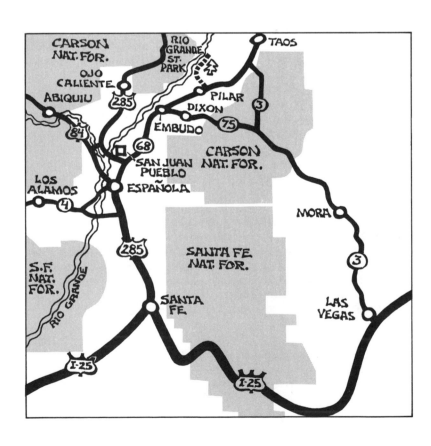

ESPAÑOLA

Population, 10,800

(C-6)

Elevation, 5,590

The Española Valley is the cradle of Spanish civilization in New Mexico. Five miles (eight kilometres) north of Española, across the river from San Juan Indian Pueblo, Don Juan de Oñate established the first capital of New Mexico in 1598. The site is marked by a simple cross on top of an unexcavated mound of the pueblo the Spaniards took over. The fertile soil of the Española Valley had already made it the heart of the northern Pueblo Indian country. Six pueblos are within 20 miles (32 kilometres) of Española.

Santa Cruz, about a mile (1.6 kilometres) east of Española on NM 76, is the second oldest *villa* in New Mexico. It was officially founded in 1695, although there had been around a thousand settlers living in the vicinity before the rebellion of 1680. Holy Cross Church contains examples of early religious art, and during the 18th century this was one of the most important churches in New Mexico. NM 76 continues from Santa Cruz through the small mountain villages on the High Road to Taos (see *Chimayo and the Mountain Villages*).

Three miles (4.8 kilometres) south of Española on NM 5 is Santa Clara Pueblo, and in the Jemez Mountains west of the pueblo are Puye Cliff Dwellings and the Santa Clara fishing lakes and recreation area (see *Native Americans*).

US 84 leads north from Española 23 miles (37 kilometres) to the village of Abiquiu, settled in 1747 on the site of an abandoned Tewa pueblo ruin. It was a *genizaro* village of Indians who had been captured by Plains Indians, rescued by the Spaniards through trade with their captors, and Christianized to live as Spaniards. They were usually of mixed blood and often had lost their tribal identity. Today the village is best known because the world-famous artist, Georgia O'Keeffe, lives there. The brilliant colors of the cliffs and mesas near Abiquiu have provided inspiration for many of Miss O'Keeffe's stark, hauntingly beautiful paintings.

The highway continues beyond Abiquiu through some of the most brilliant sandstone formations in the state. Red, ochre, creamy white, they paint swaths of color across the landscape. Echo Amphitheater, with a nature trail and picnic area, is set in the midst of this unbelievable geology that millions of years ago was a humid, steamy swamp, inhabited by reptiles and dinosaurs. Children and adults alike love to shout into the canyon walls and get an eerie response.

Ghost Ranch, 14 miles (22.5 kilometres) north of Abiquiu on US 84, is owned by the United Presbyterian Church and used as an educational facility, ecumenical study and conference center, and conservation experiment area for local residents. The National Forest Service maintains Ghost Ranch Museum on the highway, a free public museum with exhibits of dinosaur fossils, Indian artifacts, and live native animals found in the area.

NM 68 northeast from Española goes to Taos through the deep volcanic gorge cut by the Rio Grande. Even though the narrow valley is hemmed in by black lava walls, the soil is fertile, and small riverside villages, such as Embudo, Pilar, Velarde and Dixon, are almost hidden in fruit — especially apple — orchards. During the summer and fall, fruit and chile stands along the highway are like edgings of flowers along a pathway.

At Embudo, NM 75 turns east through Dixon and Carson National Forest, connecting with NM 3, a scenic mountain route to Taos. NM 3 continues across the mountains through Mora and several other interesting old Spanish villages to Las Vegas.

US 285 goes north of Española to Ojo Caliente, where Indians, Spaniards and Anglos have bathed in the hot springs for centuries. This route continues through the national forest to Tres Piedras and on to Antonito, Colorado.

Española offers good motel and restaurant facilities.

ESTANCIA VALLEY   (6-D and E)

East of Albuquerque, beyond the Sandia and Manzano mountains, which run north and south about 80 miles (130 kilometres), is the Estancia Valley, once the bed of a great inland sea. From an airplane you can see gray-white beads strung along the valley like pearls — salt beds of the extinct lakes. When it rains they collect pools of water, but most of the year they are dry.

In prehistoric times Indians went to the dry lakes for supplies of salt. As nomadic Indians from the mountains and plains moved into the area, they, too, went to the salt beds. When the Spaniards entered New Mexico, they mined the salt and sent it by oxcart caravans to Mexico — New Mexico's first mining export.

Several pueblos were on the east side of the mountains, and

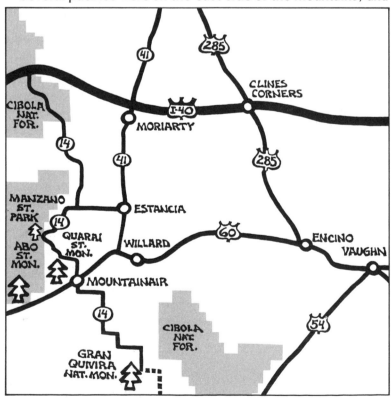

the Spaniards built three magnificent mission churches to serve them (see Abo, Quarai and Gran Quivira in *Missions and Churches*).

Estancia means large estate or resting place, a name used by cattlemen during the 1800s when they grazed their livestock on the rich grasses of the valley. In the 20th century the area was opened for homesteading, and Stanley, Estancia, Willard and Moriarty were established. Wells were dug, windmills stood like sentinels, small frame houses were built and fields of beans, grains and other dryland farm crops were soon planted.

The New Mexico Central Railway ran down the valley from Stanley to Willard where it joined the Atchison, Topeka and Santa Fe, and quantities of beans and potatoes were shipped out. But the rains stopped and drought took over. During those dust bowl days and the Depression, many farmers moved on. But a few stubborn ones stayed on and bought their neighbors' lands.

There are still some good crops of hay, wheat and corn grown in the valley, irrigated by deep wells, but most of it has been restored to grazing land. Here and there across the plains you can still see a sagging, lonely shack, weathered silver-gray, beside the broken triangle of wooden windmill. These are the only reminders of the homestead era, unless you go to a rodeo or community social gathering in one of the valley towns. There you will find the pioneer spirit still strong in the second and third generation settlers. Not much remains of the town Stanley except for a few abandoned buildings. Estancia and Willard still have schools, business buildings, homes, churches, schools and parks. Moriarty is a tourist service town along I-40, as is Clines Corners, farther east, which was founded in 1934 on old US 66.

The homestead era was important in New Mexico. Land along streams and springs was homesteaded as the nuclei of large cattle ranches. Much of the arid farmland opened to homesteading should never have been plowed, but the Homestead Act accomplished its purpose: it settled the West.

FARMINGTON   (A-3)

Population, 40,200   *Elevation, 5,390*

This fast-growing city is the center of an area richly endowed with oil, gas and coal for the energy-hungry world. As the name implies, there is fertile agricultural land along the San Juan, Animas and La Plata rivers, which come together at Farmington. The town was settled in 1879 as a trade center for homesteaders, farmers and ranchers in the area. In the days of the open range, large herds of cattle were grazed on the plateaus and hills, and disputes often arose between cattlemen and homesteaders.

Farmington is the commercial center of the Four Corners Area, the only place in the United States where four states meet. Here coal gasification plants and thermoelectric power projects produce energy for a large part of the Southwest.

San Juan College, many parks, churches, new residential

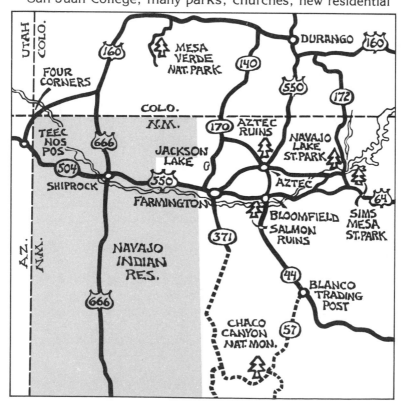

163

and commercial areas attest to Farmington's fast growth of recent years.

US 550, a paved road, goes west from Farmington about 50 miles (80 kilometres) to the Four Corners Monument. In this land of craggy mesas and wind-sculptured rock formations, New Mexico, Arizona, Colorado and Utah come together. The spot is marked with a marble platform with steps leading up on four sides. In the center a small tower rises with the outline of each state etched into the side facing that state, and on the floor of the monument, in each of the four sections, the seal of that state.

On the way to Four Corners, 29 miles (47 kilometres) west of Farmington, is the town of Shiprock on the Navajo Reservation. Visible from NM 666, a few miles south of the town, is the legendary mountain of the Navajos, Shiprock.

Many years ago, so the story goes, The People were beseiged by enemies, and a giant bird carried them on its back to this place of safety. When the bird settled to earth it turned to stone (some stories say it landed on the stone), and they called it Tse bida'hi, their sacred Winged Rock. Anglo settlers thought the giant upthrust of volcanic rock resembled a mystical ship in full sail across the desert sands and they named it Shiprock.

Continuing west of Shiprock toward the Four Corners, the road enters Arizona and the Navajo village of Teec Nos Pos, famous for a type of Navajo rug with intricate designs.

Three miles (4.8 kilometres) west of Farmington, NM 17

Shiprock.

turns north to the Jackson Lake fishing and waterfowl area. Canoeing, picnicking and fishing for bass, catfish and trout are permitted at the lake, but no overnight camping.

Navajo Lake State Park, 40 miles (64 kilometres) east of Farmington, is New Mexico's largest lake, formed by a dam on the San Juan River. The park includes the entire 28 miles (45 kilometres) of lake from the Colorado line to the dam, and, below the dam, three and one-half miles (five and a half kilometres) of river reserved for quality trout fishing. The deep blue waters of the lake offer fishing, water-skiing and boating. Miles of irregular shoreline let hikers, geologists and archeologists explore the rugged canyons and mesas. Pine River Recreation Site near the dam has an 1,800-foot (550-metre) launching ramp, 170 covered slips, tie-down sites for hundreds of boats, and a complete marine supply store. The state park system operates the visitor center and the picnic and campgrounds, with complete services for campers and other travelers.

Simms Mesa at the south end of the dam has a boat ramp, campground and picnic area, but no modern accommodations. The dirt road leading to it is rough when dry and slick when wet. Before trying this road with anything but a four-wheel-drive vehicle, make local inquiry.

Waterfowl, deer and bird hunting are available in season in the entire area near the dam, and at the lake, some of the best fishing in the state for crappie, bluegill, channel cat, brown and rainbow trout, northern pike, coho and kokanee salmon. Below the dam, the San Juan River is reserved for fly fishing.

East of Farmington on US 64 near Bloomfield is the Salmon Ruins archeological site (see *Bloomfield*).

Mesa Verde National Monument, in Colorado about 75 miles (120 kilometres) north of Farmington, contains ruins of pit houses, pueblos and magnificent cliff dwellings that trace the life of prehistoric Indians in the Four Corners country from the time of Christ to about AD 1300.

Contemporary with Mesa Verde, in many ways rivaling and in some ways surpassing it, was Chaco Canyon, now an important national monument about 60 miles (96 kilometres) south of Farmington (see *Parks and Monuments*).

Farmington offers a good choice of motels and restaurants, gas stations and grocery stores, and other travelers' facilities.

FORT SUMNER (F-8)

Population, 1,640   *Elevation, 4,030*

See *Santa Rosa* map

Fort Sumner began in 1862 as the site of the fort built to supervise thousands of Navajos and several hundred Apaches in an ill-conceived attempt to teach them to be farmers. The spot is now Fort Sumner State Monument and has a visitor center and museum (see *Parks and Monuments*). Little remains of the fort.

Once a favorite hangout of Billy the Kid, who met his death here, Fort Sumner is a quiet restful town today, though its Western heritage seems very near. It is a trading center for the farmlands along the Pecos River and the huge cattle ranches in the area.

Some of the Old West lives again during the town's annual Old Fort Days around the middle of June when they stage a bank holdup, a parade, barbecue, and several other entertainments. There is a new rodeo grounds near town.

Behind the Old Fort Museum, a private enterprise, is a graveyard where lie the remains of some of the most famous names in New Mexico history — Billy the Kid and his two buddies in the Lincoln County War, Tom O'Folliard and Charlie Bowdre, and the land baron, Lucien Maxwell, and his son Pete.

Eighteen miles (29 kilometres) northwest of the town of Fort Sumner, a dam on the Pecos River has created Sumner Lake State Park. Park facilities include a boat ramp, drinking water, restrooms and shelters. The lake is stocked with pike, bass, bluegills and channel catfish.

There are tourist facilities in Fort Sumner, more in Santa Rosa and Clovis.

Billy the Kid's grave.

GALLUP   (D-2)
Population, 21,000   *Elevation, 6,515*

When the Atlantic and Pacific Railroad reached the present site of Gallup in 1881, a village of sorts began, but it was not officially founded until 1891. It was named for the paymaster on the railroad, who was more important to the workers than the company president or any historical figure.

Travelers on the main line of the Santa Fe Railway, which bought the A & P many years ago, have always been impressed with the spectacular red rock formations east of Gallup, and photographs of the area have long been used as promotional shots for the railway.

A few years after the founding of Gallup, rich coal deposits were found north of the city, and mining has drawn workers from many European countries, giving Gallup a cosmopolitan population. It also became a trade center for the Navajos,

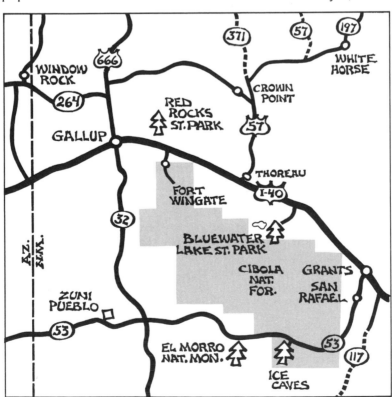

whose huge reservation is north and west of Gallup, and for the Zunis to the south. Indian jewelry and rugs are warehoused and wholesaled at Gallup, and the big trading posts are tourist attractions in themselves. In addition, almost every shop, store, motel, restaurant and filling station sells Indian arts and crafts.

The annual Inter-Tribal Indian Ceremonial is held the second week in August. From simple beginnings in 1922 when Navajo dancers performed in a pool of light from carbide lamps on tin lizzies parked in a ring, the Ceremonial has grown to a major event. The Navajo Tribe is still the host group, but dancers from most New Mexico tribes, other states and several foreign countries perform for four days before thousands of visitors.

The Ceremonial has excellent new facilities at Red Rock State Park 10 miles east of the city on NM 566. Set in a breathtaking natural amphitheater of sandstone cliffs, the Ceremonial takes on added beauty and significance.

All-Indian rodeos take place in the afternoons and dances are in the evening (except on Sunday when the program is reversed: dances in the afternoon and rodeo at night to accommodate photographers). An exhibit hall is open all four days of the Ceremonial, showing some of the finest Indian arts and crafts in the world. The prestigious show is sponsored by the Indian Arts and Crafts Association, a national Indian organization concerned with maintaining high standards in workmanship and ethics.

On Friday and Saturday mornings a parade winds through downtown Gallup, one of the highlights of the Ceremonial. Photography is permitted at the parade and the Ceremonial grounds. Next to the Ceremonial grounds is Red Rock State Park and campground, with restrooms, showers, hook-ups and drinking water. On I-40, Gallup has a wide range of motel and restaurant facilities.

Fort Wingate, south of I-40 about 12 miles (19 kilometres) east of Gallup, is older than Gallup. The fort was in two other locations before being placed here permanently in 1868. During World War II, Fort Wingate was enlarged greatly to become a munitions depot, a purpose it still serves. Driving along the interstate, you can see rows of mounds stretching across the foothills like symmetrical ant hills.

Cibola National Forest begins just south of Fort Wingate and has fishing lakes, campgrounds and miles of hiking trails through tall timber and aspen trees.

Window Rock, tribal headquarters for the Navajo Tribe (see *Native Americans*), is eight miles (13 kilometres) north of Gallup on US 666 and 20 miles (32 kilometres) west on NM 264, just over the border into Arizona. The original tribal buildings are of red sandstone set at the base of a monolith through which time, wind and water have worn a large hole — Window Rock. From Window Rock, roads lead north and west across the Navajo Reservation to such points of scenic and historic interest as Canyon de Chelly, Monument Valley, Navajo National Monument and Hubbell Trading Post National Monument. Over a thousand miles (1600 kilometres) of paved road cross the reservation, but many more thousands are unpaved and risky when wet. It is a large, lonely land of over 16 million acres (6.5 million hectares) and is not for the timid tourist, but it is a rewarding experience for those who value solitude, grandeur and brilliant almost abstract landscapes.

NM 32 goes south from Gallup to join NM 53 that leads east around the Zuni Mountains of Cibola National Forest or west to Zuni Pueblo (see *Native Americans*). Pinnacles and mesas of banded pink and buff sandstone thrust up through forested foothills in this colorful country. The paved highway leads past the old farming and ranching community of Ramah (a Navajo reservation) to El Morro National Monument (see *Grants,* and *Parks and Monuments*) before rejoining I-40 at Grants. This portion of Cibola National Forest is relatively unexplored, but several Forest Service roads lead to camping and picnic areas.

Gallup offers travelers a wide choice in hotel, motel and restaurant accommodations.

GLENWOOD
Population, 150

(H-1)
Elevation, 4,700

Where the San Francisco and Whitewater rivers join in a narrow valley between two bulky mountain ranges lies Glenwood, a year-round vacation town. In the 1870s, when gold and silver were discovered in the Mogollon Mountains, mining camps sprang up, and cattlemen and homesteaders began to settle in the area. Apaches made life precarious until 1885. Some of the mines were active until World War II, and ranching and farming continue to be important in Glenwood.

Five miles (eight kilometres) northeast of town a dirt road leads to the mouth of Whitewater Canyon where the stream rushes from the mountains. During mining days water was piped down to the mill at the mouth of the canyon, where a few piles of stone still mark the site. A catwalk was laid above the pipe for repairmen, and years later the Forest Service made an

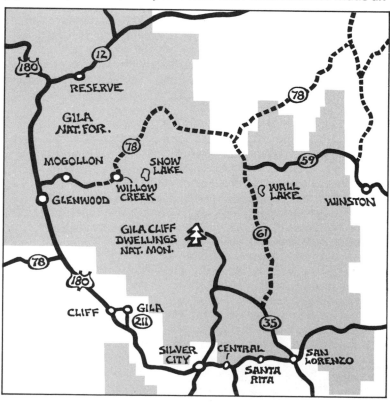

improved walkway so visitors could experience the thrill of walking through the narrow canyon — like a fly on the face of the cliff, 30 feet (nine metres) above the tumbling stream. Recent floods have badly damaged this canyon and its trails to the Gila Wilderness are closed until possibly 1983 or later. In the meantime, backpackers who formerly used this access trail into Gila Wilderness should consult Gila National Forest rangers in Silver City or the district ranger stations. Picnicking is still permitted in the glen of big Arizona sycamore trees by the stream at the entrance to the beautiful canyon.

Established in 1924 as the first wilderness in the United States, the Gila contains almost half a million acres (202,000 hectares) of forests, meadows, lakes, streams and trails where man may go only on foot or horseback. It lies within the Gila National Forest, and trails lead in from campgrounds around the perimeter. Forest Service maps are available at the district ranger station a mile south of Glenwood. A permit should be obtained there or elsewhere in the Gila National Forest before going into the wilderness.

Two miles (three kilometres) beyond US 180, on the road to Mogollon (NM 78), a little dirt road turns north along Mineral Creek to Cooney Tomb. This was once the trail to the mining towns of Cooney and Claremont (nothing left). In 1880, James Cooney, who had made the first strike in the Mogollon mining district, was riding from Alma to Cooney to warn the miners that Apaches under Victorio were on the warpath — but the Indians ambushed him on the way. A few days later friends found his body. They blasted a hole in a large boulder, and made a most unusual crypt.

Mogollon had the longest and most colorful life of all the mining camps in the area. The mines closed in 1942, but a few hardy souls still live there. Silver Creek runs down the street, where many weathered buildings hint of past glories. One or two stores sell arts and crafts, antiques and relics of the area. Ruins of mine shafts, powder houses, mills, plants and tailings dumps are in every canyon, attesting to the fact that once Mogollon mines produced $3 million a year in gold and silver.

NM 78 continues from Mogollon into the national forest, part of the Outer Loop around the Gila Wilderness. The first campground is about 10 miles (16 kilometres) up the road, another one eight miles (12 milometres) farther, and three more at Willow Creek. Forest Road 142 branches off to Snow Lake, a cold, high mountain lake where trout fishing is usually good. Trails lead into the wilderness from the primitive campground, as they do from all the campgrounds along the way.

NM 78 continues east across the mountains to Beaverhead, where a paved road (NM 59-52) continues to Winston, Cuchillo and I-25 near Truth or Consequences. NM 78 (unpaved) continues northeast to US 60 near Magdalena.

Near Beaverhead, NM 78 connects with NM 61, which goes south (a rough, rocky road) past Wall Lake to NM 36. Another interesting route through the Gila National Forest is to leave NM 78 about 15 miles (24 kilometres) north of Willow Creek and take Forest Road 141 to Reserve. This road is across high park-like benches of the Mogollons, where fat cattle graze the meadows and piney ridges.

Of utmost importance to anyone planning a trip into this remote, beautiful area is road information, which should be obtained at the time at the nearest ranger station. The road from Glenwood to Mogollon was paved at one time, but big chunks are broken out of the sharp curves, making a scary few miles. Beyond Mogollon it gets worse. Most of it has been graded and graveled, and is usually safe enough, but it is strictly a dry weather road, open only from April to October — or less, if there are unseasonal storms. Some roads are limited to trailers under 17 feet (5.18 metres), and along some routes it is well over 200 miles (322 kilometres) between service stations. This is adventurers' country, worth every minute of it, but not recommended for tenderfeet.

US 180 through Glenwood is the scenic route from El Paso to Phoenix, and there are one or two small motels, restaurants and a lodge in Glenwood, and all tourist facilities in Silver City (which see) 65 miles (105 kilometres) south.

Pleasanton, four miles (six kilometres) south of Glenwood, is an old farming and ranching community settled by Mormons in 1879. Thirty miles (48 kilometres) farther south are Cliff and Gila, farming and ranching communities on the historic Gila River, once the boundary between the United States and Mexico.

Prehistoric Indian ruins of the Mogollon Culture abound throughout this area. The Mogollon Culture existed from about 300 B.C. to around A.D. 1500. Unauthorized digging and pot hunting are forbidden by state and federal law, but regional museums and informative material at Gila Cliff Dwellings National Monument (see *Parks and Monuments*) explain something about the little-known culture. Kwilleylekia Ruins at Gila are on private land, but the owners maintain a small museum and offer guided tours and lectures of the partially excavated site which contained 300 rooms and was four stories high.

Little Fanny Mine, Mogollon.

GRANTS (E-3)
Population, 16,000

Elevation, 6,460
See *Gallup* map

In 1882 Grants began as a station where the Santa Fe's steam engines stopped to refuel with coal. When US 66 was built, it followed approximately the same route. Grants became a trade center for ranchers and farmers in the area and a tourist stop on the famed Route 66. Lumbering on Mt. Taylor has also been a sizable industry for years, but today Grants is recognized as the uranium capital of the country, and the uranium industry has caused booming growth.

Tawny-red cliffs and pinnacles of sandstone highlight the landscape, and in the distance the symmetrical, timbered slopes of Mt. Taylor rise. At 11,300 feet (3,445 metres), this is the highest point of the volcanic range of mountains 44 miles (70 kilometres) long. Mt. Taylor, often snowcapped, is one of the four great sacred mountains of the Navajos, marking the four corners of their traditional world. Cibola National Forest covers most of this range, and two forest campgrounds are a few miles north of Grants.

East of Grants a recent — perhaps 1,000 years old — forbidding river of lava flows on either side of the highway, a blue-black mass frozen for eternity in ripple lines, or broken into chunks with razor-sharp edges. Sinkholes are emerald with algae-skimmed water and reeds. The lava is to look at, not to walk on. Shoe soles would be shredded in no time.

Ten miles (16 kilometres) east of Grants, NM 117 turns south, threading its way between the edge of the lava flow and high sandstone cliffs on the other side. In places the lava and sandstone recede, leaving broad meadows where cattle graze. Prehistoric Indians, probably the ancestors of the Acomas, once lived on these mesas, as many archeological sites indicate. This road continues a scenic 78 miles (125 kilometres) to Quemado and US 60, through several large cattle ranches. Much of the road is unpaved and washboard, though it is scenic and little traveled.

NM 53 turns south at the west edge of Grants and runs parallel to the west side of the lava flow, but farther from it. Here you are not so much aware of the geologic formations as of the vast, open sky and clear air. Three miles (almost five kilometres) from Grants on NM 53 is the old Spanish village of San Rafael, its red adobes slowly melting into the earth. No sign remains of the fort that served as headquarters for Kit Carson and his troops when they were pursuing Navajos in 1862.

Twenty-two miles (35 kilometres) beyond is the Perpetual Ice Cave, privately owned and open to the public for a small admission fee. A solid wall of pale blue-green ice forms the wall confronting visitors who enter the cave by a wooden stairway. In some areas, frost crystals and icicles hang from the ceiling like stalactites, and lines in the wall clearly show where annual layers of ice have been added. The ice continues to grow in a temperature that never varies from 31 degrees F (—.5C). The ice cave is in the midst of volcanic formations, the most impressive being Bandera Crater, a symmetrical cone of brown and black cinders rising several hundred feet high.

This same road continues over the Continental Divide to El Morro National Monument, about 40 miles (64 kilometres) southwest of Grants (see *Parks and Monuments*). NM 53 continues in a loop, connecting with NM 32 near Zuni, then north to Gallup and I-40.

Sixteen miles (26 kilometres) west of Grants a paved road turns south into the Zuni Mountains (Cibola National Forest) to Bluewater Lake State Park. Surrounded by wooded hills, the lake has good boating, water-skiing and swimming in summer, and ice fishing is popular in the winter. The lake is stocked with rainbow trout and catfish. A campground, picnic units, showers, cafe, small store, boat ramp, service dock and rentals offer complete recreation facilities. Ojo Redondo Campground is about 12 miles (19 kilometres) south of Bluewater.

Travelers to Crownpoint for the Navajo rug auctions or to Chaco Canyon National Monument (see *Parks and Monuments*) may reach their destination from Grants. Take I-40 west about 30 miles (48 kilometres) to Thoreau, turn right into NM 57 and continue 28 miles (45 kilometres) over paved road to Crownpoint. To Chaco Canyon, continue to the right for 23 miles (37 kilometres), then left into 39 miles (63 kilometres) of unpaved road to Chaco Canyon. It is about 120 miles (193 kilometres) from Grants to Chaco.

Grants offers a choice of motels, restaurants, service stations and other services for travelers.

175

HOBBS (I-10)
Population, 35,200 *Elevation, 3,625*

Hobbs is one of the newer towns in New Mexico. Part of the Llano Estacado, or Staked Plains — that great flat plateau that sweeps down the eastern side of New Mexico — it has been cattle country since the days of the Texas longhorn cattle drives of the 1860s and 1870s. The first settlement in the area, Monument, was 15 miles (24 kilometres) south of Hobbs at the site of the only waterhole in the area. The Hobbs family were said to be the first homesteaders in the area in 1907.

An oil company was exploring the area in 1927, and, just before their lease expired, they struck oil. Old #1, drilled in January 1928, turned out to be the first in one of the richest oil fields in the Southwest. A tent city sprang up overnight, but Hobbs soon became a vigorous, permanent town, headquarters for the high-yield oil and gas producing area sur-

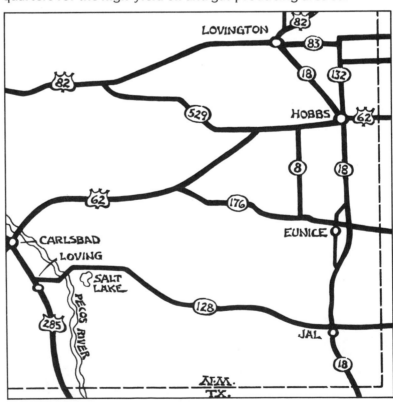

rounding it, with about 90 percent of the state's petroleum.

New Mexico Junior College and the College of the Southwest are in Hobbs. Some of their activities are of interest to the public, such as the lecture series and the artist series in the library at College of the Southwest, where a Southwestern artist is featured each month.

Hobbs consistently produces outstanding athletic teams, and sports of all kinds are popular, including golf and swimming at public facilities.

The Confederate Air Force Museum in a hangar at Hobbs Airfield is dedicated to acquiring and preserving all military aircraft built between 1939 and 1945. B-24 and B-17 Army Air Corps pilots were trained at Hobbs Air Base during World War II. After the war the base was converted to an industrial and recreational park where the junior college, hospital, golf course, rifle range, public campground and several other recreational facilities are located.

Lovington, Eunice and other towns in the Hobbs area were, like Hobbs, part of the Llano Estacado cattle country, and are still large producers of livestock, feed grains and other crops, but are also part of the rich oil empire of southeastern New Mexico.

A variety of travel accommodations may be found in Hobbs.

Museum of antique airplanes.

JAL

Population, 2,860

(J-10)

Elevation, 3,030

See *Hobbs* map

In the far southeastern corner of New Mexico at the intersection of NM 18 and NM 128 is a town with the unusual name of Jal. In a state where most "j's" are given the Spanish pronunciation "h", this leads to some confusion, but the name Jal is not Spanish. In the late 1880s, a cattle company in Texas, wanting to expand westward where the gramma grass was knee-high to a cow, established their headquarters at the only water hole in the area, in Monument Draw just over the border in New Mexico.

They stocked the range with thousands of head of cattle from the John A. Lynch ranch in Texas. The cattle bore his brand, J A L, which extended from shoulder to hip — and must have made for a painful branding! Cowboys and settlers referred to the area as Jals. When a town began to develop in the early 1900s, it was natural to call it by the same name.

In the middle 1920s oil and gas were discovered in the area, and Jal is now an important oil, gas, farming and ranching center.

Jal Lake in the city's main park is built in the shape of the old J A L brand, and is used for boating and fishing for blue gill, rainbow trout, black bass and catfish. Public tennis courts and other public facilities are in the park.

Just seven miles (11 kilometres) east and nine miles (14.5 kilometres) south of Jal is its big brother, Texas.

Jal is cow country.

JEMEZ SPRINGS (C-5)
Population, 480

Elevation, 6,306

See *Los Alamos* map

This cool, quiet mountain village serves thousands of travelers who regard the Jemez Mountains as one huge playground.

On NM 4 between Los Alamos and Jemez Pueblo, Jemez Springs is a cluster of homes, vacation cottages, tourist businesses and several retreat houses of the Catholic Church all spread along a colorful canyon where it widens out enough to permit small fruit orchards and fields of alfalfa.

Servants of the Paraclete, a Catholic order dedicated to the spiritual and physical refreshment of priests, has its headquarters at Jemez Springs. Gray and black robed priests walking along the roadway add a serene, pastoral quality to the village. Their main chapel, Via Coeli, next to the highway, is usually open to the public.

Jemez State Monument (see *Parks and Monuments*), containing the ruins of a mission church, is directly across the road from Villa Coeli.

For at least 20 miles (32 kilometres) up the canyon, hot mineral springs bubble up through the cold waters of the river, and at a covered fountain in Jemez Springs visitors may drink the water that has been considered therapeutic for centuries.

A mile (1.6 kilometres) beyond the village is Soda Dam, a barrier of sodium deposits built up through eons across the river. The gray-white mass forms a dam 40 feet (12 metres) high, stretching from canyon wall to canyon wall, at least 300 feet (92 metres). The river has forced a hole in it, letting the water cascade through in a waterfall, forming a deep pool, a favorite place for bathers and trout fishermen. A ranger station near Soda Dam is a good place to pick up maps and information.

The highway goes over one end of the dam and continues through the forest to 11 recreation sites in the Santa Fe National Forest. Battleship Rock, a huge mesa of basalt pointed like the bow of a ship, has a picnic and camping area at the base. A few miles farther are Indian Head and Dark Canyon picnic areas.

La Cueva Picnic Area is at the junction of NM 4 and NM 126. This large cool area of meadows and forests along San Antonio Creek was named for several caves (*cuevas*) in the cliffs above it. Trails lead up to the caves, where smoke-blackened ceilings testify to their use long ago.

NM 126 is paved to Fenton Lake, about ten miles (16 kilometres), an old favorite for camping, boating and fishing. On the way are two more large forest campgrounds, Horseshoe Spring and San Antonio. After Fenton Lake the road is unpaved and continues about 30 miles (48 kilometres) through the mountains to Cuba, on the western side.

At La Cueva where NM 126 turns west, NM 4 turns east to Los Alamos, 31 miles (50 kilometres), passing more campgrounds, all near fishing streams and forest trails.

The highway to Los Alamos skirts the perimeter of Valle Grande, the true heart of the Jemez Mountains. Now a lush green valley bisected by meandering streams, this is the caldera of a once-raging volcano — perhaps the largest on earth. The Jemez volcano built these mountains and its ashes built the Pajarito Plateau, now carved into canyons where prehistoric Indians built their cave homes.

Valle Grande, 18 miles (29 kilometres) long and 12 miles (19 kilometres) wide, is rich with nutritious grasses. Winter snows are deep and quiet at this altitude. The highway runs along the edge of the forest, looking over the pastoral valley where cattle graze contentedly, looking like ants from such a distance.

In the fall this drive through the Jemez Mountains is glorious with the living gold of aspens spilling down the mountainside. The route can be reversed, coming from Santa Fe or Los Alamos on NM 4.

Stores in Jemez Springs stock supplies for picknickers, campers, hunters, but there are no motels or restaurants.

LAS CRUCES

Population, 51,000

(J-4)

Elevation, 3,896

The City of Crosses was named in memory of travelers on El Camino Real who were ambushed by Apaches a few miles north of the present site of the city. Weathered crosses stood for years as reminders of the harsh realities of travel in colonial and territorial days. Three modern crosses stand near the intersection of Solano and Main streets.

Las Cruces is in the Mesilla Valley, where the Rio Grande flows through south-central New Mexico. The oldest settlement in the valley was Doña Ana, nine miles (14.5 kilometres) north of Las Cruces, in 1839. Ten years later Las Cruces was founded. By then the war with Mexico had made this a part of the United States, and citizens of Doña Ana and Las Cruces who wished to remain citizens of Mexico started a new settlement across the Rio Grande from Las Cruces, which they

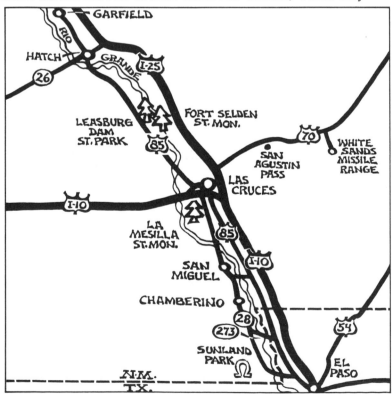

named La Mesilla. However, after the Gadsden Purchase was completed in 1854, by which the United States acquired a strip of land across the southern boundary of the states, Mesilla turned out to be in the United States after all.

When the railroad came in 1880, bypassing La Mesilla, Las Cruces quickly became the leading town of the three early settlements and today is a vigorous, growing city, largest in southern New Mexico, set off by the striking backdrop of the jagged Organ Mountains to the east.

Fertile Mesilla Valley soil supports extensive world-renowned commercial pecan orchards, cotton fields and farms that grow onions, alfalfa, chile and several other fruit and vegetable crops. Other facets of the economy of Las Cruces are cattle ranching, tourism, retirement and employment at White Sands Missile Range.

Much of the social, cultural, educational and recreational life of Las Cruces revolves around New Mexico State University, with many activities open to the public (see *Colleges and Universities*).

Because of the mild climate, tennis, swimming, golf, horseback riding, rockhounding, hiking and exploring are year-round activities in Las Cruces. The city maintains many public recreation facilities. An attractive mall down Main Street is the scene of almost weekly sidewalk markets or craft shows. In late September the Southern New Mexico State Fair takes place at the fairgrounds.

The village of La Mesilla (locally called Old Mesilla), two miles (3.2 kilometres) south of town, is a state monument (see *Parks and Monuments*) and most of the interesting shops and restaurants around the plaza are in buildings of historic significance.

Fort Selden State Monument is 18 miles (29 kilometres) north of Las Cruces. Along the Rio Grande less than a mile away is Leasburg State Park, with camping and picnicking facilities (see *Parks and Monuments*).

Old US 85 continues north past the Fort Selden turnoff through rich farm country to Hatch and Garfield. Hatch justifiably claims to be the chile capital of the world.

Legends of buried treasure add romance to the stark, rocky Organ Mountains east of Las Cruces. Padre La Rue, supposedly a French priest, was said to have led a small colony of people from Mexico in 1797 to find a gold mine he had heard of. One legend says he found rich placer mines on the west side of the Organ Mountains near San Agustin Springs and Pass (US 70 to Alamogordo), and another folk tale led to the controversial investigations at Victorio Peak on the east side of the Organs. Buried treasure or not, considerable mining has been done in the Organs and around Las Cruces, and mineralogists claim it is the best rockhounding country in the world. Check with local rock shops for good places to look, since much of the Organ Mountains is included in White Sands Missile Range and not open to the public.

The most southerly Indian Pueblo group in New Mexico is the Tortugas (Turtle) Tribe who live in a small village about four miles (6.4 kilometres) south of Las Cruces. Believed to have been part of the Isleta people who fled with the Spaniards during the rebellion of 1680, the group may have been joined by a few members of the Piro tribes who had already abandoned their pueblos near Socorro, and by a few Mansos from Mexico. Today Tortugas is an almost entirely Hispanic village, but their Indian ancestry is obvious in the Tiwa chants they sing at fiestas. December 10-12 is their Fiesta of Guadalupe when they perform dances and make a pilgrimage to the top of nearby A Mountain. On June 24 they celebrate San Juan Day with dances. Both celebrations are open to the public.

NM 28, running parallel to I-10 from Las Cruces to El Paso, goes through country reminiscent of Las Cruces' Mexican heritage. It follows the route of El Camino Real and the Chihuahua Trail. Foot soldiers, colonists, padres, conquistadores and caravans of ox carts traveled this route. All signs of the trail have long since been washed away by the unpredictable river, or plowed under cotton fields and pecan orchards, but a sense of antiquity pervades the area. The villages of La Mesilla, San Miguel, Chamberino and La Union lie along the way.

Either this route or I-10 leads to Sunland Park, New Mexico's most southerly racetrack, on the outskirts of El Paso, Texas. Racing season is on weekends from the first week in October through the first week in May — the only winter racing season in the state. Close to Las Cruces, El Paso and Juarez, there is plenty to do in this sun country when the horses aren't running.

Las Cruces offers excellent accommodations for travelers.

LAS VEGAS (D-7)

Population, 16,000 *Elevation, 6,435*

History is visible in Las Vegas. From its beginning as a Mexican settlement, through the exciting days of the Santa Fe Trail and the growth of the cattle and sheep industries, Las Vegas was one of the most important towns in the territory. Many historic buildings remain, an unusual blend of pueblo architecture with Queen Anne and Victorian styles. An excellent guide to historic sites and buildings in the area is available at the chamber of commerce.

In 1835 settlers from San Miguel del Bado, an important stop on the Santa Fe Trail, petitioned and were given the Las Vegas Land Grant. When General Stephen Watts Kearny led the American Army of the West into New Mexico, Las Vegas was the first village they reached. On August 15, 1846, General Kearny climbed to the roof of an adobe building on the

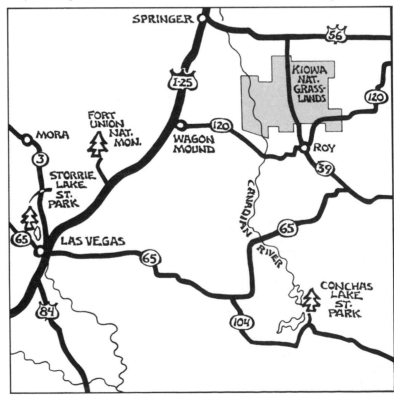

plaza and proclaimed that New Mexico was part of the United States. A few days later the flag was raised over the Palace of the Governors in Santa Fe.

Beginning in 1821 when Mexico became independent of Spain, trade across the Santa Fe Trail mushroomed. Until Las Vegas was established, the first New Mexico settlement was at San Miguel del Bado, about 20 miles (32 kilometres) southwest, where the trail crossed the Pecos River. Soon after the American occupation, Fort Union was built north of Las Vegas, and became the gateway to New Mexico. It was the major supply depot and military base in the Southwest, and Las Vegas became the major frontier town. It was known as the only place between Missouri and Santa Fe where weary stagecoach travelers could sleep in a bed.

When the railroad reached Las Vegas in 1879 the town became a shipping center and headquarters for the great cattle and sheep ranches in northeastern New Mexico. Elegant hotels, huge mercantile stores and wool warehouses were built. Many buildings and homes still standing attest to the prosperity of the era. The Plaza Hotel and the Ilfeld Building on the plaza in Old Town are outstanding examples of the architecture of the period. The old Exchange Hotel, built in 1851 on the southwest corner of the plaza, was a stagecoach stop and for a few weeks was the capitol of New Mexico while the Confederates occupied Santa Fe in the spring of 1862.

Montezuma Hotel, five miles (eight kilometres) up Gallinas Canyon (NM 65) was built in 1880, a 77-room stone hotel. Two years later the Santa Fe Railroad bought it and added a 300-room luxury hotel. It was destroyed by fire more than once but was rebuilt each time to cater to wealthy tourists from the east who came for curative baths, ice skating, gambling, riding and hunting.

New Mexico Highlands University, established in 1893, is the hub of academic and cultural life in the area. A spring fiesta, usually May 5, weekly lectures, theatrical productions and concerts on the campus are community affairs. A golf course and tennis courts are for public use.

Forty percent of Teddy Roosevelt's Roughriders in the Spanish American War of 1898 were from New Mexico, largely from the Las Vegas area, and a city museum next door to the chamber of commerce has an interesting collection of souvenirs and mementos of that campaign, as well as items relating to the pioneer days in Las Vegas.

Storrie Lake State Park, five miles (eight kilometres) north of town, offers water-skiing, boating, fishing, camping and picnicking. McAllister Lake and Waterfowl Area, about eight miles (12.9 kilometres) southeast of Las Vegas, sometimes rewards fishermen with large rainbow trout, and it is a prime wintering refuge for waterfowl. Primitive camping and boat launching facilities are located at the south and west ends of the lake.

Ice skating is still a popular winter sport in Gallinas Canyon near Montezuma. NM 65 continues about five more miles (eight kilometres) up the canyon to the base of the legendary Hermit's Peak in Santa Fe National Forest. Several guest ranches and resorts are in the mountains northwest of Las Vegas. Seven campgrounds in the national forest have trails leading to fishing streams.

NM 3 and NM 94 continue past Storrie Lake to many small, interesting villages in the foothills of the mountains, such as Sapello, Tierra Monte, La Cueva, Mora, Cleveland and Holman. Place names such as Gascon and Ledoux are reminders that several French settlers came into this beautiful mountainous area. At La Cueva are remains of a large adobe, water-powered grist mill and warehouse. Four miles (6.4 kilometres) farther, at Mora, settled by Spaniards in 1818, are remains of a grist mill built by the famous fur trader and mountain man, Ceran St. Vrain in 1864. Wheat was grown in the mountain valleys to produce flour for Fort Union.

Four miles (6.4 kilometres) southwest of Mora on NM 94, at Ledoux, a two-and-a-half-mile (four-kilometre) dirt road leads to Morphy Lake State Park. The road is narrow and rough, recommended only for four-wheel-drive vehicles, even in good weather, but leads to one of the most scenic parks in the state. The lake fills a small basin surrounded by dense forests of pine. Primitive camping and picnic sites are provided (see *Parks and Monuments*).

From Mora NM 38 leads 18 hard-surfaced miles (29 kilometres) through scenic foothills to the old Spanish village of Guadalupita and Coyote Creek State Park. Stream fishing for trout, hiking, camping and picnicking may be enjoyed in this secluded place (see *Parks and Monuments*).

NM 3 continues beyond Mora to Sipapu Ski Area, 48 miles (77 kilometres) northwest of Las Vegas (see *Winter Sports*).

West of the junction of NM 94 and NM 105, 22 miles (35 kilometres) northwest of Las Vegas, are two mountain resort areas. One has a lodge, golf course, private fishing waters and a landing strip, the other is a working guest ranch. At Rociada, a mining town in 1883, access trails lead into the Pecos Wilderness Area.

Southeast of Las Vegas, I-25 passes within sight of several villages whose stone and crumbling red adobe walls speak of 18th-century Spanish colonial roots. Settlers began moving into the area around 1750.

US 84 south from Las Vegas parallels cattle trails used when thousands of head of Texas longhorns were driven north to stock the ranges of New Mexico, Colorado, Wyoming and Montana in the 1860s and 1870s. The old towns of Anton Chico and Dilia on the Pecos River were founded sometime after the Anton Chico Land Grant was made in 1822.

Nineteen miles (31 kilometres) north of Las Vegas, I-25 sweeps past a large white ranch home on the right where a flag can usually be seen flying above the trees. Now the Doolittle Hereford Ranch, this historic place began as a 20-room house and stage station built by Samuel B. Watrous in 1849. At the junction of the Sapello and Mora rivers, the land was fertile and well watered and had been a natural stopping place on the Santa Fe Trail. Within a few years a village had grown up around the stage station. Several old buildings remain in Watrous today, across the highway from the ranch.

Four miles (6.4 kilometres) beyond Watrous a road leads eight miles (13 kilometres) to Fort Union National Monument, the most important fort in the Southwest for many years (see *Parks and Monuments*).

Wagon freighters, cattle barons, railroad builders, homesteaders, miners, gamblers, barroom girls, school teachers and cowboys have written the history of the frontier west in the Las Vegas area.

Las Vegas offers motels, restaurants and other services for travelers.

LINCOLN
Population, 50

(H-7)
Elevation, 6,500

See *Carrizozo* map

The Spaniards called it "The Little Town by the Pretty River," a serene, pastoral name that may have suited it when they settled there in the early 1850s. But within a few years the town was the scene of violence that shook the territory.

In 1869 the name was changed, in honor of the president, to Lincoln, county seat of the new county of the same name, which included the present counties of Lincoln, Chaves, Lea, Eddy, half of De Baca, most of Otero and Roosevelt, and parts of Socorro, Torrance and Curry counties. Fort Stanton had been founded upstream a few miles in 1855, and after the Civil War great herds of Texas longhorns were brought into New Mexico to feed soldiers at the forts. Lincoln was on a branch of the trail that came up the Pecos, and became the leading town in the area.

Fierce competition developed between ranchers and merchants in Lincoln for beef contracts at Fort Stanton, erupting in 1878 in five months of violence and bloodshed known as the Lincoln County War. It was a complicated situation involving John H. Tunstall, an English rancher and merchant; Alexander McSween, a young Scottish attorney, and John Chisum, a cattleman, who were pitted against L. G. Murphy, James Dolan and several other established merchants who would not tolerate competition for the lucrative beef contracts. The Murphy-Dolan faction had powerful political friends known as the Santa Fe Ring. When Tunstall was shot and killed in February 1878, his cowboys, including Billy the Kid, swore revenge. They killed several members of the posse that had murdered him. The Dolan store and the Tunstall-McSween store in Lincoln became headquarters for the opposing factions. Fighting continued until July 19, 1878, when, after a three-day battle in Lincoln, the McSween house next to the store was burned, and five men, including McSween, were killed.

Lew Wallace was sent to replace Samuel B. Axtell as territorial governor to clean up the unsavory political situation in Santa Fe and to end the Lincoln County War. He accomplished both missions.

Billy the Kid, though on the side of what most people consider the "good guys" in the Lincoln County War, continued his career as an outlaw and cattle rustler until December 1880, when he was captured by Sheriff Pat Garrett. In April 1881, he was convicted of murder at La Mesilla, and taken to the courthouse in Lincoln to await hanging. On April 28, he made a dramatic escape from the Lincoln County Courthouse, killing two guards. In July he was traced to the Maxwell ranch at Fort Sumner, and shot by Pat Garrett.

Because so much of old Lincoln town remains, it has been preserved as a historic district and is a state monument administered by the Museum of New Mexico. The old courthouse is a good regional museum containing many relics, books, photographs and records of the Lincoln County War. Even the hole made in an adobe wall by the bullet Billy the Kid fired into one of the guards is still there. Across the street is the Wortley Hotel where the other guard was having lunch when the Kid escaped. As the guard ran toward the courthouse, the Kid shot and killed him, and held the rest of the town transfixed as he made his escape.

The Wortley is still an operating restaurant and hotel. A long veranda, a dining room furnished with enormous oak sideboards and tables, and guest rooms with brass beds and marble-top tables, provide an authentic environment for visitors in this historic town. Reservations are advisable.

Old Lincoln Days takes place the first weekend in August each year, featuring the reenactment of the Kid's escape, parades, fiddlers' contests and arts and crafts displays. Another highlight is a Pony Express race from White Oaks to Lincoln, 41 miles (66 kilometres) through the Capitan Mountains, where horsemen carry mail postmarked by the two towns — the only time all year this happens. Stamp collectors vie as keenly for the right to mail a letter as riders do to win the race.

Eight miles (12.9 kilometres) west of Lincoln is Capitan, and Smokey Bear Historical State Park. Interpretive displays in the museum deal with the prevention of forest fires, the goal that a little bear cub with burned feet came to symbolize nationally. It was within sight of Capitan, in Lincoln National Forest, where Smokey himself was originally rescued from a forest fire in 1950.

Also in Capitan, the Smokey the Bear Stampede takes place on July 3 and 4, and the Lincoln County Fair and Rodeo on the weekend before Labor Day.

Baca Campground in Lincoln National Forest has primitive camping facilities. It is at the foot of the Capitan Mountains, a few miles north of Lincoln.

LORDSBURG

Population, 5,400

(J-1)

Elevation, 4,350

See *Silver City* map

Visitors entering New Mexico from the west on I-10 come first to the town of Lordsburg, county seat of Hidalgo County, the sparsely populated bootheel of New Mexico. Lordsburg was founded in 1880 when the Southern Pacific Railroad went through. Tourism, mining and agriculture are the bases of the economy now. Mild winter climate, pure air, vast skies, brilliant sunsets and sunrises, and always the mirage-like suggestion of mountains on the horizon make Lordsburg an attractive place to visit or to live in.

Around 1850, pioneers bound for the goldfields of California followed an Apache trail about two miles (3.2 kilometres) south of Lordsburg, where Mexican Springs afforded a precious water hole in the dry land. In 1858, when the Butterfield Trail was established, it followed this same trail and continued west approximately along the present route of I-10. At the place where the route crossed the Peloncillo Mountains, near the border of Arizona, the town of Steins was founded. The adobe ruins here, visible from the highway, are in the process of being restored.

Of more permanent nature was the town that grew at Mexican Springs, first named Grant, then Ralston and finally Shakespeare. Silver was discovered in the nearby Pyramid Mountains in 1870, and the new mining district became the victim of false promotions, fraudulent claims, salting a mine with diamonds, and other roughshod practices, but silver did, indeed, exist in the mountains, and beginning in 1879 a great deal of ore was shipped (see *Ghost Towns*).

South of Lordsburg, toward the empty bootheel of New Mexico on NM 338, is the village of Animas, settled by Hispanic people in 1843. Some of the people who work at the nearby copper smelter in the company town of Playas now live in Animas. Southwest of Animas, via NM 9 and US 80, almost on the Arizona line, is the small village of Rodeo, once a shipping point for cattle.

The bootheel country farther south is a land of great distances broken by jagged lines of desert mountains. Mysterious and unknown, this is the least explored part of New Mexico. Three ranges of mountains run down the bootheel, traversed by few trails and fewer roads. Once the stronghold of Apaches as they moved back and forth between New Mexico and Mexico, it is now inhabited by a few cattle ranchers and an occasional javelina or dove hunter. A portion of Coronado National Forest, which is mostly in Arizona, includes the Peloncillos in New Mexico, but has no designated campsites. One dirt road crosses the Peloncillos along a route once known as Geronimo's Trail, but this is strictly a dry weather road, and local inquiry should be made before venturing on it. The site of Geronimo's surrender is several miles north of the trail and can be reached only by foot trail or by a dirt road from Apache, Arizona.

A map of the Coronado National Forest, available at regional headquarters of the U.S. Forest Service in Albuquerque, is advisable for anyone wishing to explore this remote part of the state.

A state Welcome Center supplying tourist information is at the port of entry on I-10 west of Lordsburg. Motels, restaurants and other services are in Lordsburg.

Shakespeare ghost town.

191

LOS ALAMOS   (C-5)
Population, 19,500   *Elevation, 7,410*

Los Alamos sparkles like emeralds after a summer rain and smells like wet pine needles. Spread along the tops of five mesas, it has flower-lined streets, neat lawns and modern homes and buildings. Heavy stands of timber cover the mesas and mountains surrounding the town. Bridges span the deep canyons, and tie the city together.

Most towns and villages in New Mexico rely on antiquity and adobe for charm, but Los Alamos is interesting for the opposite reasons.

By the end of 1942 the United States had reached the momentous decision that it must immediately establish a research site to work on producing an atomic bomb. The highly secret work was called Project Y of the Manhattan Project. Isolation was the first requisite for the site, but such factors as

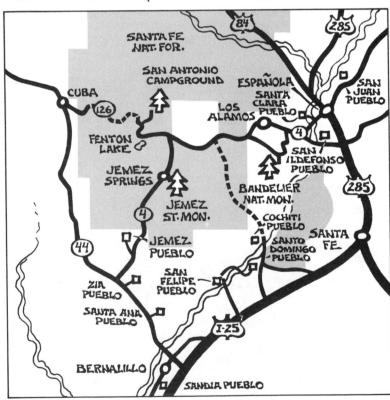

room for, or access to, testing ground, a good climate, access to roads and railroads, available utilities, immediate housing and remoteness bore on the decision to choose Los Alamos Ranch School for Boys on the eastern slope of the Jemez Mountains. It was hidden in the mountains, but was 34 ground or 20 air miles (55 or 32 kilometres) from Santa Fe.

Until the first atomic bomb was detonated in southern New Mexico on July 16, 1945, the work at Los Alamos was cloaked in almost total secrecy. Everyone knew something was afoot up there, but except perhaps for a few professional spies, no one knew exactly what. After the war Los Alamos remained a closed city until 1957, and it was another decade or more before residents were able to buy the houses they lived in. The original 54 buildings that belonged to the boys' school had long since been put to other uses. Additional apartment buildings and barracks-type housing were built quickly, and when pressure lessened many single family dwellings were built.

The big log building that was school headquarters became a lodge for visiting scientists and officials and is now a museum in the central business district.

Since the end of the war research has branched out into many nonmilitary uses from the Anderson Meson Physics Facility for cancer treatment, to studies on air pollution, geothermal energy and solar heating.

Los Alamos may look like any other clean American city lucky enough to be in the mountains, but there are differences. Almost everyone works at Los Alamos National Scientific Laboratory or its support facilities. The ratio of Ph.D.s is higher than on most college campuses.

Museums include Bradbury Science Hall and the Los Alamos Historical Museum. Musical and cultural events occur throughout the year, and several arts and crafts fairs are held, the major one being the first weekend in August. A branch of the University of New Mexico was established in Los Alamos in 1973.

About 20 miles (32 kilometres) from Los Alamos on NM 4 is Bandelier National Monument, which preserves cliff dwellings and ruins of a large pueblo that were inhabited between A.D. 1200 and 1500 (see *Parks and Monuments*).

Los Alamos offers the traveler motels and restaurants, and golfing may be enjoyed on a public 18-hole course.

LOVINGTON
Population, 12,200

(I-10)
Elevation, 3,910

See *Hobbs* map

On the great Staked Plains of southeastern New Mexico, Lovington was founded in 1903 as a homesteaders' and cattlemen's center. It was named for R. F. Love, who homesteaded the plot of land where the townsites were laid out. Cattle and sheep ranching and irrigated farming continue to be important industries in the Lovington area, but when the big oil strikes occurred around 1930, Lovington's future changed course dramatically.

Lea County, of which Lovington is county seat, is the leading oil-producing county in the United States. Of the 11 billion barrels of oil originally estimated to have been in New Mexico, about three-fourths are under Lea County.

Lovington is a clean, attractive city of many new homes and buildings. The Lea County Fair takes place the second week in August with a good rodeo, parade and agricultural exhibits.

Lovington has motels, restaurants and other services.

Early days of Lovington's oil boom.

New Mexico Travel Division

MAGDALENA   (G-4)

Population, 625   *Elevation, 5,575*

See *Socorro* map

Magdalena, 27 miles (43 kilometres) west of Socorro on US 60, was a famous cattle town when it was the railhead of the Magdalena Livestock Driveway that came from St. Johns, Arizona, and Horse Springs, New Mexico, across the San Agustin Plains. The railroad is gone now and the depot and Ilfeld warehouse stare emptily across the track bed, evoking memories of those days when hundreds of thousands of cattle went through this town every year. A block south of the main street the old hotel, a two-story brick building with what was once a fancy veranda on all sides, succumbs sadly to the inevitability of time. An Old Timers' Reunion, soon after the Fourth of July each year, recalls the early days of Magdalena with a parade, fiddling contest, rodeo and dances.

Kelly, a mining ghost town, is on a dirt road two miles (3.2 kilometres) southeast of Magdalena (see *Ghost Towns*).

About 23 miles (37 kilometres) west of Magdalena in the midst of the plains, giants from outer space march in a row to the horizon. Dish-shaped antennas mounted on structures as high as a nine-story building, weighing 214 tons (192.6 tonnes) each, make up the VLA (Very Large Array), the world's largest radio telescope. When completed, 27 such antennas, set on 38 miles (61 kilometres) of railroad track, will search the skies for objects beyond the Milky Way.

There is a restaurant or two in Magdalena, but most travel accommodations are in Socorro.

MESCALERO (I-6)
Population, 2,234 *Elevation, 6,650*
See *Carrizozo* map

Nestled in the pine-covered foothills and green valleys of the Sacramento Mountains of southeastern New Mexico, this small town is headquarters for the Mescalero Apache Tribe. Some tourist services are available here, but the tribe's major tourist facility is the luxurious new lodge, Inn of the Mountain Gods, a few miles farther north on US 70 near Ruidoso (see *Native Americans*).

Mescalero is the scene of the tribe's celebration over the Fourth of July each year when they hold the Maidens' Puberty Rites Ceremonial, accompanied by the Mountain Spirits Dance, powwow and rodeo. Parts of the ceremony are for Indians only, but most of it is open to the public. Several cool, shady campgrounds and a fishing lake are on the reservation.

Other facilities for travelers may be found in Alamogordo.

Mescalero Apache Mountain Spirit Dancers.

New Mexico Travel Division

196

MORIARTY (E-6)

Population, 800

Elevation, 6,200

See *Estancia Valley* map

Best known to travelers along US 66 and later I-40 as a good place to stop and stretch and have a bite to eat, this highway town began, like others in the Estancia Valley, as a homesteaders' town. It was named for an Irishman who homesteaded here in the 1880s, hoping the climate would cure his rheumatism. Apparently it did, for he spent more than 50 more years following the active life of a sheep rancher.

A drive north on NM 41 goes through the heart of the Estancia Valley homestead country, to the old Spanish village of Galisteo, and joins I-25 in the mountains a few miles east of Santa Fe. This drive of less than 50 miles (80 kilometres) goes from plains to mountains, through country traveled by prehistoric men, Spanish conquistadores and American pioneers.

Clines Corners on I-40 east of Moriarty is a large tourist service center at the interchange with US 285, the main route to Santa Fe from southeast New Mexico and Texas.

Farm on the eastern plains.

197

MOUNTAINAIR   (F-5)
Population, 1,150   *Elevation, 6,495*

See *Estancia* Valley map

On US 60 in the red bluff and piñon country at the south end of the Manzano Mountains, Mountainair is on Abo Pass, a long gentle rise between the Rio Grande and the Estancia Valley. The town was settled in 1901 as a center for ranchers and farmers in the area, but travelers had been using this route for centuries.

When the Spaniards under Oñate settled New Mexico in 1598, an expedition went east of the Manzano Mountains and reported finding large numbers of Indians they called Las Humanas. Several pueblos were in the foothills, and over the next 50 years Franciscan fathers directed the construction of four large mission churches and one or two smaller ones to serve them (see *Missions and Churches*).

During this period the fierce Plains Indians were becoming more numerous and, acquiring the horse and gun of the Spaniards, became superb warriors. The peaceful Pueblos were no match for them. Even before the last mission was completed at Gran Quivira, the Pueblo people had deserted their villages and gone over Abo Pass to find refuge with the Pueblo Indians of the Rio Grande Valley.

Mountainair is in the midst of this ancient Indian country. Quarai lies to the north, Abo to the west, and Gran Quivira to the south.

During the 1860s and 1870s a cattle drive trail went from Socorro and the San Agustin Plains through Abo Pass to the big ranches in the northeastern part of the state. The Santa Fe Railway goes through Mountainair, a busy freight line between Clovis and the main line at Belen.

Soon after the turn of the century, several settlements were started east of Mountainair, along the railroad. Homesteaders were flocking in from the East and Midwest to try dryland farming, but after the drought most of the land reverted to grazing land, or to irrigation by deep wells. Such towns as Willard, Estancia, Encino and Vaughn were started then. Those that were railroad towns remained active centers, others became shadows of what they once were.

Limited motel and restaurant facilities are in Mountainair.

PECOS   (D-6)
Population, 600   *Elevation, 6,925*

See *Santa Fe* map

Pecos town is on the river it was named for, on NM 63 just
north of I-25, 20 miles (32 kilometres) east of Santa Fe. It is in
one of New Mexico's most scenic and historic areas.

From its headwaters high in the Sangre de Cristo Mountains
the historic Pecos River tumbles down the mountains. Near
the town of Pecos, it leaves the mountains and continues
through old Spanish villages, then southeasterly, larger and
slower, irrigating thousands of acres of cropland, providing
recreation, feeding waterfowl. It then winds into Texas and finally into the Gulf of Mexico.

The Pecos River shaped the history of much of New Mexico.
NM 3 leaves the interstate about 40 miles (64 kilometres) east
of Santa Fe and goes through San Miguel del Bado, Pueblo,
Sena and Villanueva. San Miguel was the port of entry for New
Mexico on the Santa Fe Trail. Here the trail crossed the Pecos
and merchants had to stop and pay duty on goods they brought
into the province. This was the last civilization eastbound travelers saw until they reached Franklin, Missouri. It was their
last chance to buy fruits, vegetables or other comforts. More
than one corrupt provincial politician made his fortune on
taxes collected here. Several old adobe and stone buildings remain in San Miguel, some of which probably date back to the
Santa Fe Trail days. A large stone church, well cared for and
maintained, rises above the rest of the village. It was built
about 1806.

The paved road continues south another nine miles (14.5
kilometres) to Villanueva State Park, near a Spanish colonial
village of the same name (see *Parks and Monuments*). Stone
and adobe walls and tin roofs sloping down the hill toward the
river have a curious old-world look to them. The state park offers picnicking, camping, hiking, a playground and some fishing along the river. In the village church, made of stone and
seeming more Mexican than Spanish, is an unusual tapestry
made by women of Villanueva and depicting the history of the
community. The paved road continues 20 miles (32 kilometres) south to connect with I-40.

Pecos National Monument, within sight of I-25, preserves
ruins of a great mission church and a multistoried pueblo that
was one of the largest and most important at the time the
Spaniards entered New Mexico (see *Missions and Churches,
Parks and Monuments*).

North of Pecos the road (NM 63, paved) continues upstream past vacation cabins, campgrounds, and through Santa Fe National Forest to Cowles, where dozens of trails lead into the forest and Pecos Wilderness Area. Ten Forest Service campgrounds are located along the road and at the end of it.

One mile north of Pecos is Monastery Lake, a popular and accessible fishing area. Set in a wide valley cut by the river as it begins to leave the mountains, the lake is surrounded with grasses and shrubs, but along the river cottonwoods, willows and birches provide shade, and on the hillsides conifers grow. Immediately north of the lake is Lisboa Springs Fish Hatchery, the New Mexico Game and Fish Department's oldest unit. A self-guiding tour through the hatchery lets visitors see the huge rainbow trout brood fish. Monastery Lake, the hatchery and Bert Clancy Fishing and Wildlife Area about ten miles (16 kilometres) farther upstream are all owned and operated by the Department of Game and Fish. At the latter are extensive camping and picnicking facilities, combined with good fishing in a forest setting.

All traveler facilities may be found in Santa Fe, 20 miles (32 kilometres) west.

Pecos Wilderness.

PORTALES

Population, 12,300

(F-10)

Elevation, 4,010

See *Clovis* map

Cowboys driving cattle north up the old Fort Sumner Trail camped at a place where springs came from a series of caves resembling a porch across the front of a pueblo-style house, so they named them Portales (porches) Springs. In 1898, when the railroad came through, a settlement was started near the springs, which took the same name. A few years later Portales was incorporated as the county seat of Roosevelt County. The city lies on the high plains of eastern New Mexico, but is in a valley where irrigation produces bountiful crops of Valencia peanuts, grains, sweet potatoes, corn and cotton.

Eastern New Mexico University was founded in Portales in 1934 as a two-year college, but since 1946 has been a four-year liberal arts university. Much of the cultural and recreational life of the community revolves around the university with its musical and dramatic presentations, several museums, golf, tennis and swimming (see *Colleges and Universities*). The Roosevelt County Historical Museum is also here.

Oasis State Park, six miles (9.7 kilometres) northwest, off NM 467, offers camping and picnicking around the shores of a small fishing lake. The setting is in a grove of cottonwoods with shifting sand dunes and uninterrupted vistas.

Near the towns of Milnes and Crossroads, about 30 miles (48 kilometres) south of Portales, and Floyd, 16 miles (26 kilometres) west, the New Mexico Department of Game and Fish operates several restoration areas where lesser prairie chickens have made a dramatic comeback from near-extinction. In sandhills and shinnery oak thickets, the charming little bird has reproduced well, and now provides good hunting for sportsmen.

The Roosevelt County Fair takes place at the fairgrounds in Portales the third or fourth week in August each year.

Good visitors' accommodations are offered in Portales.

QUEMADO
Population, 300

(F-2)
Elevation, 6,890

Quemado is the first town visitors come to when entering New Mexico from the west on US 60. Even with its small population it is the second largest town in Catron County, an area of almost 7,000 square miles (18,130 square kilometres) that has only about 2,000 people. Each person in Catron County has three-and-a-half square miles of elbow room. Some of the terrain is high sagebrush grazing land, but most of it is mountainous.

About five miles (eight kilometres) east of the present town a spring used to rise in a little draw, attracting both Indians and early white travelers to camp — but not at the same time. It became the custom to burn off the grass and brush around the campsite, the better to watch for enemies, thus the place became known as Rito Quemado, Burned Creek.

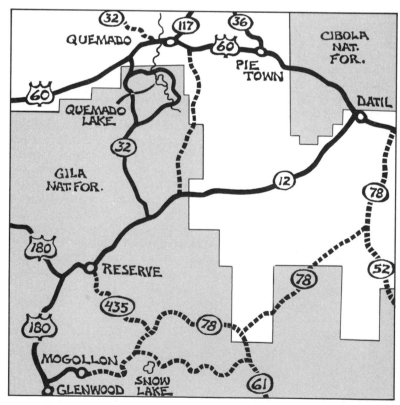

At the east end of Quemado, a cluster of old adobe buildings remains from the original settlement. In the center of town are a few abandoned adobe buildings that once housed dance halls and saloons, reminders of the Saturday nights when cowboys, ranchers and homesteaders came to Quemado. The branch of the Magdalena Cattle Drive Trail that originated in Arizona came through Quemado, and many a weary cowman has revived his spirits there.

A good paved road goes directly south of Quemado to Quemado Lake in Apache National Forest. Trout fishing, boating, camping, picnicking and hiking are available at this uncrowded lake, formed by a dam across Largo Creek. Ponderosa pine, pinon and juniper trees grow in this transition zone. A new store and campground, owned by a ranching family who run cattle in the surrounding mountains, provides boat and equipment rentals, supplies, and all hook-ups and facilities for campers.

The area around Quemado is now almost entirely taken up by large cattle ranches, but during the twenties and thirties many homesteaders moved in. They soon learned it was impossible to earn a living on 160, 320 or 640 acres (65, 130 or 260 hectares) of the high, cold, arid land, and gradually they moved away, their weatherbeaten cabins stark reminders of dreams that died. Some are used as line cabins on the ranches.

Pie Town, 22 miles (35 kilometres) east of Quemado, a block off the highway (US 60), was once a homesteader trade center, and a busy highway town. A few people still live there, but many of the log and adobe buildings are slowly sinking into oblivion. The Diamond T Ranch near Pie Town hosts the Pie Town Polo Tournament every August, when polo players from ranches over the state come to compete. A dance and Western barbecue follow the polo games. There are limited motel and restaurant accommodations in Quemado. And, yes, pies are usually available in Pie Town.

RATON
(A-8)

Population, 9,600

Elevation, 6,666

See *Capulin* map

Raton is the northern gateway to New Mexico, set in the foothills of the Rockies at the south end of Raton Pass on I-25. This was once the mountain or main branch of the Santa Fe Trail. In 1866, "Uncle Dick" Wootton, mountain man, Indian scout, Santa Fe Trail freighter and cattleman, bought land on the Maxwell Land Grant that included the trail over the pass. He felled trees, blasted rock and built bridges to make the route more passable for wagons, then built a house and toll-gate on the border between New Mexico and Colorado. Travelers who didn't want to pay the toll could make a 100-mile (161-kilometre) detour to the east. Wootton's place is identified along the railroad, and a picnic area is on the pass not far away.

When the railroad came through in 1879, the company bought the toll road, and the line follows approximately the same route today. Raton was founded at the site of Willow Springs, a stop on the Santa Fe Trail. The town quickly developed as a railroad, mining and ranching center for the northeastern part of the territory.

Along two blocks of First Street, once the main business street of Raton, are buildings of interesting Victorian architecture, reminiscent of the town's early days. Some have been restored and put to new uses. The focal point of this development is the Palace Hotel, an impressive stone structure that houses an elegant restaurant. Stained glass, thick carpets, fine crystal chandeliers, paintings and other art objects create an ambience of leisurely grace that distinguished that period.

Thoroughbred and quarter horse racing are at La Mesa Park on the south end of town on weekends from mid-May until mid-September. A municipal golf course is in the foothills at the west edge of town. In mid-July each year the Jaycees hold a rodeo that draws contestants and spectators from afar.

NM 526 goes north of Raton to Sugarite Canyon Park and Picnic Area, and a few miles farther to Lake Maloya where boating, fishing, hiking and picnicking may be enjoyed. The paved road continues to Sugarite ski basin, 14 miles (23 kilometres) from Raton (see *Winter Sports*). The ski area itself is actually across the line in Colorado, but can be reached only from Raton.

The scenic drive to the ski area goes past old mines and the rubble of houses that were part of Raton's robust mining history. All the mountainous areas north, west and south of Raton once resounded with the clang of pick and shovel, but most of the ghost towns are on private land and inaccessible to visitors. Sugarite, however — a cluster of foundations on the way to the ski area — is alongside the highway, and may be examined by the curious. Extensive coal mining is still done at York Canyon Mine southwest of Raton, which ships out thousands of tons a month on a specially built rail line — on a train that never stops.

Another scenic drive goes over Johnson Mesa, a volcanic tableland east of Raton. NM 72 branches off NM 526 six miles (9.7 kilometres) from town and quickly climbs to the top of the mesa, passing the site of Yankee, another old coal mining town. The mesa is an expanse of verdant grasses and lakes homesteaded in the early part of this century. The homesteads were gradually combined into large cattle ranches. It is cold on top of the mesa, which rises to above 8,600 feet (2,621 metres), and few ranchers remain there the year round. But in the summertime it is a pastoral scene of fat cattle and horses leisurely grazing the tall grass. Deer and wild turkey confidently strut in the canyons along the escarpment where pine trees and dense brush grow. The road was paved once upon a time, and is all right in good weather, but there are large chuck-holes, and in the winter it is closed entirely. It runs the 30-mile (48-kilometre) length of the mesa, then drops down to Capulin and Folsom near the east base (see *Capulin*).

A few miles southwest of Raton on US 64 is the national headquarters of the National Rifle Association. Each spring they sponsor a Santa Fe Trail Rendezvous. Members dress in clothing of 125 years ago, use muskets in contests, camp in teepees, and cook over campfires, bringing back a hauntingly real picture of the Old West.

Raton has more than 20 motels and many restaurants, but on racing season weekends, reservations are advisable.

RED RIVER
Population, 250

(B-7)
Elevation, 8,750

See *Taos* map

In spite of its relatively small permanent population, on any weekend in ski season or in summer, you're likely to find 4,000 to 5,000 people in Red River, all having fun. It is a town devoted exclusively to recreation and tourism.

Ski runs come down almost to the main street of the village, and skiers can walk from most lodges to the lifts. Complimentary buses, however, make continuous runs from all lodges, condominiums and motels to the ski slopes. Red River Ski Area is in Red River, and Powder Puff Ski Area is at the west end of town (see *Winter Sports*).

Because of the high elevation with its cold temperatures, and snow-making machines that can give nature a nudge, Red River is frequently the first ski area in the state to open. Other winter sports are almost as popular as skiing: cross-country skiing, snowmobiling, snowshoe hiking and ice skating. All equipment and clothing are available to rent at several shops in Red River. The ski areas operate complete schools, including ski ballet.

In summertime fishing is popular in Red River, which flows through town, and in other mountain streams in the vicinity. The chairlift takes people to the upper slopes for sightseeing and hiking. Jeep tours on old mine roads are popular all summer and into the fall when the aspen forests turn to gold. Horses are available to rent for individual rides or to accompany organized trail rides. A skating rink and game arcades, square dancing every week, and live entertainment in several restaurants provide fun all year, most of it family oriented.

Among the special events that occur in Red River are a square-dance festival over Memorial Day weekend and a July 4 celebration that includes a men's and women's tug-of-war across Red River, quick-draw and horseshoe-pitching contests, a parade and tennis. Enchanted Circle-Wheeler Peak Bicycle Race and Tour is a 100-mile (161-kilometre) route that begins and ends in Red River, circling around through Questa, Taos, Gorge Bridge, and Eagle Nest. It takes place early in September and is open to contestants from anywhere in the world. Most of the route is through mountains and forests, with a side trip to Rio Grande Gorge near Taos, and it is a spectacular scenic drive.

The last weekend in September and the first few days of October is the time of the Aspencade Festival, when jeep tours take visitors to see the changing colors in the mountains. Square dancing and an arts and crafts fair also take place during this time. In late fall hunting is good in the surrounding mountains for deer, bear, elk and wild turkey. Guide and pack trips may be arranged out of Red River.

Red River was first prospected in about 1870 by miners from E-Town, across the mountains to the east, and several good mines were found in the area. When the rich strikes played out, the town lapsed into near oblivion. About 1925 it came to life again as a resort community, and a few years later a large molybdenum mine opened between Red River and Questa.

NM 38 between Red River and Questa runs mostly through Carson National Forest. There are seven forest campgrounds and several privately owned campgrounds along the way. A few miles east of Questa, a dirt road turns northwest to Cabresto Lake and campground. This scenic high mountain country is not heavily traveled, and offers good fishing, hunting and hiking. Except for the last mile and a half (2.4 kilometres), the road is graded and graveled, but during wet weather, local inquiry should be made about road conditions.

Restaurants, lodges, condominiums and motels of all kinds are in Red River, yet during ski season or any holiday weekend in the year reservations are essential.

Red River Ski Area.

RESERVE (G-2)

Population, 500   *Elevation, 5,749*

Reserve used to be three separate villages, settled by Spanish farmers from the Rio Grande Valley sometime after the Civil War. Upper, Middle and Lower Frisco Plazas eventually became one. The name was changed to Reserve after the U.S. Forest Service was established and forest reserves surrounded the villages. Only at Lower Plaza does anything remain of the old villages. A large adobe mercantile store faces a field that was once a plaza, and along another side is a row of adobe houses with pitched roofs, resembling mountain villages of northern New Mexico.

It was at one of the Frisco Plazas where the legendary sheriff of Socorro County (which at that time included Catron County), Elfego Baca, held off a gang of drunken cowboys for a day or two. He was holed up in a shack that was riddled with bullet holes. Even a broom handle standing in one corner looked like a piccolo. He escaped injury because the floor was below ground level. When he emerged unscratched, the astonished cowboys and villagers bestowed upon him a reputation of invincibility that endured throughout his long and colorful career as a lawman and lawyer. Walt Disney made a movie based on his life, "The Nine Lives of Elfego Baca."

Reserve is surrounded by the Apache and Gila National Forests and is headquarters for hunters, fishermen, backpackers. Forest Road 141 begins at Lower Frisco Plaza and connects with several other graded but unpaved roads that crisscross the forests. There is a highway sign at the beginning of Forest Road 141 that is a favorite of many travelers. It says, "This is not NM 12 to Silver City. Go back one-half mile."

Forest Road 141 joins NM 78, which leads to Snow Lake, Willow Creek and other campgrounds on the perimeter of the Gila Wilderness. It is 50 miles (80 kilometres) from Reserve to Willow Creek. The road is mostly graded on high benches of park-like meadows surrounded by big timber. From Willow Creek to Mogollon, about 15 miles (24 kilometres), the road was once paved, but little evidence is left. The same is true for the nine miles (14.5 kilometres) from Mogollon down to US 180. All these roads are passable in good weather, however, and parts are a real pleasure to drive. The forest roads are usually open from April to mid-September, but weather conditions change from year to year, and local inquiry should always be made. District ranger stations are at Reserve and

Glenwood, a good place to get information and maps. State highway maps do not show forest roads (see *Glenwood* and *Mogollon* for more information on this area).

NM 12 turns sharply west at Reserve, going through colorful Starkwether Canyon and across timbered plateaus seven miles (11 kilometres) to join US 180. Twenty-one miles (34 kilometres) northwest of this junction is the old Mormon settlement of Luna. A big mercantile store and several other buildings still look much as they did when they were built. The town was settled in 1885 in a pastoral mountain valley on the San Francisco River. Because this had been the lambing pasture for the big flocks driven to California by a Mr. Luna from the Rio Grande valley the Mormons named it for him.

Though the Apaches attacked ranches and mining camps throughout the area, legend says they never attacked the Mormons because it was their custom to pass food and supplies to the Indians through a window in the store where the settlers gathered in time of danger. Most of the families in Luna today are descended from the early settlers, including the people who run the store.

Two Apache National Forest campgrounds are just off US 180 south of the junction with NM 12. Cottonwood is six miles (9.7 kilometres) south of the junction, and Pueblo Park is 11 (18 kilometres). At the latter, rockhounds report that bytownite, which resembles a yellow diamond, is easily found.

A big log building across the street from the courthouse houses a restaurant, but motel accommodations are limited.

ROSWELL

Population, 47,325

(H-8)

Elevation, 3,750

This lovely city in the Pecos Valley was not even dreamed of that day in 1867 when the pioneer cattleman, Charles Goodnight, held a large herd at a spring near there. Other cattlemen and settlers followed Goodnight's trail, and they saw that the Pecos could be controlled to irrigate the entire valley. Within a year a township was laid out and lots sold.

Roswell has always been a stable town, its economy based on agriculture and livestock. Residential streets, tunnels of shade flanked by brick and frame homes, are reminiscent of the Midwest where most of the early settlers originated.

New Mexico Military Institute at Roswell is recognized as one of the better academies in the Southwest (see *Colleges and Universities*). The Roswell Museum and Art Center began as a scientific museum housing the work of Dr. Robert Goddard,

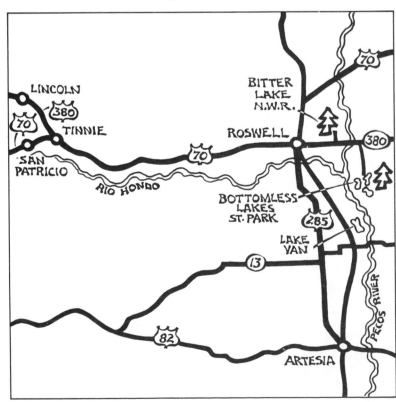

who proved in 1926 that rockets were feasible, and did much of his experimentation near Roswell. Permanent collections now include works of several internationally known artists who have lived in New Mexico. The large Peter Hurd collection includes lithographs as well as oils. The Hurd home is a ranch at San Patricio about 50 miles (80 kilometres) west of Roswell. Perhaps more than any other artist, Hurd has captured the haunting beauty of the plains country, the windmills, isolated ranches, barbed wire fences and lonely cowboys.

Bottomless Lakes State Park, 16 miles (26 kilometres) southeast of Roswell by way of US 380 and NM 409, was one of the first state parks in New Mexico. It is a series of very deep lakes with most recreational facilities near Lea Lake, where swimming and boating are permitted. Some of the smaller lakes are stocked with trout. The park is open all year and has complete camping facilities, boat rentals, restaurant and gift shop (see *Parks and Monuments*).

Bitter Lake National Wildlife Refuge, about 10 miles (16 kilometres) east of Roswell, off US 380, was established in 1937 to protect lesser sandhill cranes, at that time a dwindling species. The cranes have made a remarkable recovery, and controlled hunts are now permitted. No recreational facilities are at the refuge, but who can forget watching in the misty dawn as thousands of the big birds fly out of the marshlands along the Pecos to their feeding grounds, or when they return, silhouetted against a rosy sunset? Thousands of other waterfowl winter at Bitter Lake, and more than 200 species of other birds either winter or live there the year around.

Roswell has good motel and other tourist facilities.

RUIDOSO (H-6)
Population, 9,000

Elevation, 6,900
See *Carrizozo* map

This beautiful year-round resort town is on the site of Dowlin's Mill, a grist mill built in the early 1880s on a fast-flowing stream that ran down from the high mountains to the west. The stream was called Ruidoso — noisy — and the village took the same name.

On weekends and holidays from Memorial Day through Labor Day, sleek thoroughbreds and quarter horses thrill large crowds at Ruidoso Downs. The world's richest horse race, the All-American Futurity Quarterhorse Race, with a million-dollar purse — almost four times as large as the Kentucky Derby — is held on Labor Day, climaxing the colorful season. In conjunction with the Futurity is the All-American Yearling Sale, with several hundred colts bringing premium prices.

Winter sports season follows soon after racing season. Sierra Blanca Ski Area on the Mescalero Apache Reservation (see *Native Americans*) is a major winter sports area. It is reached by taking NM 37 north from Ruidoso, then turning west at Alto on NM 532, a total of 16 miles (26 kilometres) from Ruidoso to the base of the slopes. The road is paved but fairly steep. Sierra Blanca, at 12,003 feet (3,659 metres), is the highest peak this far south in the United States. Facilities at the base include restaurant, complete rentals, warming lodge and tavern. Enclosed gondolas operate up the mountain summer and winter (see *Winter Sports*).

Because a number of professional artists have chosen to make their homes there, Ruidoso has become known as an art center. Activity is focused on a place called the Art Center, a group of galleries and shops where fine collections of contemporary and Western art are shown. During the summer, classes in arts and crafts are taught to students from all over the world, and a summer music and art camp for high school and college students is nearby.

Lincoln National Forest, which surrounds Ruidoso, provides opportunities for unlimited outdoor recreation. On NM 37 at the edge of town is a cluster of four campgrounds on Cedar Creek. On the road to the ski area two recreation sites are a short distance off the highway, both above 9,000 feet (2,743 metres) in elevation, offering grand vistas of the mountains and valleys. A few miles farther is another large camping area.

NM 37 continues north from Alto about five miles (eight kilometres) to a dirt road that leads to Bonito Lake, a large, fully developed fishing and camping area in the pines. NM 37 turns north before reaching Bonito Lake and goes to Nogal Lake, formed by a natural spring in a grassy meadow. The road to Bonito is paved part way, the rest is graded and graveled, but because of a few sharp turns near the end, it is limited to trailers under 16 feet (4.9 metres). The road to Nogal is graded and graveled from the Bonito turn-off to the lake. From there to US 380, between Capitan and Carrizozo, it is paved.

In the fall two kinds of hunters often go to Ruidoso. One is after bear, deer, elk or wild turkey; the other seeks the flamboyant changing of colors in aspen groves throughout the forest. Usually in early October the delicate aspens begin their show. Sometimes it happens overnight, sometimes it lasts two weeks. Green changes to chartreuse, to pale yellow, to liquid gold, sometimes to orange and pink. Ruidoso celebrates this glorious time with aspencades, an old-timers picnic, antique car rallies, mule races, dances and parades.

A wide range of accommodations and facilities are available in Ruidoso. Supper clubs, restaurants, golf courses, swimming pools, service facilities, and more than 50 hotels and lodges cater to visitors.

Three miles (4.8 kilometres) south on US 70 the Mescalero Tribe operates the luxury resort, Inn of the Mountain Gods (see *Native Americans*).

Though Ruidoso has changed in nature and grown considerably from the grist mill on the noisy river, big ponderosa pines still grow along main street, a casual Western ambience pervades the town, and the feeling of a small mountain village is not lost.

SANTA FE (D-6)
Population, 52,530   *Elevation, 7,000*

The rest of the country may not know that New Mexico is a state of the Union, but everyone knows about Santa Fe. Millions of words have been written about the historic old city, and the adjectives have been used and used again: unique, charming, cosmopolitan, livable, intriguing. In spite of more growth than most Santa Feans would like, the city core has kept its architectural integrity and the radiance of sunlit streets with lilacs hanging over adobe walls.

Santa Fe was founded in 1610, making it the oldest capital city in the United States. It has always been a seat of government. During Spanish rule, 1598 to 1822, Santa Fe was the capital of an isolated and neglected province, jealously forbidden by the mother country to have commerce or communication with the French, English or American settlements in the

East. With Mexican independence, trade opened up, and overnight the Santa Fe Trail was born. Thousands of tons of merchandise came over the trail to people hungry for manufactured goods. At the same time a social and economic climate was being established that made acquisition by the Americans easy in 1846.

Santa Fe bears her years with dignity and grace. Old homes and buildings speak of the past. Newer buildings respect traditions, often out-santa-feing the older places. A drive or walk down any street is an architectural experience.

Churches are some of the most interesting buildings in Santa Fe. Among them are St. Francis Cathedral, Loretto Chapel, Cristo Rey, San Miguel, Our Lady of Guadalupe and the First Presbyterian Church (see *Missions and Churches*).

The state government complex is centered around the capitol building, shaped like a Zia sun symbol, a circle with rays extending out in four directions. Territorial style architecture distinguishes most of the government buildings and many homes in Santa Fe. This is an adaptation of pueblo-style architecture and is characterized by a row of bricks around the firewall. Milled woodwork trim on doors and windows and posts rather than vigas also characterize this later style, which resulted when Fort Union built a brick kiln and the railroad made it possible to ship more material.

Santa Fe is a city of art and artists; some have made it their permanent home, others have stayed briefly, but it touched their lives. Incredibly blue skies, clear mountain air that intensifies light and shadow, the brilliant and varied landscape of high desert and mountains, and the subtle blending of Indian, Hispanic and American cultures, all work together to produce a creative environment felt immediately by artists and artisans. Galleries are found all over town, but are concentrated in the plaza area and several downtown streets. The best known is Canyon Road, a street that follows an old trail that meandered up the Santa Fe River. Many of the homes here have been converted to galleries, studios and workshops. Several restaurants are also on Canyon Road. To capture the feel of the ancient city visitors should discover the plaza area and Canyon Road on foot.

The Palace of the Governors occupies the north side of the plaza. It is the oldest public building in America in continuous use and is a state monument as well as the historical division of the Museum of New Mexico. Indian craftsmen sit on blankets under the portal in front, selling jewelry and pottery (see *Parks and Monuments*).

Also on the plaza is the New Mexico Museum of Fine Arts, whose permanent collection is representative of New Mexico masterpieces since the beginning of the art movement in New Mexico in 1898.

Two other outstanding museums in Santa Fe are the Museum of International Folk Art and the Wheelwright Museum, both on the south side of town, just off Old Santa Fe Trail. At the former, exhibits include folk art collections of every kind from all over the world. The latter is devoted to the history, art and culture of the Navajo people.

The Santa Fe Opera, five miles (eight kilometres) north of town on US 84-285, is recognized for its superb music, sets and costumes and especially for its magnificent outdoor setting. High on a hill, the sweep of the open roof lets in the stars. Lights of Los Alamos sparkle beyond the stage, and, during many performances in the July-August season, thunder and lightning become part of the score.

Summer also brings the Santa Fe Chamber Music Festival. Throughout the year, the Orchestra of Santa Fe gives excellent performances.

Many programs of good quality in the fields of drama, music and education are presented at the College of Santa Fe, St. John's College, Armory for the Arts, St. Francis Auditorium (part of the Fine Arts Museum on the plaza), and at several smaller theaters. The Rodeo de Santa Fe takes over with Wild West fun in mid-July each year. At the end of July, Hispanic arts and crafts are displayed and sold in open street stalls during Spanish Market, a tradition carried on for more than 50 years. Even older is the spectacular Indian Market, which takes place the third weekend in August each year on the plaza and shows the work of more than 300 top Indian artists and craftsmen from all over the country.

The biggest celebration in Santa Fe is the Fiesta de Santa Fe, commemorating the triumphant reentry of General Diego de Vargas and his conquistadores when they reconquered New Mexico in 1692 after the Indian rebellion of 1680. Since 1712 the event has been celebrated, and in modern times the pageantry of costumed horseback riders, religious processions and parades has thrilled visitors. It begins with the burning of Zozobra, Old Man Gloom. The giant caricature writhes and groans in agony as he goes up in fireworks and smoke. The fiesta takes place in mid-September.

Destinations for trips out of Santa Fe include eight Indian pueblos in fewer than 40 miles (64 kilometres), where feast days and ceremonial dances occur frequently during the summer and occasionally the rest of the year (see *Native Americans*). Two guest ranches within 10 miles (16 kilometres) of the city offer complete Western resort facilities — horseback riding, hiking, swimming, tennis and restaurants.

Santa Fe is at the foot of the Sangre de Cristo Mountains,

St. Francis Cathedral.

217

the southern end of the Rockies. Santa Fe National Forest provides opportunities for camping, picnicking, hiking, backpacking, fishing, skiing and all other outdoor recreation. The ski area is 16 miles (26 kilometres) from downtown (see *Winter Sports*). On the way are Hyde State Park and several campgrounds, often used as headquarters for backpacking trips into the Pecos Wilderness, which borders on the ski area.

The drive east from Santa Fe on I-25 follows approximately the same route as the Santa Fe Trail. If you take the Pecos exit about 20 miles (32 kilometres) east, the route follows a stretch of old US 85 through the area where the Confederate troops were driven back in March 1862, during their almost-successful western campaign. A stone marker denotes the battlefield, and the ruins of an old adobe way station, a corral and a well mark a place that was a stop on the trail.

Six miles (9.7 kilometres) east of Santa Fe, US 285 turns south from the freeway to Lamy, as close as regular transcontinental passenger rail service ever came to Santa Fe. The old railroad station still stands, and a saloon of early vintage has been turned into an elegant restaurant and bar.

A few miles farther, NM 41 turns to Galisteo, an old Spanish village on the site of an earlier Indian pueblo. A private museum in the owner's old hacienda lures visitors to the quiet village. When the Spaniards came in the 1500s there were four large pueblos in the Galisteo Basin, and the main route north, used by both Indians and Spaniards, left the Rio Grande near Santo Domingo, swung east around the mesa, up through the pueblos in the Galisteo Basin, then across the plateau to Santa Fe. This route is approximately the same as the one followed by the Santa Fe Railway today.

Santa Fe is in the heart of an area unusually rich in history. The city and its environs on all sides give visitors a taste of antiquity, a sense of rich cultural mix, and an array of scenery that delights the eye and lifts the heart.

Excellent motel and restaurant accommodations are in Santa Fe.

SANTA ROSA   (E-8)
Population, 2,800   *Elevation, 4,600*

Known as the City of Lakes, Santa Rosa is in eastern New Mexico where I-40 crosses the Pecos River. Grasslands undulate like waves of the ocean across the landscape. First settled around 1865 by Hispanic settlers on land grants, the town was named several years later in honor of Santa Rosa de Lima, the first canonized saint in the new world. Don Celso Baca, a prominent early settler, built a chapel dedicated to Santa Rosa in 1879.

The Southern Pacific Railroad came through in 1901, changing it from a quiet village to a trade center for the surrounding farm and ranch country.

Because of the many lakes in the area, recreation in Santa Rosa is largely concerned with water. Near the southern city limits, on NM 91, James Wallace Memorial Park offers free

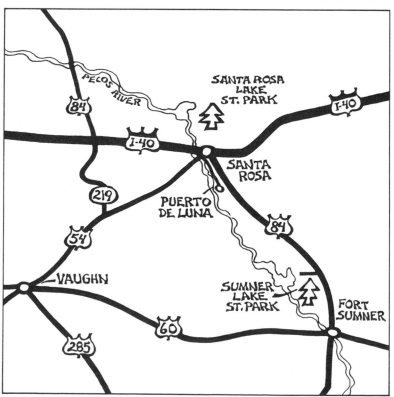

fishing, camping and picnicking. At Park Lake, another city park, is the largest free swimming pool in the entire country. Playgrounds, tennis courts, basketball courts and baseball facilities are all free.

The mysterious Blue Hole, one block from Park Lake, is 60 feet (18 metres) in diameter and 81 feet (25 metres) deep. It is stocked with large, colorful goldfish, and, because of its amazing clarity, is a favorite with scuba divers.

Several other lakes, all formed by artesian springs, offer scuba diving and rustic settings for nature study, and for pondering the folk tales that say the lakes are protected by the Golden Carp, as big as a shark, who rules the lakes and creeks in the area. The Golden Carp is said to sing a siren-like song under the fairy tale bridge over El Rito Creek.

Los Esteros State Park, a few miles up the Pecos, offers good fishing, boating and camping (see *Parks and Monuments*).

Old Puerto de Luna, 10 miles (16 kilometres) south on NM 91, was a campsite for the Coronado Expedition in 1541 at a place where they could cross the Pecos. It began to be settled by farmers and sheep men around 1862, but life was precarious because of frequent raids by Comanches and Kiowas from the plains. Large cattle drives on their way from Texas to northern New Mexico, Colorado and Wyoming often went through Puerto de Luna. Stores, a grist mill, hotel and saloons were opened, and for a short time Puerto de Luna was the county seat of Guadalupe County.

When the railroad bypassed Puerto de Luna, going through Santa Rosa instead, the town began to decline. Two historic points of interest in this ghost town remain today. The church of Nuestra Señora del Refugio, built in 1882, is of Byzantine architecture, the result of French priests serving the parish at the time. And a bridge across the Pecos is believed to be in the exact spot chosen by Coronado to build a wooden span when his army passed through in 1541.

Santa Rosa has motels, restaurants and other facilities to meet travelers' needs.

SILVER CITY (I-2)

Population, 13,200　　　　　　　　　　　　*Elevation, 5,900*

How many towns do you know of that have a 55-foot-deep ditch for a main street? In July 1895, two days of rain caused floods to rush down Silver City's main street, tossing boulders as big as houses against anything that stood in its way. When the deluge was over, stunned residents saw, instead of a street, a chasm running through their town, with halves of houses hanging over the edge. Eventually bridges were built across the ditch to rejoin the two parts of town, but the chasm continues to be called Main Street.

In 1870, silver was discovered in a mountain valley marsh, and a townsite was quickly laid out. Silver strikes had already been made over the hill at Pinos Altos, and 45 miles (72 kilometres) southwest at Shakespeare, so within days the new town of Silver City was swarming with miners and camp fol-

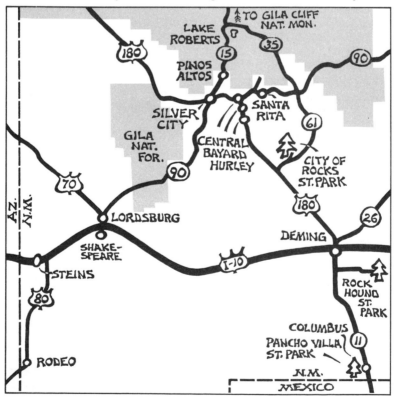

lowers. Before long it became the trade center and shipping point for mining camps in the area. Big cattle ranches were established throughout the district, and today the mining and cattle industries are still the main economic bases of Silver City, though it is copper, not silver, that is mined now.

Silver City was never a boom-and-bust town. It had a solid, substantial growth from the beginning, which makes it unusual among mining towns of that period. The discovery of a type of clay that made good bricks had a profound influence on the architecture and permanence of the buildings. The downtown business district and many of the homes in the historic zone are of late Victorian style, often combining the best qualities of brick and adobe construction.

The city museum on the corner of Broadway and Pinos Altos Road was built as a home in 1881 by a miner who struck it rich in the Georgetown mines east of Silver City. The house has served as a rooming house, hospital, recreation center, fire station, and now a museum. It features exhibits of geological, archeological and regional historical interest.

Western New Mexico University, opened in 1893, is on the edge of the historic zone, and much of the cultural and civic life of the town revolves around the campus (see *Colleges and Universities*).

Silver City holds a traditional Fourth of July celebration every year featuring rodeo and parades.

Sixteen miles (26 kilometres) east of Silver City on NM 90, the Kennecott open pit copper mine at Santa Rita is a man-made, mile-wide Grand Canyon. Forty-ton power shovels crawling along the horseshoe bends, deep in the pit, look like toys. A visitors' observation point is open during daylight hours with recorded information, and a mine museum is open during the summer. Another huge open pit copper mine, owned by Phelps Dodge, 11 miles (18 kilometres) south of the city on NM 90, has a viewpoint on the crest of a hill overlooking the mine. A tour covers the geology and history of the area and the operation of the mine.

Six miles (9.7 kilometres) north of Silver City on NM 15 is Pinos Altos, a mining town that already had 3,000 inhabitants when Silver City was founded. It was attacked time and again by Apaches, and when the ores began to play out, the town died. Several old adobe buildings have been restored, including the first schoolhouse, built before the Civil War, which now houses a good local museum. The man who owns it is the grandson of the builder and first teacher. At a restaurant, saloon and opera house across the street, melodrama is offered during the summer. A fine collection of Mimbres pottery, artifacts, and a rare collection of photographs of most of the old mining towns in southwestern New Mexico are on display in the opera house.

The road that goes to Pinos Altos (NM 15) continues through Gila National Forest to the Gila Cliff Dwellings National Monument (see *Parks and Monuments*).

NM 15 returns to a junction with NM 35, and continues through the mountains past Lake Roberts and Bear Canyon

Gila Cliff Dwellings National Monument.

Dam where boating, fishing and camping are available. The road follows the Mimbres River out of the mountains, through a valley once inhabited by the Mimbres branch of the Mogollon Culture, whose fine pottery was distinguished by stylized animal figures and geometric designs. The road joins NM 90 a few miles east of Silver City, making a complete circle trip known as the Inner Loop, 76 miles (122 kilometres), all paved.

NM 90 goes east from Silver City over the Black Range to Truth or Consequences, a two-lane paved road with many curves, but not heavily traveled. Forests, scenic overlooks, and the old mining towns of Kingston and Hillsboro (see *Truth or Consequences*) make it a scenic, if slow, route.

Nine miles (14.5 kilometres) east of Silver City is Central, and just south of there is Bayard, residential communities for miners working in the Santa Rita mines. The site of the old military installation, Fort Bayard, is a little north of Central, now occupied by neat rows of white buildings housing a state hospital. The military base was established in 1863 to guard settlers and pioneers against Indian attacks.

City of Rocks State Park is off US 180 between Silver City and Deming (see *Deming* and *Parks and Monuments*).

Silver City is the largest town in the four counties of southwestern New Mexico that combine talents to promote that region for visitors. Catron, Grant, Hidalgo and Luna Counties are sparsely populated and unfamiliar to many people in the state. This is a land for outdoors people, for explorers, for history and geology buffs, or for those who like time and space to think long thoughts and see long vistas.

All accommodations are available in Silver City.

SOCORRO

(G-4)

Population, 8,059

Elevation, 4,617

Wh
hen the Spaniards entered New Mexico, they left the
Rio Grande a few miles north of Las Cruces, where the river
made a sharp bend to the west through an impassable volcanic canyon. They struck due north with their oxcarts and
horses across a forbidding desert they later named *Jornada
del Muerto* (Route of the Dead Man). They met the river again
about 70 miles (113 kilometres) north, where there were
several Piro Indian pueblos. Because the Indians gave the
Spaniards grain and other supplies, Oñate named the spot
Socorro, which means help or aid.

The first Spanish mission was built in the area in 1628, but
abandoned in 1680. Most of the inhabitants went south with
the Spaniards during the Pueblo Revolt of 1680, and
established another village there named Socorro del Sur. The

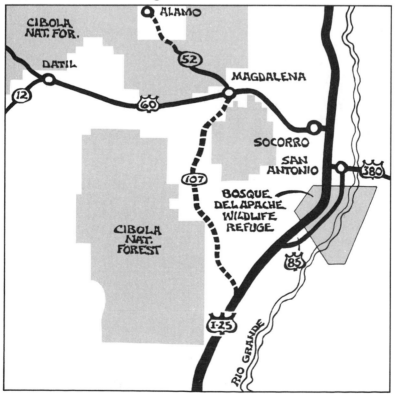

original village was not resettled until around 1815.

Socorro is in the midst of a rich mining area and was the scene of intense activity from about 1867 to 1890. Many buildings remain of the Spanish, Mexican and American periods, mostly near the plaza, a block off US 85. The chamber of commerce publishes a walking or driving tour of the major historic sites, beginning with San Miguel Mission and including an opera house and several old homes near the plaza, the Valverde Hotel (famous in the 1920s for its cuisine and accommodations), and the old brewery, a busy place during mining days.

In early April an arts and crafts fair is held with about 75 artists and craftsmen participating. The Conrad Hilton Golf Tournament is held in June each year. Players tee off from the top of a rugged peak at the edge of the campus golf course at New Mexico Institute of Mining and Technology (see *Colleges and Universities*) . August 10 to 12 the Fiesta de San Miguel honors the patron saint, and the end of August is the time for the big Socorro County Fair and Rodeo, which lasts four days.

San Antonio, an old village 12 miles (19 kilometres) south of Socorro on US 85, is the birthplace of Conrad Hilton. The home where his parents ran a small hotel, and where young Conrad carried bags from the depot a block away, is still standing in good condition, but is not open to the public. It is on the south end of town about a block west of abandoned buildings that were once the center of town.

US 85, which parallels I-25, continues 15 miles (24 kilometres) beyond San Antonio to the Bosque del Apache Wildlife Refuge. From late November to mid or late February, thousands of sandhill cranes, snow geese, Canada geese, ducks and other waterfowl and birds may be seen here. A few whooping cranes are also at the refuge, part of a program to bring them back from near-extinction by placing whooping crane eggs under sandhill cranes. The whoopers, considerably larger and pure white, stand out from the thousands of gray sandhills.

It is a thrilling sight to stand at sunset and watch thousands of the big birds silhouetted against the western sky as they settle down for the night. Again at dawn they leave to go to their feeding grounds to the north. Many other forms of wildlife inhabit the refuge, and foot trails lead through the woods and along the waterways. Picnicking is permitted, but not overnight camping. The nearest motels are in Socorro. There is no admission charge to the refuge.

Two portions of Cibola National Forest lie southwest of Socorro. The first is reached by seven miles (11 kilometres) of dirt road that leaves US 60 15 miles (24 kilometres) west of Socorro, and leads to camping and picnic facilities at Water Canyon. The other section is reached by continuing west on US 60 12 miles (19 kilometres) west of Magdalena, and south on NM 52, a graded and graveled road that connects with roads leading into the Gila National Forest (see *Glenwood*). There is one forest campground on NM 52. Both these roads are dry weather roads.

Socorro has motels, restaurants, and other facilities for travelers.

Bosque del Apache Wildlife Refuge.

SPRINGER

Population, 1,800

(B-8)

Elevation, 5,800

See *Cimarron* map

When the railroad was built across northeastern New Mexico in 1879, camps for workers were established every 20 or 30 miles (32 or 48 kilometres). Some camps vanished as soon as the next one was established. Others, like Springer, remained to become important shipping points along the line.

On the Cimarron River, Springer was in the rich grasslands of the Maxwell Land Grant, surrounded by vast ranches. Cattlemen were eager for the railroad to arrive so they could ship beef to slaughter houses and packing companies in Kansas City and Chicago.

Overnight the cattle industry was big business in New Mexico, and Springer was headquarters for the northeastern part of the territory. Holding and loading pens were built along sidings. Hotels, boarding houses, livery stables, saloons and stores sprang up within weeks. The streets were dusty and noisy with the clump of booted heels and the shouts of cowboys as they worked with the cattle.

In 1882, Springer was made county seat of Colfax County and a handsome courthouse built. The county seat moved to Raton in 1897, but the courthouse remains on Springer's main street, housing the Santa Fe Trail Museum.

W.W. Mills, a controversial and important attorney during the 1880s, built a 32-room mansion of adobe and frame with such innovations as an elevator, a ruby glass transom and delicately carved woodwork. The house is not open to the public, but can be seen from the street. A big stone livery stable, built in 1882 on the main street, and a block of old buildings down a side street bear evidence of the important role Springer played in the early days.

In early September each year, the Colfax County Fair and Rodeo are held in Springer with such activities as a cow-chip throwing contest, tractor pull and barbecue.

Lying in the basin where the Cimarron, Ponil, Vermejo, Canadian, Rayado and Ocate rivers drain from the Sangre de Cristo and Raton mountains, there are many lakes, usually stocked with trout, bass, pike, catfish, perch and crappie.

Springer Lake, four miles (6.4 kilometres) northwest in rolling grasslands, has primitive picnicking and camping facilities.

Charette Lakes, 23 miles (37 kilometres) southwest of Springer on NM 569 (dirt road), are on a high mesa where the view extends to a distant horizon in all directions. Camping and picnicking are permitted around the lower of the two lakes.

Miami Lake is on NM 199 about 13 miles (21 kilometres) west of Springer. This road continues to Rayado where Lucien Maxwell first lived when he bought the land grant, but it is now part of Philmont Boy Scout Ranch (see *Cimarron*). The road turns north to join US 64 at Cimarron, all paved except the 10 miles (16 kilometres) between Miami and Rayado.

Thirteen miles (21 kilometres) north of Springer, just off US 85, is Maxwell, about the same age as Springer, and also a shipping point for the cattlemen and farmers of the early days. The Maxwell National Wildlife Refuge, four miles (6.4 kilometres) northwest of town, was established in 1966 to provide a resting and feeding sanctuary for migratory waterfowl. Almost two dozen small lakes make up the refuge, but Lake Thirteen, largest of the group, attracts the majority of the birds.

Twenty-three miles (37 kilometres) east of Springer on US 56, then 12 miles (19 kilometres) north is the Dorsey Mansion State Historical Monument (see *Parks and Monuments*).

Motel facilities in Springer are limited. Raton, 39 miles (63 kilometres) north, has full travelers' accommodations.

Buffalo still roam the plains.

TAOS (B-6)

Population, 3,100   *Elevation, 6,965*

Taos is magic. White sunlight and lavender shadows, air sparkling like champagne, high plateaus reaching to a distant blue haze, the pungent odor of sagebrush, mountains hovering like benevolent gods . . . are part of the magic of Taos.

Artists found that mystical quality in Taos, beginning with J.H. Sharp on his first visit in 1885. E.L. Blumenschein and Bert G. Phillips came in 1898, and in 1912 these formed the nucleus of the Taos Society of Artists, a prestigious group that brought world-wide recognition to Taos as an art center. More than 80 galleries are in Taos today.

Musicians, writers and craftsmen are also drawn to Taos, and many types of programs, concerts, lectures, art films and theatrical productions are offered frequently. The Taos School of Music and the New Mexico Music Festival present chamber

concerts during the summer.

Taos Indian Pueblo, two miles (3.2 kilometres) north of town, is probably the most visited and photographed of all the pueblos. Two large multistoried communal dwellings face each other across the plaza, separated by a clear, running stream that flows down from the high mountains on the east. The pueblo is open to visitors with the payment of a small fee. Photography for an additional fee is permitted in the plaza area except during certain ceremonial religious days (see *Native Americans*).

The Spanish village of Taos was settled in 1617 near the pueblo. Through the years, even after American occupation in 1846, Taos was the meeting ground for Indians of the Rio Grande Valley and nomadic tribes from the mountains and plains, Spanish settlers and soldiers, American and French beaver trappers or mountain men, and traders from the Santa Fe Trail. Twice a year they converged on Taos for the great trade fair, when buffalo hides and beaver pelts, grain, flour, blankets, baskets, pottery, scarce metal objects, horses, bullets, Indian captives and Taos Lightning, a potent and popular whiskey, changed hands rapidly. The rest of the year, Plains Indians made life risky for the rest of them, but during the trade fair there was a gentleman's truce. From those years of contact, the Taos Indians acquired characteristics of the Plains Indians that the other Pueblos never adopted, such as long braids and some of the dances.

The American flag flies day and night in the plaza in Taos in recognition of the patriotism of a few Taos pioneers, including Kit Carson. Rebels took the flag down during the Civil War, but Yankees nailed it to the tallest pine tree they could find, and guarded it with rifles day and night.

The restored Kit Carson home is now a museum just off the plaza on Kit Carson Road. The famous scout and frontiersman called this home for 24 years. A state park on North Pueblo Road, a few blocks north of the plaza, is dedicated to his memory. The park includes grassy picnic areas, a playground and pleasant walkways for daytime use only (no camping), and the cemetery where Kit Carson and several members of his family are buried. Many other prominent Taos names can be found on headstones (see *Parks and Monuments*).

The Governor Bent House on Bent Street preserves the home of the first governor of New Mexico appointed by the

Americans in 1846. He was murdered during an uprising a few months after the American conquest. The home contains a museum and gallery.

Ledoux Street is lined with studios and galleries of working artists, many of which are open to the public, and is the location of the Harwood Foundation Museum and Library, owned by the University of New Mexico. The classic pueblo-style building houses an excellent Southwestern library, a collection of paintings by early Taos artists, and a fine collection of Spanish furniture and crafts.

The Millicent Rogers Memorial Museum houses an outstanding collection of Indian and Spanish colonial arts and crafts in a lovely pueblo-style hacienda. The house itself is as much a part of the museum as are the items within it. Located on a

Taos Pueblo.

gentle rise, the house looks across the valley to the Sangre de Cristos. To reach it, go north on NM 3 about four miles (6.4 kilometres) to just before the junction with US 64. At the museum sign, make a hard left on a dirt road that goes about a half-mile to the museum.

Of all the creative people to call Taos home, none is more famous than the English writer, D.H. Lawrence. Brought to New Mexico by his wealthy patroness, Mabel Dodge Luhan, Lawrence spent three happy summers in a simple ranch home on land given him by Mrs. Luhan, about nine miles (14.5 kilometres) north of town on NM 3, and six miles (9.7 kilometres) up into the mountains. A large sign indicates the turnoff. After Lawrence's death in France, his widow, Frieda, brought his ashes back to the ranch and enshrined them there. She is buried in front of the small white shrine. At her death, the ranch was willed to the University of New Mexico. It is used for special seminars and for writers-in-residence, but the shrine is open to the public. The six miles of dirt road from the highway to the ranch may be slick when wet.

The Mabel Dodge Luhan house in Taos is now used as a summer school for teaching crafts and Southwestern subjects. Across a field is a morada, a meeting place for the Penitentes, a Spanish Catholic brotherhood, which is being restored by a private foundation. The Penitentes will continue to use the morada during Holy Week, but it will be open to the public the rest of the year. The same foundation is also restoring the Padre Antonio Martinez house two miles (3.2 kilometres) southwest of the plaza, a fine example of early 19th-century Spanish colonial architecture and construction.

Ranchos de Taos is a small village about two miles (3.2 kilometres) south of Taos. Though Taos has grown to its edges, the village retains its own character. Several old adobe buildings cluster around a plaza, and on one side is St. Francis of Assisi Mission Church, a classic and famous example of early Spanish mission architecture (see *Missions and Churches*).

Rio Grande Gorge Bridge on US 64 about 15 miles (24 kilometres) northwest of Taos spans the deep gorge cut by the river through the high volcanic plateau west of the Sangre de Cristos. The bridge hangs 650 feet above the turbulent river that is at the bottom of a deep black gorge. Picnic shelters and tables are at the west end of the bridge.

Five miles (8 kilometres) south of Taos, a rough, unpaved

road leaves NM 68 and goes across the plateau several miles before it hairpins down the steep canyon walls to the river and Rio Grande Gorge State Park (see *Parks and Monuments*). Four developed camping areas are in the canyon along the river where trout fishing is usually good. It can be reached from the south by turning west at Pilar on NM 96 (unpaved).

From Taos Junction Bridge north to the Colorado line, 48 miles (77 kilometres), the Rio Grande is classed as a wild river, corresponding to a wilderness area in a national forest. Four miles (6.4 kilometres) of the tributary Red River are included in the classification. This was the first officially designated wild river in the country. It flows through a deep, rocky gorge cut by the river through the volcanic plateau, hundreds of feet deep in places. For rafters and kayakers the turbulent water ranges from Grade II (mild rapids) to Grade VI, most dangerous of all. Boulders as big as houses and drops of 15 feet (five metres) are common in that stretch of the river. No vehicular roads are along the river, but several campgrounds on the east rim accommodate vehicles, and trails lead to the river where there are primitive campgrounds for hikers, boaters and fishermen. The trails to the river are steep and rocky. Some of the best trout fishing in the state is downstream from Big Arsenic Springs in the canyon.

Directly east of Taos rise the Sangre de Cristo Mountains, most of which are in Carson National Forest. US 64 going east toward Eagle Nest and Cimarron follows the canyon of Rio Fernando de Taos, and crosses the mountains at Palo Flechado Pass. Half a dozen forest campgrounds are in the first 10 miles (16 kilometres), and lodges, resorts and commercial campgrounds are farther along the route.

NM 3, turning east from US 68 at Ranchos de Taos, goes through the mountains and joins NM 75 a few miles east of Picuris Pueblo. The route sweeps through stately forests, and the vista point atop U.S. Hill looks north to the highest peaks of the New Mexico Rockies. This route connects with NM 76 — the High Road to Taos (see *Chimayo and the Mountain Villages*).

A 90-mile (145-kilometre) circle trip north of Taos loops around this portion of the Rockies, seldom losing sight of Wheeler Peak, 13,161 feet (4,011 metres) high — highest in New Mexico. Take NM 3 north of Taos to Questa; turn east on NM 38, following Red River canyon to the village of Red River (see *Red River*), cross over Bobcat Pass, drop down to US 64 at Eagle Nest (see *Eagle Nest*). The road loops west over Palo Flechado Pass to Taos. The highway is all paved, and forest and commercial campgrounds, motels, lodges and restaurants along the way provide ample accommodations.

Whether your taste leans to art galleries or the wildness of a river, Taos has something to offer. If possible, make your visits during spring or fall when it will be less crowded. There are many lodges, motels, resorts, clubs, condominiums and restaurants in Taos, but during peak winter and summer seasons reservations are advised.

Church at Ranchos de Taos.

TRUTH OR CONSEQUENCES

(I-4)

Population, 7,500   *Elevation, 4,260*

In 1950 the radio personality, Ralph Edwards, offered instant and everlasting publicity to any town in the country that would change its name to Truth or Consequences, the name of his popular radio show. Hot Springs, New Mexico, won over a number of other towns. Several times a few residents have pushed for changing it back, but "T or C" sticks.

True to his word, Ralph Edwards comes back to T or C every May for the Ralph Edwards Fiesta. He leads the parade, participates in tournaments, contests, jeep tours, barbecues and parties. He has made many warm friendships in T or C. A park named for him and a wax statue of him in the museum indicate he is T or C's favorite adopted son.

Mineral waters bubble up in springs throughout the area, and for many years people have gone there to drink and bathe

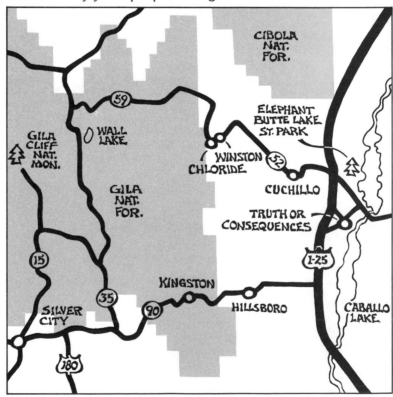

in the waters, especially in the winter, when the permanent population is sometimes doubled by visitors. A dozen bath-houses accommodate those who seek the therapeutic effects of the springs. On one of the main downtown streets, Geronimo Springs is enclosed in a pagoda-like structure where anyone may drink the mineral water free. Geronimo Springs Museum, of regional historical interest, is next to the springs.

Elephant Butte Dam on the Rio Grande, five miles (eight kilometres) northeast of T or C, was completed in 1916, the largest man-made dam in the world at that time. It backed up a lake several miles long, which has become popular for water sports and vacation homes. A state park includes extensive camping areas, marinas and docking areas (see *Parks and Monuments*). The old lodge at the south end of the lake has a dock, lounge, cabins, store and post office. The new inn near the dam has a restaurant, pool, and superb view of the lake. The golf course is nearby. Many motels and restaurants are in the town itself.

Twelve miles (19 kilometres) south of T or C is Caballo Lake State Park at another dam on the Rio Grande. Here, too, are all facilities for camping, picnicking, boating, water-skiing, rental boats, marinas and fishing supplies.

T or C is headquarters for big game hunting in the area. North, west and east of the city deer, elk, bear, cougar, oryx, ibex and barbary and big horn sheep may be hunted in season.

During the last half of the 1880s, several mining towns sprang up in the mountains near T or C. Most had brilliant, but brief, careers, and their crumbling or weathered wood ghosts doze peacefully in the sun. NM 90, which turns west at Caballo, goes over the Black Range to Silver City, a scenic drive through the heart of the mining country. Hillsboro, once the county seat and supply center for mines in the area, is now a restful little village where artists, writers and retirees live. The ruins of the old courthouse and several other buildings attest to a busier, rowdier past. In August the Black Range Art Exhibit and Sale takes place in Hillsboro, and in early September the Apple Festival is held. An interesting museum is in Hillsboro.

Kingston, a few miles farther west, had a similar mining history in the 19th century, but now rests quietly in the foothills, home to a few dozen people. A cemetery on the west side of town has many colorful headstones and crosses marking graves of early settlers.

Seven miles (11 kilometres) north of T or C, NM 52 leads northwest to three other old ranching and mining towns, Cuchillo, Winston and Chloride. Cuchillo is a quiet little Hispanic farming community dating back to the early 1880s. Winston, once called Fairview, and Chloride, two miles (3.2 kilometres) west on a dirt road, were both started in 1880 when rich silver strikes were made in Cuchillo Canyon. Chloride is a virtual ghost town now, and Winston has a few families of ranchers living in it. A few false-fronted buildings with faded lettering remind visitors of the exciting, often dangerous, lives the early settlers lived. The paved road continues through Winston into Gila National Forest to connect with the Outer Loop. Pavement ends at Beaverhead (see *Glenwood*).

T or C offers all facilities for travelers.

Elephant Butte Lake.

TUCUMCARI   (D-9)
Population, 7,500   *Elevation, 4,085*

Originally called Six Shooter Siding, Tucumcari began in 1901 when two railroad lines met there. The Rock Island was building west, and the El Paso & Southwestern was going northwest to the coal mines at Dawson near Raton. Tucumcari is still a railroad town, and the depot is a good example of the arches and arcades of California-Spanish architecture popular early in this century. Ranching, farming and cattle-feeding are also important industries, as is tourism. The location on I-40 and proximity to major water recreation areas attracts many travelers to Tucumcari.

Tucumcari Lake, a natural lake on the east edge of town, was a watering place for prehistoric animals, and evidence has been found that stone age game hunters, Spanish conquistadores, roving bands of plains and mountain Indians, pioneers,

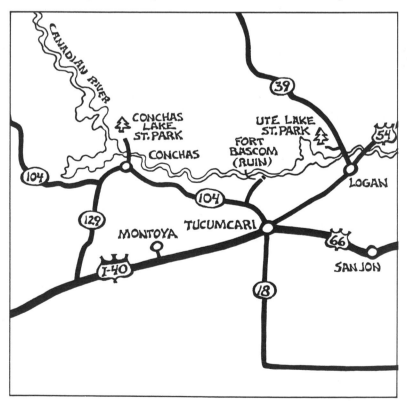

outlaws and cattlemen have all passed by here. The lake attracts thousands of migratory waterfowl each year.

Tucumcari Historical Museum occupies an old two-story brick building and contains thousands of early Indian artifacts, gems and minerals, an old bottle collection, and several authentic reconstructions of Western vignettes, such as a school room, hospital room and a sheriff's office.

The Lions Club Rodeo usually follows the Fourth of July holiday, and the 4-H Horse Show and Rodeo is the latter part of the month. A Piñata Festival the first week in September lasts four days and is held in the Four Seasons Mall, an older downtown street that has been converted into a mall. Pageants, parades, crafts show, antique cars, contests and races, music and food booths provide entertainment.

Boating, fishing, swimming, water-skiing and camping are available at Ute and Conchas lakes. Conchas Lake, 30 miles (48 kilometres) northwest of Tucumcari on NM 104, is 25 miles (40 kilometres) long, holding back the waters of the Conchas and Canadian rivers. A resort, modern marinas and fully developed campsites offer year-round recreation.

Ute Lake, at the town of Logan, 33 miles (53 kilometres) northeast on US 54, has complete accommodations for travelers. At the junction of Ute Creek and the Canadian River, Ute Lake is unique in that the water level is not drawn down each spring for irrigation. It is an excellent spawning water for walleye pike. Both lakes are in shortgrass prairie country of eastern New Mexico, broken by red clay and sandstone formations (see *Parks and Monuments*).

On the bank of the Canadian River, four miles (6.4 kilometres) north of Tucumcari on NM 104, then four miles (6.4 kilometres) northeast on a dirt road, are the ruins of Fort Bascom, established in 1863 as an outpost for troops who were trying to protect the frontier against roving bands of Cheyenne, Arapaho, Kiowa and Comanche tribes from the plains. Only a few piles of rubble indicate outlines of the barracks.

The village of San Jon, 25 miles (40 kilometres) east of Tucumcari on I-40, has a small museum and reconstruction of a brush arbor and dugout such as early pioneers used. The name is probably a corruption of *zanjon* which means deep gully.

Tucumcari has many motels and restaurants.

TULAROSA

Population, 3,300

(I-6)

Elevation, 4,520

See *Alamogordo* map

There are two Tularosa Rivers in New Mexico, one in the southwestern part of the state and one in the south central. The town of Tularosa is on the latter and takes its name from the marshy lands along the river where reddish-brown reeds grew.

Spanish settlers began farming here about 1860, but, until the Civil War was over and soldiers could be stationed at forts, life was precarious. The town lies in the Tularosa Basin at the western base of the Sacramento Mountains, about 15 miles (24 kilometres) from the Mescalero Apache Indian Reservation. Flowing down from the high mountains of the reservation, the river creates a valley of rich farmlands and orchards. Yet almost within sight of Tularosa are the extremes of desert desolation, and beauty: the black of a long malpais called Valley of Fires and the white of White Sands (see *Parks and Monuments*).

Along two or three blocks of the older part of town, buildings with ornate facades, fancy woodwork and pressed tin trim are reminders of days when the town was, perhaps, a little busier than it is today. Alamogordo, 13 miles (21 kilometres) south, outpaced it some years ago, but Tularosa has kept the charm of a quiet farming town. The simple, attractive church of St. Francis de Paula stands on the main thoroughfare through town. It was built in 1869 and is lovingly tended. On the first full weekend in May each year, townspeople stage a four-day Rose Festival, and the following weekend, parishioners celebrate the St. Francis de Paula Fiesta and the Spanish beginnings of Tularosa with pageants, food booths and Spanish dances creating a festive atmosphere.

In April each year special religious services commemorate the Battle of Round Mountain. Ten miles (16 kilometres) northeast of Tularosa, where US 70 enters the Mescalero Apache Indian Reservation, a low, symmetrical hill rises above the piñon-juniper foothills. Here in 1868 cavalrymen from Fort Stanton were attacked by a war party of Apaches. The outnumbered soldiers held on until men of Tularosa came to their rescue. There was only one death and one injury, but settlers believed the victory protected them from further attacks, and they show their gratitude annually.

Alamogordo, 13 miles (21 kilometres) south, offers travel accommodations.

241

VAUGHN
Population, 867

(F-7)
Elevation, 5,965
See *Santa Rosa* map

This town on the high plains of eastern New Mexico is at the intersection of US 285, 54 and 60, and where the Santa Fe and Southern Pacific railroad lines meet. Many a traveler has sought warmth here during winter storms, and found it, not only in the form of shelter, but in the people who reflect the self-sufficiency of living in lonely places.

Vaughn was established in the early part of this century as a shipping point for the large cattle and sheep ranches in the area, and was named for a civil engineer who helped build the Santa Fe Railway through Vaughn.

The town is divided into east and west sides, with the newer restaurants and motels being on the west side.

Santa Fe Railway.

242

WAGON MOUND   (C-7)
Population, 600   *Elevation, 6,200*

See *Las Vegas* map

To travelers bound for the West on the Santa Fe Trail, a volcanic mesa shaped like a long, sagging-in-the-middle covered wagon was a welcome sight. It meant that at the foot of the distant Rockies lay Fort Union, offering protection, shelter and rest. Unfortunately, this last landmark at the end of the trail was frequently a dangerous one. It was a natural place for ambushes, for here the Cimarron Cutoff and the Main or Mountain Branch of the trail met. Attacks and ambushes gave Wagon Mound a bloody reputation until after the Civil War.

When the railroad came in 1879, a new townsite was laid out and named Pinkerton, but common usage preferred Wagon Mound. The geological formation stands out as prominently today along I-25 as it did on the Santa Fe Trail. Wagon Mound grew to be a merchandizing and shipping center for large cattle and sheep ranches that developed in northeastern New Mexico during the past century. Except for a roadside diner and service stations, business has since moved to other towns along the highway, such as Las Vegas and Springer.

Thirty-four miles (55 kilometres) east of Wagon Mound on NM 120 is the town of Roy, which came into being around 1902 when homesteading opened settlement of the grasslands of eastern New Mexico. About five miles (eight kilometres) before reaching Roy, the highway crosses the Canadian River at a scenic and historic site, where the old trail wound down into a deep canyon slashed through red cliffs. Roy served the needs of cattle and sheep ranchers as well as homesteaders until the 1930s when drought and the Depression almost wiped out the town. The same fate befell many other dry-land farming towns in New Mexico. Roy never completely died, but parts of its old main street look like a Western movie set.

Ten miles (16 kilometres) north of Roy on NM 29 are Kiowa National Grasslands and Chicosa Lake State Park (see *Parks and Monuments*). This was once a watering stop on the Goodnight-Loving Trail. Camping and picnic units, water and primitive sanitary facilities are here. Impersonal, and of a magnitude to make all but the bravest cover, the high plains country has always been there beyond the mountains to challenge the nomadic Indians, conquistadores, buffalo hunters, wagon freighters and cattlemen. The high plains are just one of the many faces of enigmatic New Mexico.

INFORMATION SOURCES

NEW MEXICO MAGAZINE
Bataan Memorial Building
Santa Fe, NM 87503
827-2642

STATE AGENCIES

BUREAU OF MINES
AND MINERAL RESOURCES
Socorro, NM 87801
835-5420

MUSEUM OF NEW MEXICO
(State Monuments Division)
PO Box 2087
Santa Fe, NM 87501
827-3241

NEW MEXICO GAME
AND FISH DEPARTMENT
Villagra Building
Santa Fe, NM 87503
827-2143

NEW MEXICO PARKS
AND RECREATION DEPARTMENT
141 East De Vargas
Santa Fe, NM 87503
827-2726

NEW MEXICO STATE POLICE
Alamogordo, 437-1313
Albuquerque, 842-3082
Clovis, 763-3426
Española, 753-2277
Farmington, 325-7547
Gallup, 863-9353
Las Vegas, 425-6771
Las Cruces, 522-2222
Roswell, 622-7200
Santa Fe, 827-2551
Socorro, 835-0741

NEW MEXICO TOURISM
AND TRAVEL DIVISION
Bataan Memorial Building
Santa Fe, NM 87503
827-5571

FEDERAL AGENCIES

BUREAU OF LAND
MANAGEMENT
Federal Building
Santa Fe, NM 87501
988-6243

NATIONAL PARK SERVICE
Old Santa Fe Trail
Santa Fe, NM 87501
988-6340

FOREST SERVICE
Federal Building
Santa Fe, NM 87501
988-6643

FISH AND WILDLIFE SERVICE
Federal Building
500 Gold Avenue, SW
Albuquerque, NM 87102
766-6546

(Telephone area code for state: 505)

244

TRIBAL OFFICES

JICARILLA APACHE
PO Box 313, Dulce, NM 87528
(505) 759-3242

MESCALERO APACHE
PO Box 176, Mescalero, NM 88340
(505) 671-4495

NAVAJO TOURIST DEPARTMENT
Window Rock Arizona
(602) 871-4941

ACOMA
PO Box 309, Acomita, NM 87034
(505) 552-6606

COCHITI
PO Box 70
Cochiti Pueblo, NM 87041
(505) 465-2244

ISLETA
PO Box 317, Isleta Pueblo, NM 87002
(505) 869-3111

JEMEZ
PO Box 78, Jemez Pueblo, NM 87024
(505) 834-7359

LAGUNA
PO Box 194, Laguna Pueblo, NM 87026
(505) 552-6654

NAMBE
Route 1, Box 117-BB, Santa Fe, NM 87501
(505) 455-7692

PICURIS
PO Box 228, Peñasco, NM 87553
(505) 587-2519

POJOAQUE
Route 1, Box 71, Santa Fe, NM 87501
(505) 455-2278

SANDIA
PO Box 608, Bernalillo, NM 87004
(505) 867-2876

SAN FELIPE
PO Box 308, Algodones, NM 87001
(505) 867-2439

SAN ILDEFONSO
Route 5, Box 315-A, Santa Fe, NM 87501
(505) 455-2273

SAN JUAN
PO Box 1099, San Juan Pueblo, NM 87566
(505) 852-4400

SANTA ANA
PO Box 37, Bernalillo, NM 87004
(505) 867-3301

SANTA CLARA
PO Box 580, Espanola, NM 87532
(505) 753-7326

SANTO DOMINGO
Santo Domingo Pueblo, NM 87052
(505) 465-2240

TAOS
PO Box 1846, Taos Pueblo, NM 87571
(505) 758-8626

TESUQUE
Route 1; Box 1, Santa Fe, NM 87501
(505) 983-2667

ZIA
General Delivery, San Ysidro, NM 87503
(505) 867-3304

ZUNI
PO Box 339, Zuni Pueblo, NM 87327
(505) 782-4481

INDEX